THE PRACTICE MANAGER'S LAW HA

THE PRACTICE MANAGER'S LAW HANDBOOK

A READY REFERENCE TO THE LAW FOR MANAGERS OF MEDICAL GENERAL PRACTICES

ARTHUR BROWN

Blackwell Science

© 2000 Blackwell Science Ltd
Editorial Offices:
Osney Mead, Oxford OX2 0EL
25 John Street, London WC1N 2BS
23 Ainslie Place, Edinburgh EH3 6AJ
350 Main Street, Malden
  MA 02148 5018, USA
54 University Street, Carlton
  Victoria 3053, Australia
10, rue Casimir Delavigne
  75006 Paris, France

Other Editorial Offices:

Blackwell Wissenschafts-Verlag GmbH
Kurfürstendamm 57
10707 Berlin, Germany

Blackwell Science KK
MG Kodenmacho Building
7–10 Kodenmacho Nihombashi
Chuo-ku, Tokyo 104, Japan

The right of the Author to be identified as the
Author of this Work has been asserted in
accordance with the Copyright, Designs and
Patents Act 1988.

First published 2000

Set in 10/12 pt Century
by DP Photosetting, Aylesbury, Bucks
Printed and bound in Great Britain at
The Alden Group Ltd, Oxford and Northampton

DISTRIBUTORS

Marston Book Services Ltd
PO Box 269
Abingdon
Oxon OX14 4YN
(*Orders:* Tel: 01235 465500
           Fax: 01235 465555)

USA
Blackwell Science, Inc.
Commerce Place
350 Main Street
Malden, MA 02148 5018
(*Orders:* Tel: 800 759 6102
           781 388 8250
           Fax: 781 388 8255)

Canada
Login Brothers Book Company
324 Saulteaux Crescent
Winnipeg, Manitoba R3J 3T2
(*Orders:* Tel: 204 837-2987
           Fax: 204 837-3116)

Australia
Blackwell Science Pty Ltd
54 University Street
Carlton, Victoria 3053
(*Orders:* Tel: 03 9347 0300
           Fax: 03 9347 5001)

A catalogue record for this title is available
from the British Library

ISBN 0-632-05549-9

Library of Congress
Cataloging-in-Publication Data
Brown, Arthur (Thomas Arthur)
    The practice manager's law handbook: a
ready reference to the law for managers of
medical general practices/Arthur Brown.
       p. cm.
    Includes index.
    ISBN 0-632-05549-9
    1. Medical laws and legislation—Great
Britain.   2. Physicians—Malpractice—Great
Britain.   3. Medical offices—Risk
management—Great Britain   4. National
Health Service (Great Britain)   I. Title.

KD2945.B76 2000
344.41′041—dc21

                                00-034258

For further information on
Blackwell Science, visit our website
www.blackwell-science.com

Contents

List of figures

Explanatory diagrams and illustrations are included in the handbook as below:

Chapter 6

Chapter 7

Chapter 8

Chapter 9

Chapter 10

Preface

With the benefit of hindsight it can be said that the year 1990 was a crucial year in the NHS. It marked the start of the greatest changes seen in primary medical care since the beginning of the NHS in 1946.

Two significant factors leading to these dramatic changes lay in the alteration of the financial and administrative operation of primary care. First there was fund-holding in its various guises, later to be replaced by the formation of primary care groups and trusts. The second was the Citizen's Charter with its underlying requirements of open government and 'value for money' in all public spending. These administrative requirements have now developed into the complex arrangements of the Health Ombudsman and the Commission for Health Improvement. Additionally, a variety of quality systems are being imposed throughout all sectors of the NHS, including the primary care sector.

Quite apart from the clinical consequences of these changes, they have resulted in medical general practices being brought within the same legal framework as any other professional partnership such as lawyers, accountants, etc. The only difference is that the financial arrangements for doctors are dissimilar to the others.

Every doctor in general practice must now take note of the legal rights of different classes of people such as:

- patients
- employees
- visitors to the surgery
- suppliers of goods and services to the practice
- anyone who is the subject of information recorded in the practice

to ensure that these rights are not infringed in any way. Additionally, doctors must have a general knowledge of their own rights and how to seek redress when they are wronged.

All of these matters affecting the business side of the practice are in addition to the established duties and responsibilities of the doctor when acting in a professional capacity.

Following the 1997 general election, the new government set about introducing the laws needed to bring into effect the promises made in its political manifesto. From the election to the present time (May 2000) over two dozen acts, regulations, etc. have been enacted which have affected all businesses. Some matters are quite minor, but others such as the Employment Relations Act 1999 and the Data Protection Act 1998 will cause significant changes in the way that all businesses are managed. Other laws such as the Health Act 1999 bring about additional changes to the whole of the health sector, including general practices. A glance at Appendix A will show the range of this legislation, all of which is described in the handbook.

A practical problem facing any practice manager is that there are few, if any, textbooks containing the whole range of the laws affecting medical general practices. Particular law books will be found that deal with specific aspects of the law but the range encompassed is often too narrow for the practice manager's needs. This makes it difficult to obtain an overall view of the laws unless the reader has access to a comprehensive law library.

The author is able to draw on over ten years experience in lecturing to practice managers in the niceties of the law insofar as it affects their day-to-day duties. This handbook is the result of that experience and owes a good deal to the comments from the managers who were students. They advised me about the relative importance of different areas of the law to their daily work and this advice was gratefully accepted.

All aspects of law relevant to a general practice are covered, except for:

- financial matters, including taxation, and
- matters strictly within the professional purview of clinicians

as both of these areas of law warrant totally separate treatment.

The handbook is designed to provide a practical guide to the law in easily understandable language and does not pretend to be a formal law textbook. Descriptive illustrations are used to highlight the main features of the laws being described, but these figures do not include the finer legal details that would make them too cumbersome for easy understanding.

The basic legal points are expanded by the introduction of reports of cases heard by the courts; likewise these reports are simplified to highlight the main points. They are found in the text as shown in the case of *Hammond* below. That is to say, they are indented from the main text, the main points of the case are emphasised with italics and the name and date is given. The full reference of each case quoted is shown in Appendix A.

Managers are strongly urged to keep formal, accurate records of all matters that could form the basis of a future dispute. The contents list of the handbook shows which areas of activity are most likely to be vulnerable. The records should be kept for at least five years and those involving contentious matters for even longer: for instance, employer's liability insurance certificates must now be kept for 40 years. The problem concerning the retention of records was shown in a recent case.

> A health authority had a policy of destroying patients' X-rays after three years, even those of patients known to be contemplating legal action. The judge said that *this practice was wholly unacceptable as it showed a cavalier disregard for the rights of patients to have access to their records.*
>
> Hammond *v.* West Lancashire Health Authority (1998)

Please note that in law (the Interpretation Act 1978) when the terms 'he', 'him' and 'his' are used, they must be taken to read 'he or she', 'him or her', 'his or hers'.

For the convenience of expression, and no other reason, the same convention has been followed in this handbook.

If the reader requires further information about any particular topic in the handbook, the sources of the materials used together with the locations of other sources of information are shown in the appendices. They should provide a suitable starting point for further research work when used together with conventional law books.

Practice managers are not usually trained lawyers, but they should be able to find out where and how the law affects the practice. In appropriate cases formal legal advice should be sought, and the diligent manager should be able to provide the lawyer with all the records covering the event that he needs (as mentioned above).

Alexander Pope said 'A little learning is a dang'rous thing.' and this is particularly true in matters of the law. This handbook is only intended to give you a 'little learning' nonetheless it is enough for you to identify problems and know when you should seek legal help.

Arthur Brown
May 2000

Part I
An Overview of the Law

- Introduction to the law and its sources
- Legal liability and what it means in different circumstances
- Public law and private law

Chapter 1
Introduction to the Law

Basic principles of the law

The laws of England and Wales come from a variety of origins; Scottish law is quite different. Laws are necessary because they provide the framework of our social conduct. Without laws, everyone could 'do their own thing', and modern society would be impossible. Laws cover many aspects of conduct, several of which will be relevant in the context of a medical general practice.

Perhaps surprisingly some laws have an ancient history. For instance, part of the law on murder is over 1000 years old being part of what is called English common law. However, other parts of the common law are much more recent in their origin.

Parliament makes most modern law by the creation of Acts of Parliament or statutes as they are also called. In recent times important laws have originated in the European Union, being authorised by the European Communities Act 1972. Examples exist in the health and safety and sex discrimination laws.

Figure 1.1 shows the sources of law in England and Wales concerning those areas of law most likely to affect a medical general practice. Even this simplified illustration shows how complicated the law can be and in consequence how difficult it is to interpret it correctly. There are many more aspects of both public and private laws than are shown in the diagram. Those illustrated are probably the most likely to affect a practice manager.

Legal liability

Sometimes, what people think of as being a 'wrong' is not a legal wrong, so some bad or unjust actions cannot be taken to a court of law for settlement. Even some of the 'rights' that people claim to have are not recognised by the law, and, similarly, they can not be taken to the courts for enforcement.

An example of this confusion occurred in cases of 'stalking' – when someone, usually a man, has followed and harassed another person, usually a woman. Until 1997 the law gave no protection to the victim but with the passing of a new statute (the Protection from Harassment Act 1997) victims can seek protection from the courts. Another example relates to privacy as many people feel that they have a 'right' to personal privacy. However, no privacy law exists, so when an individual's privacy is invaded, no protection is provided by the law. However if the breach of privacy involves breaking a particular law, such as the Data Protection Act or the common law duty of confidentiality, then the law is available for use.

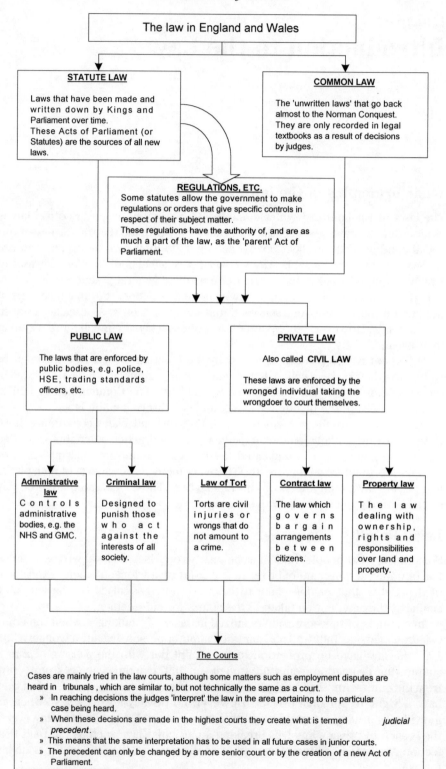

Figure 1.1   The law in England and Wales

To know the law about any particular topic the lawyer has to be aware of:

- The relevant statutes
- Any regulations made under the statutes
- Any common law principles that apply
- The details of any cases forming a judicial precedent that are applicable

Figure 1.2   To know the law

The principle of legal liability is illustrated in Figure 1.3. There are different forms of legal liability; those most important to the practice are shown in Figure 1.4.

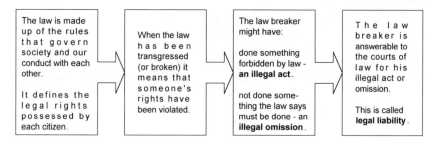

The law is made up of the rules that govern society and our conduct with each other.

It defines the legal rights possessed by each citizen.

When the law has been transgressed (or broken) it means that someone's rights have been violated.

The law breaker might have:

done something forbidden by law - **an illegal act**.

not done something the law says must be done - an **illegal omission**.

The law breaker is answerable to the courts of law for his illegal act or omission.

This is called **legal liability**.

Figure 1.3   Legal liability

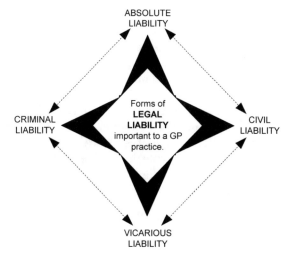

ABSOLUTE LIABILITY

CRIMINAL LIABILITY

Forms of **LEGAL LIABILITY** important to a GP practice.

CIVIL LIABILITY

VICARIOUS LIABILITY

Figure 1.4   Forms of legal liability

Criminal liability

This happens when a person has broken the criminal law in some way – by exceeding the speed limit or at the other extreme by murdering someone. The purpose of the law is to punish the wrongdoer in some way, perhaps by a fine or imprisonment. The punishment aims to dissuade others from committing the same crime.

Civil liability

This happens when the civil law has been broken, for example, by carelessly injuring someone, not keeping to the terms of a contract, etc.

The purpose of the law is to give the victim redress by awarding compensation or perhaps by ordering the wrongdoer to right the wrong in some way.

Absolute liability

The principles of absolute liability and vicarious liability are applicable to both criminal and civil laws.

Absolute liability means that in some cases, irrespective of whether or not they were deliberate or reckless (crime), or negligent (tort), the person responsible is fully accountable to the law. The law places a duty on the person concerned to ensure that particular forms of conduct do not occur.

An example of absolute liability affecting a practice is the duty of the employer to ensure the safety of employees at their place of work. Another example lies in the laws of consumer protection that define the terms of strict liability when a defective product causes damage or injury to the customer or his property.

Some laws refer to *strict liability* which is technically different, but for our purposes can be considered the same as absolute liability.

Vicarious liability

Vicarious liability occurs in both criminal and civil law. It is the responsibility that employers have for the acts or omissions of employees done *in the course of employment*. The principle is illustrated in Figure 1.5.

The principle is illustrated in the following terms. If, for example, an employed driver drives negligently and injures another person, then the employer will be vicariously liable. However, if another person employed as a clerk drives the company car without permission, and injures a third party, then the employer is probably *not* liable. In the second example the driving is being performed outside the scope of the clerk's employment. The 'third party' involved in vicarious liability could be another employee, as in the following case.

> A notorious practical joker played a prank on another employee that resulted in injury. *As the employer knew the history of these pranks but had taken no steps to stop them, he was, in consequence, vicariously liable.*
>
> Hudson *v.* Ridge Manufacturing Co Ltd. (1957)

Within the practice, the doctor partners will have vicarious liability for the actions of all employees including the practice manager. Therefore, if during his work the practice manager is negligent and causes injury to a patient, the doctor will be vicariously liable.

If damages are awarded against an employer as a result of his vicarious liability, he can sue the employee to recover the money paid. In reality this would be

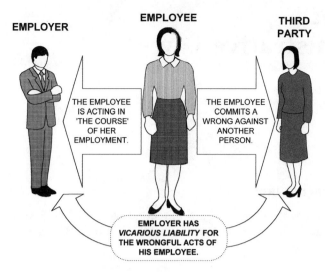

Figure 1.5   Vicarious liability

unusual because employers will normally have insurance cover against such eventualities.

Although the principle of the law is simple, the practicality is very complicated because there is a wide range of cases setting various judicial precedents. As a consequence, in any other than the most simple cases, legal advice should be sought as soon as practicable.

Chapter 2
Administrative Law

Administrative law

Administrative law is that area of law that controls official bodies. Of interest to practice managers are the laws that control the National Health Service and the medical profession.

The National Health Service

The beginnings of the National Health Service go back to the publication of the Beveridge Report in 1942 – the middle of World War II. The report related to the provision of all forms of social security, including health care, in post-war Britain. It envisaged that all citizens would have access to comprehensive medical care both at home and in hospital. The phrase used to explain the aim was 'from the cradle to the grave'.

The wartime coalition government accepted the report in principle. This meant that the first post-war government irrespective of political party would implement its provisions. In 1945 a Labour government took office and Aneurin (Nye) Bevan became Minister of Health with the responsibility of inaugurating the new service.

The initiating statute, the National Health Service Act 1946, authorised the taking over of all hospitals, convalescent homes, etc. and consultants were offered contracts as salaried employees of the National Health Service. General practitioners who provided family doctor services were encouraged to sign contracts with the NHS. These contracts allowed them to remain independently self-employed, receiving fees from the NHS for services rendered. GPs still retain this independent contractor status.

During the ensuing 30 years or so the laws governing the NHS were amended by new statutes and an abundance of regulations made under the authority of the 1946 Act, etc. In 1977 the National Health Service Act 1977 was enacted which is a consolidating Act. This means that it gathers all the existing NHS law and presents it logically in a single statute. The 1977 Act, although subsequently altered and added to, remains the governing statute of the NHS. It authorises the existence of the service, defines its duties and places legal limits on the activities of its employees and agents.

Between 1977 and 1997 other statutes have been enacted and like the 1977 Act they have been amended in various ways. The main statutes that are currently (May 2000) in being concerning the NHS are listed on the next page.

In 1997 after the general election the new Labour government announced that the National Health Service would be restructured to meet the changing needs of society. The details of the proposed restructuring were announced in a White Paper titled *The New NHS: Modern, Dependable*, dated December 1997. During 1998 and 1999 further policy and discussion papers amplifying the reorganisation strategy were published by the Department of Health. Each paper covers a different aspect of the reorganisation of the NHS, including the following topics:

- the patient's role
- the quality of the workforce
- the quality of the service provided
- partnership with local authority social services
- quality of care and clinical excellence
- fraud.

Further legislation was enacted to give legal authority to the proposals, but note that in the 1997 White Paper it was said:

'This White Paper ... forms the basis for a ten year programme to renew and improve the NHS through evolutionary change rather than organisational upheaval'.

Therefore not all the reorganisation proposals will be implemented in the short term.

The current (May 2000) major statutes governing the NHS are:

- National Health Service Act 1977 (as amended)
- Health Services Act 1980
- National Health Service and Community Care Act 1990
- Health Service Commissioners Act 1993
- Health Authorities Act 1995
- National Health Service (Primary Care) Act 1997
- Health Act 1999

As well as the foregoing, other statutes also refer to NHS matters when their subject matter affects the service in some way or other. In addition there are many regulations made under the authority of these Acts that provide the detailed rules for implementing their provisions.

Following the introduction of the Scottish Parliament and the Welsh Assembly there are variations in the administration of the NHS in Scotland and Wales when compared with England. However, the main health care principles are unaltered.

To try to describe the multitude of legal provisions concerning the NHS is beyond the scope of this handbook. However, following are subheadings of some of the bodies within the service that affect general practices, together with a very brief résumé of the governing legal principles in each instance.

The Secretary of State for Health

The Secretary of State for Health, usually referred to as the Health Secretary is in control of the Health Service and is answerable to Parliament for its efficient functioning. His duties, as laid down in statute, comprise the promotion of a comprehensive health service designed to secure improvement:

- in the physical and mental health of people
- in the prevention, diagnosis and treatment of illness, and
- in the effective provision of health services.

Health services shall be provided free of charge except in cases where charges are permitted by law. The services to be provided are:

- hospital accommodation
- the accommodation needed for other services provided
- medical, dental, nursing and ambulance services
- facilities for the care of expectant and nursing mothers and young children
- facilities for the prevention of illness, the care of persons suffering from illness and the aftercare of persons who have suffered from illness
- any other services required for the diagnosis and treatment of illness.

Besides the above list the Health Secretary must also:

- provide for the medical inspection of pupils at LEA, etc. schools and for the medical treatment of such pupils
- arrange for the giving of advice on contraception, the medical examination of persons seeking advice on contraception, the treatment of such persons and the supply of contraceptive substances and appliances
- provide for the dental inspection of pupils at LEA, etc. schools, for the dental treatment of such pupils and for their education in dental health.

The Health Secretary may also:

- provide invalid carriages for disabled persons and on request may provide another vehicle
- arrange to provide accommodation and treatment outside Great Britain for persons suffering from respiratory tuberculosis
- provide a microbiological service, which may include the provision of laboratories, for the control of the spread of infectious diseases
- arrange research into any matters relating to the cause, prevention, diagnosis or treatment of illness.

Administration of the National Health Service

The responsibilities for ensuring that the duties of the Health Secretary are implemented are devolved to various administrative bodies within the NHS, as shown in Figure 2.1.

The NHS Executive operates through regional offices, controlling Health Authorities, who in turn supervise and administer Primary Care Groups within which general practices will operate.

National Health Service Executive

The Executive is the body responsible for administering the policies decided by the Secretary of State for Health. It undertakes the strategic management of the Service, and its duties include:

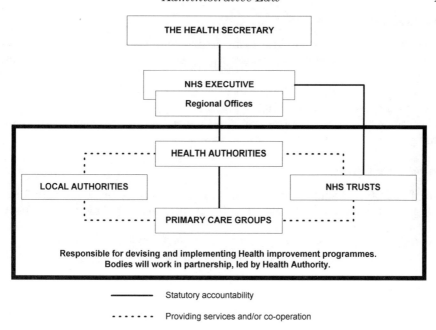

Figure 2.1 NHS administration

- strategic planning
- policy development
- responsibility for overseeing NHS Trusts
- research
- resource allocation to Health Authorities
- pay and staffing policies for the National Health Service
- public health matters.

Health Authorities

Health Authorities act as the links between primary care groups and the NHS Executive providing strategic management at a local level. Their duties include:

- assessing the health needs of the population of their area
- taking the lead in developing a Health Improvement Programme in co-operation with NHS bodies and local authorities
- deciding the range and location of health care services for the population of their area
- determining the local quality and efficiency standards
- monitoring primary care groups to
  - support their development
  - supervise the allocation of resources
  - ensure that services are provided efficiently.

Primary Care Groups

A number of pilot schemes are being implemented and with the experience gained all GPs and community nurses will eventually belong to a Primary Care Group (PCG). Each PCG will develop around natural communities, taking account of the boundaries affecting local social services. Such a group is likely to cater for the needs of about 100,000 patients.

There will be a range of forms that PCGs may take, and some will develop into Primary Care Trusts (PCT). The forms will be:

Primary Care Groups

(1)   The PCG will support the Health Authority in arranging health care for its patient population. It will act in an advisory capacity to the Health Authority.
(2)   The PCG will accept responsibility for managing the healthcare budget in its own area. It will become a formal part of the Health Authority.

Primary Care Trusts

(3)   The PCG acquires Trust status and becomes established as an independent body. It is accountable to the Health Authority for arranging health care.
(4)   As (3) but the PCT accepts responsibility for providing community health services for its patient population.

As new groups emerge they will adopt whichever of the four forms is most suitable to their operation.

The duties of all Primary Care Groups include:

- contributing to the local Health Improvement Programme
- promoting the health of the local population
- in cooperation with NHS Trusts
  o   commissioning health services as appropriate
  o   monitoring the standards of the services provided
- developing primary health care by joint working across practices and assuring that quality standards are met
- integrating primary and community health care by improving cooperative working with local authority social services departments.

Although every GP practising in the NHS will be associated with a Primary Care Group, there is no specified legal form that the group must take. The National Association of Primary Care (NAPC) recommends that each group should have a constitution to define the fundamental aspects of the group's arrangements. The points covered by such a constitution will be similar to those mentioned for a deed of partnership (as described in Figure 5.2, page 50). It will be subject to the variations needed to deal with the greater numbers involved and the additional flexibility to ensure the co-operation of different practices.

Primary Care Trusts will be created by statute. In each case an Order will be made such as the Nonsuch Primary Care Trust (Establishment) Order 2000. This Order will give the Trust legal status, making it a corporate body recognisable in law. The Order will contain details of such matters as:

- the name of the Trust
- the area it is established to cover
- the number and functions of the Trust's officers and members
- the date of its operation, and
- arrangements to cover the Trust's transition to full independent operation.

One significant legal difference between a Trust and a Group that will affect managers is that a Trust is a corporate body. Consequently it will be able to take independent action such as the direct employment of staff. In contrast, in a Group each practice will have as much or as little autonomy as the group members wish to retain. Thus they will be able to employ their own staff.

A significant point about the reorganisation of primary care will be that the new arrangements will facilitate the aim of ensuring that the principles of clinical governance permeate throughout the whole NHS. Part of this will be achieved by putting responsibility on the boards of the Groups or Trusts to ensure that all the constituent practices meet the defined requirements of clinical governance.

General medical services

General (or personal) medical services are provided by the individual general practitioners and their staff. They are outlined in the 1977 Act and described in detail in the General Medical Services Regulations 1992 (as amended). All general practices should have a copy of these Regulations available for consultation.

The services to be provided include the following:

- all necessary and appropriate personal medical services of the type usually provided by general medical practitioners
- examining, giving advice and/or treatment to women on contraception matters and providing contraceptive substances and appliances to them
- the provision by doctors of child health surveillance services and minor surgery services.

Community health services

Community health services are provided for people anywhere in the community. They include health visiting, school nursing, etc. and they involve workers such as district nurses, community psychiatric nurses, physiotherapists, chiropodists and other specialised health professionals.

Local medical committee

This is a statutory committee representing all the GPs in the area of a Health Authority. As a matter of law it must be consulted by the Health Authority when it is considering matters concerning GPs. The committee will play an important part regarding the new structural arrangements.

National Health Service Trusts

The Health Secretary has the power to establish bodies known as National Health Service Trusts for the purposes of:

- assuming responsibility for the ownership and management of hospitals or other establishments or facilities
- providing and managing hospitals or other establishments or facilities.

Every NHS Trust is an independent body corporate having a board of directors consisting of a chairman, executive and non-executive directors (directors who are not employees of the Trust). Each Trust has the duties and authority conferred on it by the Health Secretary. The functions can include anything that is appropriate concerning the services provided by the Trust for one or more Health Authorities.

They will become closely involved in meeting the new standards of quality and efficiency now required. They will also develop arrangements to meet the requirements of clinical governance.

NHS Trusts are legally accountable to Health Authorities and Primary Care Groups concerning the quality and efficiency of the services that they deliver. They also have a statutory duty to cooperate with Primary Care Groups and local authorities in developing Health Improvement Programmes under the leadership of the Health Authority. This requirement is a departure from the previous practice of Trusts acting independently and not sharing information with other health professionals.

It is expected that some Primary Care Groups will, in time, become NHS Trusts, operating as independent bodies corporate, and having like accountability for the services that they provide.

Quality of health treatment

'The new NHS will have quality at its heart. Without it there is unfairness. Every patient who is treated in the NHS wants to know that they can rely on receiving high quality care when they need it. Every part of the NHS, and everyone who works in it, should take responsibility for working to improve quality. This must be quality in its broadest sense: doing the right things, at the right time, for the right people, and doing them right – first time. And it must be the quality of the patient's experience as well as the clinical result – quality measured in terms of prompt access, good relationships and efficient administration.'

White Paper: *The New NHS*, December 1997

Apart from any party political considerations, the reorganisation of the NHS has been influenced by other factors that have generated public disquiet. The most significant factors seem to have been:

- accusations that the standard of treatment and the provision of medication varies from one part of the country to another
- long delays in access to treatment whilst private patients do not have similar delays
- lapses in the expected standards of treatment and care that have led to several high profile cases involving alleged incompetence by doctors sometimes associated with refusal to disclose information to the victims.

All of these factors disclose that the NHS lacks national standards and the means of ensuring that staff implement any such standards.

An additional point of importance is that in the long run poor standards are almost invariably more expensive as:

- patients return for further treatment if the initial treatment is inept and unsuccessful
- administrative costs rise in dealing with long waiting lists coupled with the concomitant complaints
- the costs and damages have to be paid following successful legal actions for negligence and other torts.

It is unsurprising therefore that the government has stated its intention of 'putting quality at the top of the NHS agenda'.

The new quality system

To implement the new system, new statutory bodies have been created and, additionally, the Health Act 1999 states:

'It is the duty of each Health Authority, Primary Care Trust and NHS Trust to put and keep in place arrangements for the purpose of monitoring and improving the quality of health care which it provides to individuals.'

The Health Authority supervising a particular PCG will be responsible for ensuring that it provides an appropriate quality of service.

Figure 2.2 shows the main features of the clinical quality system.

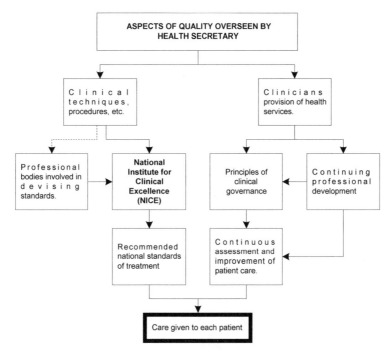

Figure 2.2   Quality overseen by government

National Institute for Clinical Excellence (NICE)

This statutory body, in cooperation with other professional bodies, will produce, gather and disseminate information for health professionals regarding:

- clinical guidelines based on relevant evidence of 'clinical and cost-effectiveness', and
- clinical audit methodologies and information on good practice.

The working of NICE is described by the government as follows:

> '...the Government will [help] to clarify ... which treatments work best for which patients and those which do not.... Clear, authoritative, guidance on clinical and cost-effectiveness will be offered to front line clinicians....'

Insofar as all clinicians (the health professionals) are concerned, two aspects of the quality system have a direct impact on each individual. Each clinician is expected to provide treatment according to the principles of clinical governance and will be expected to undertake continuous professional development.

Clinical governance

The key components of clinical governance are as follows.

- A comprehensive programme of quality improvement activity (e.g. clinical audit) and processes for monitoring clinical care using effective information and clinical record systems.
- Clear policies aimed at managing risk, including procedures that support professional staff in identifying and tackling poor performance.
- Clear lines of responsibility and accountability for the overall quality of clinical care.

These principles are mainly directed at doctors in hospitals, however Primary Care Trusts will be expected, as part of their adherence to clinical governance, to

- ensure that proper processes exist to assure and improve the quality of the clinical services they provide
- nominate a single person to lead on the development of clinical governance and take responsibility for ensuring that these arrangements are in place
- publish annual reports on
  - o what they are doing to improve and assure quality, including self-assessment of progress in implementing local clinical governance
  - o how these systems meet national quality standards
  - o the Trust's future plans for improving the quality of services.

Clinical governance and Primary Care Groups

Primary Care Groups and individual health professionals are expected to develop quality services and to demonstrate that they are so doing by way of suitable reporting arrangements. All health professionals are expected to make use of clinical governance principles to underpin local arrangements for quality assurance and development developed by Health Authorities in conjunction with Primary Care Groups.

Continuous professional development

Continuous professional development is described as:

'A process of lifelong learning for all individuals and teams which meets the needs of patients and delivers the health outcomes and healthcare priorities of the NHS and which enables professionals to expand and fulfil their potential.'

To be effective, clinical governance must be supported by the personal development of the professional expertise of all clinicians. Without such development it will be impossible to attain and maintain the quality standards that are required by clinical governance principles.

Monitoring quality standards

All quality systems must be subjected to a monitoring process (illustrated in Figure 2.3) to ensure that the required standards are maintained. In the NHS health care standards are maintained by:

- reviewing the principles to be followed
- assessing the performance of the providers of health services, and
- surveying the satisfaction levels of recipients (the patients).

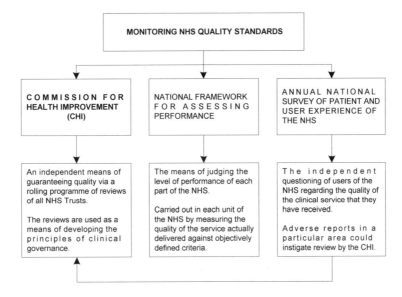

Figure 2.3 Monitoring NHS quality standards

Commission for Health Improvement (CHI)

This new statutory body has the duty of supporting and overseeing NHS activity to assure and improve clinical quality. Its core functions are to:

- provide national leadership to develop and disseminate clinical governance principles

- independently scrutinise local clinical governance arrangements to support, promote and deliver high quality services, through a rolling programme of local reviews of service providers
- undertake a programme of service reviews to monitor national implementation of national service frameworks and review progress locally on implementation of these frameworks and NICE guidance,
- help the NHS identify and tackle serious or persistent clinical problems (the Commission will have the capacity for rapid investigation and intervention to help put these right)
- increasingly take on responsibility over time for overseeing and assisting with external incident inquiries.

Although the Commission is principally concerned with clinical issues, it is also empowered to become involved in management issues where they lie behind clinical problems.

The Commission may be involved with primary care as shown in Figure 2.4.

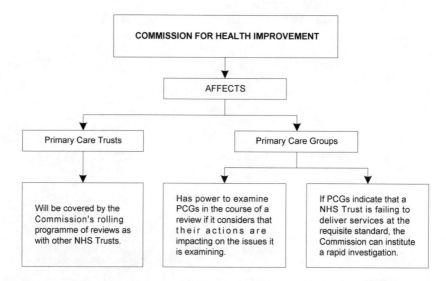

Figure 2.4   CHI and primary care

National framework for assessing performance

The performance framework is designed to provide a balanced view of the performance of NHS organisations by concentrating on six areas:

- health improvement
- fair access to services
- effective delivery of appropriate healthcare
- efficiency
- patient and carer experience
- health outcomes of NHS care.

Each of the above areas has detailed subheadings that can be used to make assessments. It is intended that the framework, to be developed over a period of ten years, will provide the defined standards expected from all parts of the NHS.

The performance framework is to be used by the Commission for Health Improvement when reviewing the efficiency of NHS Trusts. It might also be used when a Primary Care Group is making a service agreement with a particular NHS Trust.

The performance framework also provides a basis for publishing information about the results achieved by each part of the NHS.

Annual national survey of patient and user experience of the NHS

This is an innovation intended to gain opinions from the users of the NHS. A professional surveying organisation will survey patients about such matters as:

- their views on the efficiency of the medical and technical aspects of their care
- the privacy and dignity of their care, especially with regard to mixed sex accommodation in hospital
- the courtesy and helpfulness of staff.

A sample of views will be taken in each health authority area to give a comprehensive national view from a large number of patients. Results, focusing on local performances will be published so that people can assess the progress that their local services are making over time.

Complaints in general practices

The Citizen's Charter, which was introduced in 1991, laid down the general principles of service required from public service organisations together with the guarantees and redresses that victims of poor service could expect. The same principles were extended to the NHS because of the rights defined in the Patient's Charter.

Since April 1996 all GPs have been required by their terms of service to:

- devise and operate a procedure within the practice for dealing with complaints
- cooperate with the investigation of any complaints by a Health Authority.

If complaints cannot be satisfactorily resolved by the practice then the matter can be referred to the appropriate Health Authority.

If the complainant is still dissatisfied after the NHS complaints procedure has been exhausted, the matter might be referred to the Health Service Commissioner. The Commissioner also has responsibility for overseeing the correct operation of complaints procedures.

A new NHS Charter is to be published that will describe the standards of treatment and care to be expected from the NHS together with the responsibilities of patients.

Community Health Councils

These statutory bodies represent the interests of the public in the operations of the NHS locally. Councils act as a public voice in matters concerning health care and the provision of services in their area. They also give advice to patients on how they may make complaints about the services that are provided. To perform their functions they are entitled, by law, to the following:

- to receive appropriate information from the 'their' NHS authorities
- to send observers to health authority meetings
- to have access to certain NHS premises
- to be consulted in matters of strategic planning.

The Association of Community Health Councils (ACHC) publishes an annual report airing matters of national concern. In past reports ACHC has voiced strong criticisms about the obstructions put in the way of patients who wish to exercise their legal right to examine their health records.

Health Service Commissioner

The National Health Service Act 1977 instituted the office of Health Ombudsman to examine complaints about the Health Service for which no other remedy existed. In 1996 the remit was extended to include complaints made about matters in community health services. The Commissioner does not investigate complaints concerning private medical treatment. An outline of the system is shown in Figure 2.5.

The Commissioner will not seek to interfere with NHS decisions that appear to have been made properly. If such decisions are to be challenged then it must be done by way of judicial review. See page 24.

If the complaint is found to be justified the Commissioner will seek a remedy for the complainant. This could take the form of:

- an apology
- getting an improper decision changed
- repayment of any unnecessary expense incurred
- a call for changes to ensure that the matter does not recur.

The Commissioner does not award damages. If compensation is sought, the complainant must pursue the matter through the civil courts.

In the Commissioner's annual report published in June 1998 some GPs were strongly criticised. They had removed patients from their lists merely because they had made a complaint and in addition the patients were not given any reasons for the removal. The Commissioner made clear his intentions when he said:

> 'I have no powers of compulsion, but I may in future decide to name family doctors who respond (by failing to accept my findings when complaints are upheld)'.

To the present, the Commissioner has not named any of the doctors that he has criticised, but in November 1999 the first health professional was criticised adversely for the poor treatment of a patient. Following a lengthy investigation by dental experts the NHS Ombudsman recommended that the dentist concerned should revise his dental knowledge and personally apologise to the aggrieved patient. The dentist refused so to do and accordingly a national press release was issued giving the dentist's name, address and particulars of the complaint as proven (*The Times* 25/11/1999).

> **HEALTH SERVICE COMMISSIONER**

Can investigate a health authority, NHS trust, Primary Care Trust or any community health service in regard to:

» a fault in the provision of a service
» a failure to provide a service which there is a duty to provide
» maladministration
» the care and treatment provided by a doctor, nurse or other trained professional
» other complaints about GPs, dentists, pharmacists, opticians giving a local NHS service
» failing to provide information that the complainant has a right to examine -
  e.g. details of local services provided, the standards set and/or achieved, details of important decisions or proposals concerning the National Health Service.

> ### *PROVIDING*

The aggrieved person has exhausted the local complaints procedures or if the procedures are unreasonably delayed.

> ### *AND ALSO*

The aggrieved person does NOT have:

» a right of appeal or review to a tribunal regarding the complaint
» a right to a remedy in a court of law, in respect of the complaint.

(The Commissioner has discretion to hear such cases if he is satisfied that it would be unreasonable for the aggrieved person to have resorted to the action.)

Complaints may be made:
» by any person or organisation except government or local government bodies.
They must be:
» in writing by the complainant,
» made within a year of the matter complained of being known.

Reports.

After conducting an investigation the Commissioner will send a report of his findings to:

» the person who made the complaint,
» any MP who assisted in making the complaint,
» the health authority in question,
» any person who is alleged to have been involved in the action complained of,
» the Health Secretary if the complaint is against a health authority.

> **The Commissioner:**
>
> » is authorised to obtain information from such persons and in such a manner, and make such inquiries as he thinks fit,
> » has the same powers as a High Court Judge to require the attendance of witnesses and the production of documents.

Figure 2.5   Health Service Commissioner

This is obviously in line with the drive to bring greater transparency and accountability to all parts of the National Health Service. Further, it has been reported that the government is looking at the operation of Ombudsman schemes to improve the service provided for complainants.

Similar arrangements exist in Scotland and Wales which both have their own NHS Commissioners.

The medical profession

The medical profession is controlled by statute, the Medical Act 1983 that defines the principles of the training, discipline and professional conduct of doctors. Powers from the Act are delegated to the General Medical Council (GMC) and that body exercises control over and 'polices' the profession.

The Council consists of members elected by the medical profession, academics appointed from universities and lay members nominated by the Privy Council. It functions to serve professional interests but must always consider public interests as well.

Most of the work of the GMC is carried out through committees, each having a specific area of responsibility. Some of the committees receive their powers from the law, although they do not have the status of courts. For example, a newspaper can report details and speculations relating to disciplinary proceedings that would be forbidden if the matter was a legal proceeding in a court of law.

Figure 2.6 shows the statutory committees of the GMC, and a brief description of the matters dealt with by each of them. There are in addition several other committees dealing with particular aspects of the GMC's work.

The Council is probably best known for its disciplinary procedures which sometimes result in doctors being 'struck off' or being suspended for 'serious professional misconduct'. Serious professional misconduct includes the following.

- Neglect or disregard of responsibilities in the care and treatment of patients.
- Improper delegation of duties to nurses or others.
- Abuse of privileges, such as
  o issuing of false certificates when patients are not seen or not sick;
  o signing documents or making out reports that are inaccurate;
  o prescribing drugs of dependence such as opiates, hypnotics and amphetamines, except in the course of bona fide treatment;
  o questionable self-prescribing or prescribing for one's own family.
- Abuse of professional confidence, such as discussing or giving information on a patient's personal or medical history to others.
- Undue influence on patients, to gain a financial or other advantage.
- Sexual or emotional relationships with patients, or members of their families.
- Personal misbehaviour highlighted by convictions for indecent or violent behaviour.
- Convictions for drunkenness or driving when under the influence of alcohol or drugs.
- Dishonesty and improper financial arrangements.
- Improper advertising.

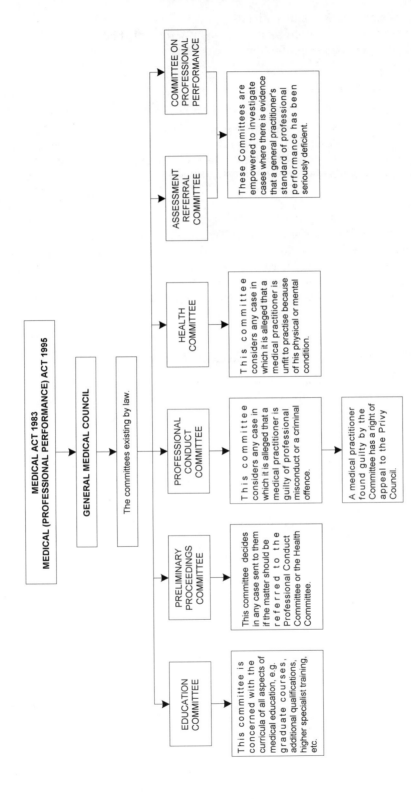

Figure 2.6 GMC statutory committees

- Canvassing and poaching patients.
- Disparagement of professional colleagues through blatant criticism to a patient, the public or professional colleagues.

Even though a GMC disciplinary tribunal is not itself a court of law, its decisions will be upheld by the courts of law. For instance, in an example involving the General Dental Council that has similar powers to the GMC regarding dentists:

A dentist was 'struck off' but carried on practising (the patients apparently did not know that he had been struck off). He was taken before the criminal court for gaining a pecuniary (financial) advantage by deception as a result of his activities (see page 147). *He was found guilty and sentenced to imprisonment.*

R *v.* Nimmo (1998)

The GMC has announced that it proposes to reform the disciplinary procedures that presently exist for the professional supervision of GPs. There has recently been much public disquiet about the apparent lack of such supervision and it seems likely that neither the public nor the government will be satisfied with mere tinkering of the existing system. Accordingly, the government might require, by statute if need be, much stricter controls than are at present proposed by the Council.

Judicial supervision of the National Health Service

In any matter of law, High Court Judges are the only interpreters of what the law means in any particular situation. The High Court will examine any decision that is made by a public body to ensure that it has been made in full conformity with the law. This process is called *judicial review.*

The bodies that are subject to review are mostly those created and controlled by statute law. These include government ministers and their departments, bodies like the NHS, Health Authorities, NHS Trusts, and all levels of local government. In each case, both what they do and how they do it can be the subject of a review. Any affected person can seek a judicial review of either the substance of a decision or the form of procedure used in making the decision for the reasons shown in Figure 2.7.

Some examples involving the NHS are as follows:

A District Health Authority refused to fund specific treatment for a child suffering a life threatening illness because the proposed treatment was experimental and was not in the child's best interests. Additionally, the expenditure of over £75,000 would not be an efficient use of the Authority's limited resources. It was said in the Court of Appeal: 'Difficult and agonising judgements have to be made as to how a limited budget is best allocated to maximum advantage of the maximum number of patients'. *In this case the Authority had not exceeded its powers or acted unreasonably in a legal sense, therefore its decision was lawful.*

R *v.* Cambridge District Health Authority, *ex parte* B (1995)

The next case involved a policy decision made by a Health Authority.

A policy was enforced that contradicted the national policy contained in a National Health Service circular and in following its own policy the Authority refused to fund

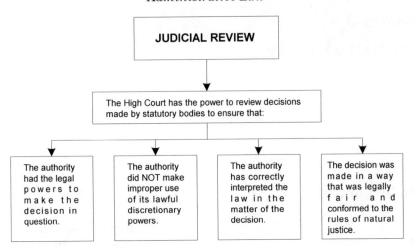

Figure 2.7 Judicial review

expensive drugs needed for a patient's treatment. *The Divisional Court held that the Authority's own policy decision was unlawful and made an order that a new policy conforming to the NHS circular must be formulated and implemented within 14 days.*

R *v*. North Derbyshire Health Authority, *ex parte* Fisher (1997)

Even the Health Secretary must act within the limits of the law.

It was held in the Divisional Court that the publication of a Department of Health Circular (1998/158) which suggested that GPs should not prescribe Viagra on the NHS was in breach of EC Directive 89/105. This Directive set out the requirements of the law in this matter. *The law could not be bypassed and the circular was therefore unlawful.*

R *v*. Secretary of State for Health, *ex parte* Pfizer Ltd. (1999)

Another case involved a dispute between a doctor and a Family Practitioners' Committee (FPC), subsequently called the Family Health Services Authority (FHSA). The Committee had responsibility for managing the contracts of GPs.

The doctor complained that his allowances had been reduced by the FPC and sought judicial review to test the legality of the decision to exclude him from the FPC list. *The High Court agreed to examine the legality of the decision. However, it was stated that if the decision was unlawful he had to sue the FPC for breach of contract by a civil action.*

Roy *v*. Kensington, Chelsea & Westminster FPC (1992)

There are many review cases included in the law reports including a large number relating to questions about when treatment should or should not be given to patients. They are outside the scope of this handbook.

General practices cannot be subject to judicial review as they are not public bodies. It is doubtful if a Primary Care Group would be subject to review, but a Primary Care Trust would certainly be a public body for the purpose of review.

However, the review of any NHS public body could call for evidence from a general practitioner involved in the events being reviewed.

Chapter 3
Criminal Law

Criminal law

There are no formal definitions of crime and criminal law. However, it can be said in practical terms that a crime is an offence against society as a whole, even though there might only be one direct victim, and it is punishable by the State. Criminal law is that area of law that defines crimes and prescribes the maximum punishments that can be imposed on offenders found guilty of committing them.

There are some important points about breaches of the criminal law that a practice manager should be aware of.

- A wrongful act or omission will not amount to a crime unless it is accompanied by a guilty intention: this means that the person concerned intended the consequences of his action. There are exceptions to this rule if the law makes the offence one of 'absolute liability' when it is not necessary to prove the guilty intention.
- The guilty state of mind means that the act was committed deliberately or recklessly and without care about the result of the action. Simply being careless or negligent (this means lacking proper care without intending to cause harm), is generally insufficient to prove a guilty state of mind, although some criminal offences, such as driving without due care and attention are based on the concept of culpable negligence.
- In legal terms, the Queen is said to be the aggrieved person when a crime has been committed, and the prosecution of the offender is undertaken in her name by an official agency. Law reports refer to the Queen as *Regina* or R. for short.
- The accused person is always innocent until proven guilty beyond all reasonable doubt. If there is any doubt, the benefit of it must be given to the accused person.
- An alleged offender is prosecuted in the criminal courts, not sued, and, if found guilty is sentenced to some form of penalty such as imprisonment, community service or a fine.
- The purpose of the punishment is to deter the convicted offender from committing future crimes and to deter others from following the same example. In serious cases, putting the offender in prison stops him from committing new offences whilst he is locked up.

The courts that try criminal cases are, in simplified form, as shown in Figure 3.1.

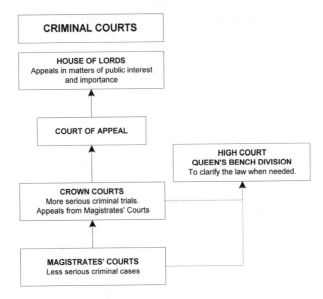

Figure 3.1 The criminal courts

Areas of crime that could affect the practice

In a general practice the sorts of crimes that you are most likely to come across will be amongst the following:

- theft, fraud, damage or assaults
- misuse of drugs
- criminal offences laid down in the Health and Safety at Work Act (see Chapter 6)
- criminal offences laid down in the Data Protection Act (see Chapter 7)
- criminal offences laid down in the Sex Discrimination Act and the Race Relations Act (see Chapter 12).

Criminal offences and general practice

There are three aspects of crime that could affect you as a practice manager:

- the organisation or staff as victims of crime
- staff committing crimes whilst at work
- staff found guilty of crime outside work.

The matter may be reported to the police who will then take all necessary action, or the matter might be dealt with by way of the practice's discipline procedures (see Chapter 13). In practical terms the decision to report to the police will largely depend upon the perceived seriousness of the offence. As a manager you must remember that both the victim and the alleged offender have got rights.

- As far as the victim is concerned you must ascertain if he wants the matter reported to the police. The relationship of trust that should exist between the employee and the employer whom you represent must not be overlooked when dealing with the victim. Sometimes the victim may demand that the matter be reported to the police and in such cases you have no option but to comply.

- As far as the alleged offender is concerned he must be treated fairly and according to the rules of natural justice (see Chapter 13). Note that you are not expected to prove that a crime was committed beyond all reasonable doubt as in the criminal courts. However, you are expected to weigh the evidence and reach a decision that is based on the balance of probabilities.

In some circumstances the alleged crime might be deemed to be gross misconduct by the employee in which case summary dismissal might be warranted (see Chapter 10). However, as a matter of prudence, it is always preferable to go through formal disciplinary proceedings, only reaching a decision after the evidence has been evaluated. If the disciplinary code allows it, the alleged offender might be suspended on pay until the matter is fully investigated and a decision reached.

If an alleged offender is dealt with by disciplinary proceedings, including any appeal procedure and he disagrees with the verdict, he still has the right to complain to an employment tribunal about the matter. The tribunal will pay particular attention to both the forms of the investigation and the punishment awarded to ensure that both were fair.

In the case of an alleged offender who consistently rejects the allegation, he might be able to sue both the complainant and the employer for defamation.

Reporting matters to the police

If the matter is reported to the police or other 'policing' body, then the procedure is straightforward as they will take responsibility for both the investigation and the subsequent disposal. On the other hand if the matter is not reported to the police but it comes to their official attention by some other means, they might still have good reason to investigate.

As a private citizen, apart from some special cases, you do not have to answer questions as a witness even though this is not necessarily a very civic minded action. However, if you are interviewed by the police and you give information that you know to be wrong or misleading, then you will commit a criminal offence. At the least this could be 'obstructing the police in the course of their duty' or more seriously 'perverting the course of justice'.

One of the exceptions when a private citizen has a duty to give information to the police concerns road traffic offences that have been committed, the law states:

> 'It is an offence for any person to fail to provide any information that he is able to give, which could lead to the identification of a driver who has committed a traffic offence, if he is required to do so by the police.' Road Traffic Act 1988, section 172

(This offence does not apply to the owner of the vehicle concerned – there is another offence for an owner failing to provide relevant information.)

Crimes committed by employees outside work

This is another area to be treated carefully. If the crime has a direct relationship to the work that the employee is employed to do, then conviction and sentence in a criminal court might be grounds for disciplinary proceedings. If the crime is quite irrelevant to the nature of the work, then disciplinary proceedings could be construed as victimisation. As far as the penalty is concerned, if it does not impede the employee in carrying out his duties, then it should be an irrelevance to the employer, see Frustration of contract in Chapter 10 (page 151).

Crimes against the National Health Service

For many years the incidence of fraud in the National Health Service has been steadily rising. The reorganisation includes steps that are being taken to try and reduce this form of crime in the NHS.

In December 1998 the document *Countering Fraud in the NHS* was published which describes the creation of a new unit within the NHS Executive titled the Directorate of Counter Fraud Services. The tasks of the Directorate are to have overall responsibility to counter fraud and corruption within:

- family health services
- health authorities
- NHS Trusts.

Examples of frauds that have been detected are given in the document and they include the following that should be known to practice managers.

Fraud committed by patients

- Patients claiming exemptions from prescription charges when they are not in fact exempt.
- Patients falsely claiming travel expenses to out-patient clinics.
- Patients falsely stating that they have lost their prescriptions and obtaining duplicates.
- Patients falsely registering with a number of doctors and obtaining prescriptions from each.

Fraud committed by pharmacists

- Conspiring with a GP and submitting bogus prescriptions for reimbursement.
- Substituting an expensive drug with a cheaper alternative, but claiming payment for the more expensive one.
- Adding items to prescriptions, or altering the amounts of the drugs prescribed to increase payments.
- Fraudulently generating fees for emergency opening.

Fraud committed by doctors:

- Issuing bogus prescriptions for residential home patients.
- Fraudulent claims for night visits.
- Fraudulent claims for mythical patients or treatments.
- Refusing to see patients at the surgery to claim night visit fees.

Fraud involving the procurement of drugs or services

- Accepting gifts as a reward for placing inflated stock orders.
- Colluding with suppliers to produce invoices for goods that are not delivered.
- Misappropriation of supplies.

Fraud committed by staff

- Claims for duty payments and hours worked, with no evidence that the work had been done.
- Forging cheque signatures and submitting false invoices to support reimbursement requests.

Most practice managers are unlikely to come across the sorts of fraud mentioned above, except for prescription fraud in its various forms. The Department of Health claims that at least £150 million per year is lost through prescription fraud that is apparently widespread.

The 1977 Act has been amended to contain two new provisions designed to deal with prescription fraud. The details are complex, but in essence they come down to two procedures:

> Anyone fraudulently failing to pay, or receiving payment towards a NHS charge will be required to pay the original charge plus a penalty charge. If the amount is not paid, a surcharge may be added and the total amount can then be recovered through the court as a civil debt.
>
> Anyone who knowingly makes a false statement, or, tendering a document or information that the person concerned knows to be false, commits a criminal offence.

Health Act 1999, section 39

For technical legal reasons, prosecutions for making a false statement as above are more likely to be successful than a prosecution using the existing law.

Vicarious liability for crime

If an employee commits a crime against a third party during his work then the employer might in some cases be vicariously liable (see page 6).

Generally speaking, most crimes that are committed will be clearly outside the defined duties of the employee, in which case there will be no question of vicarious liability. Some cases, however, could put an employer in jeopardy, most notably the following.

- Cases of sex and race discrimination perpetrated by an employee at work – whether the employer was aware of the matter or not. If the employer, on becoming aware of a complaint, takes active steps to prevent a recurrence, he might have a defence to the vicarious liability claim.
- Crimes, such as fraud, that are closely associated with the work undertaken, can present some problems. If the victim is someone other than the employer and the employee has apparent authority for his actions that enable him to carry out the fraud, then the employer might be vicariously liable.

In all cases such as these, it must first be proved that the crime was committed. It will then be a question of fact for the court to decide whether, or not, it was committed during the course of employment.

Chapter 4
Private or Civil Law

General points

If the law gives one person a *right*, it automatically imposes on all other citizens the duty of observing that right. Anyone who disregards the right may be *sued* in the civil courts by the aggrieved person to seek a *remedy*. The person bringing the action is called the *claimant* (previously known as the *plaintiff*) and the claimed offender is called the *defendant*, as shown in Figure 4.1.

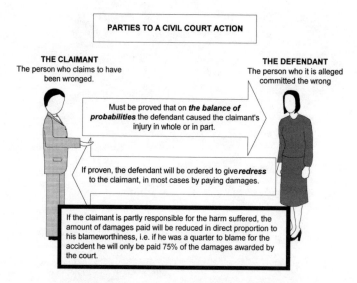

Figure 4.1 Parties to a civil action

The standard of proof in civil proceedings is different to that required in criminal cases being that of the *balance of probabilities*. In a civil case, if the defendant does not appear in court to refute any allegations that the claimant makes, then, on the balance of probabilities, the findings will favour the claimant.

Civil courts

Civil or private cases are heard before civil courts which have a different hierarchy to the criminal courts mentioned in the last chapter. In simple terms they can be shown as in Figure 4.2.

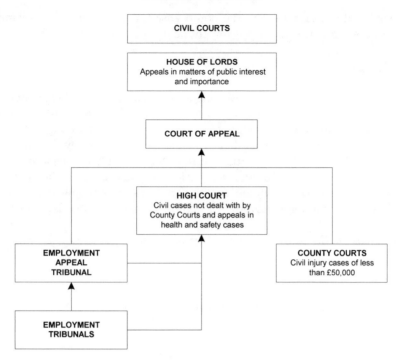

Figure 4.2   The civil courts

Redress through the civil courts

The usual remedies provided by the courts for successful litigants are as follows.

- An *injunction* is a court order requiring a person to stop doing the thing complained of, or not to undertake a particular action in the future. If the injunction is disobeyed the person concerned is considered to be in contempt of court and will be dealt with accordingly.
- Most civil actions are instigated to make the wrongdoer pay *damages* (financial compensation) for the harm that has been caused.
- Damages can be awarded to compensate the plaintiff for the harm or injury that has been suffered. In cases of a financial loss arising from a breach of contract, for instance, the damages are calculated in a way that places the plaintiff in the same position as he would have been had the wrong not been committed. In the end the plaintiff should neither suffer loss nor make a profit.
- In a case when the harm is unquantifiable such as a personal injury, etc., damages for 'pain and suffering' are usually awarded according to a tariff authorised by the High Court. In a case where the plaintiff was partly at fault, the damages when calculated will be apportioned according to the degree of blame. Thus if a plaintiff was awarded £1,000 in damages, but held to be 25% responsible for the accident he would receive £750.
- If the defendant's behaviour was such that the plaintiff suffered more than would be expected in such a case, additional sums of money may be awarded

to signify the disapproval of the court. Discrimination cases are examples where these additional damages might be awarded.

The law of tort

This part of private law covers those obligations, that we must obey, concerning someone else's person and property. Some torts are also crimes, but the law of tort provides the injured party with a personal method of obtaining redress.

Wrongdoers, or *tortfeasors* as they are called, can be sued by the victim and taken to the court to stop them causing further harm or, if harm has already been done, to either repair it or compensate for it. The purpose of tort law is to shift any loss sustained by the victim to the tortfeasor. It also gives victims the opportunity to claim compensation for non-financial harms that have been suffered.

Not all harm suffered by person is a tort that can be pursued in the courts, as illustrated in Figure 4.3.

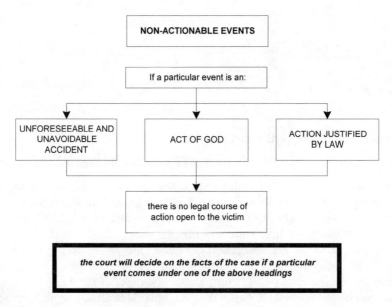

Figure 4.3 Non-actionable events

Negligence

There are many different forms of tort action, some of which will be mentioned in this handbook under the appropriate headings. However, there is a major area of tortious liability that you should be aware of under the general heading of *negligence*.

In law, negligent conduct is not the same as deliberate conduct, because the person offending does not intend the harm that results from his action. In ordinary terms it is failing to look for the consequences of an action that could harm someone. Entire legal textbooks are devoted to the subject of negligence. It follows that its treatment in this handbook is in very superficial terms that are intended to give the practice manager a nodding acquaintance with the topic.

In 1932 legal history was made when the first case of negligence was decided in a court and the following points were made then:

- you must not injure your neighbour
- you must take reasonable care to avoid acts or omissions that you can reasonably foresee would be likely to injure your neighbour
- your neighbour is any person who is so closely and directly affected by your act that you ought reasonably to realise that they are likely to be affected by your acts or omissions.

Donoghue v. Stevenson (1932)

(See also page 223 for more details of this case.)

Since the 1932 decision many cases has been decided which together have refined the definition of negligence in different situations.

The important elements of a negligence action, in the simplest of terms, are shown in Figure 4.4.

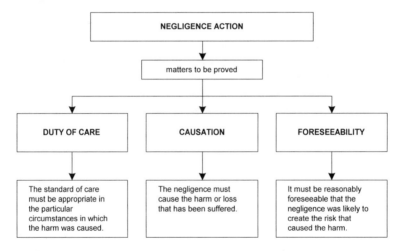

Figure 4.4 Points to prove in a negligence action

The duty of care

The law demands that we must be careful and take due precautions when doing anything that is likely to affect another person. Negligence in law can be:

- the failure to do something which a reasonable person, guided by ordinary considerations, would do, or
- doing what a prudent and reasonable person would not do.

This is called the *duty of care*. If a duty of care exists, then the court must consider what *standard* of care exists. This is discussed below.

Reasonable (or objective) standard of care normally required by law

When a duty of care exists, the standard of that duty is usually called an objective standard. This means that it is the standard that is achieved by most people undertaking the same task. There are, however, varying standards of care to be achieved, as illustrated in Fig. 4.5.

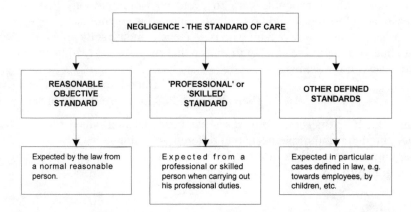

Figure 4.5 The standard of care

For example, say a learner driver, driving as carefully as he can, has an accident that a more experienced driver would have avoided, then he will be liable for any injury or damage that result. This is because he will be judged by the standard of care expected from most drivers, not his own less competent standard.

Professional standard of care

In the case of a professionally trained person such as a doctor or a lawyer, the 'reasonable person' in the definition becomes a 'reasonable person learned in the particular profession'. This standard of conduct is, naturally, higher than for a non-professional person and failure to attain it has been called gross negligence. The factors to be considered by the court in a gross negligence case against a doctor would be:

- indifference to an obvious risk of injury to health
- lack of foresight of the risk
- inattention, or failing to avert a serious risk beyond 'mere inadvertence'.

A practice nurse, acting professionally, would also be judged according to the professional standards that exist in the profession. These standards might not be as rigorous as those demanded from a doctor, but they would be considerably higher than those expected from lay persons.

Note that when doctors, nurses and other professionals are, acting outside their professional remit they are subject to the same standards of behaviour as anyone else.

Particular standards of care

There are other standards of care that apply in particular cases, examples that are relevant in a medical practice are:

- the statutory duty of an employer towards his employees to provide a safe working environment which is laid down in the law
- all reasonable adults have a common law duty of care for the welfare of children who are in their charge
- a lower standard of care is acceptable from a child who cannot be expected to have the same degree of foresight as an adult.

In many negligence cases the legal conflict arises with the question whether or not a duty of care is owed to the claimant, thus many cases defining particular precedents are examined before courts reach decisions. If there is no legal duty of care, there cannot be a case of negligence.

Causation

When a complaint of negligence is made, the claimant must prove that the act or omission was the actual cause of the harm that he suffered but this is sometimes easier claimed than proven. The very complicated principles are simplified in Figure 4.6.

Looking at the right hand side of the diagram explains why, when the claimant has claimed that an illness or condition was caused by discharges from chemical or other works, the claim was unsuccessful. In short the claimant has not been able to prove that *only* the discharges, and nothing else, caused the condition.

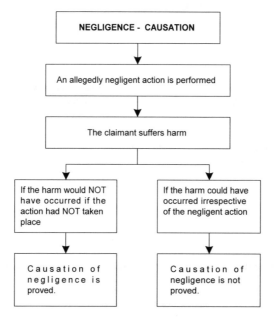

Figure 4.6 Negligence–causation

The defendant in each case would, naturally, seek to show that a number of other factors could have been the cause of the claimant's condition.

Remoteness of damage (foreseeability)

The law says that any risk must be reasonably foreseeable by a normal person. If the risk is too remote to be foreseen, negligence cannot be proven.

However, if the risk of some damage, no matter how slight can be foreseen, the extent or value of the damage does not have to be foreseeable. Thus, the acceptance that there is a risk of slight damage might make the tortfeasor liable, even though the eventual damage caused is quite disproportionate to the perceived risk.

Overview of negligence actions

A person who complains of negligence must prove to the court:

(1) The defendant owed the claimant a duty of care.
(2) That the defendant has breached that duty of care.
(3) That the claimant has suffered some injury or damage as a result of the breach of the duty of care.
(4) The risk of damage was not so remote that it could be ignored.

Around each one of these points there might be considerable legal argument depending on the individual circumstances of the case.

Likelihood of litigation

It is a fact of life that as people become more aware of their rights they become more willing to enforce them. Compensation claims in the USA for civil claims have increased annually in recent years and the same willingness to litigate for compensation seems to be developing in this country. Quite apart from the

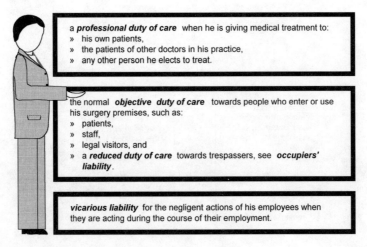

Figure 4.7   Negligence liability of a general practitioner

primary reason of good health care, both clinical and administrative procedures in the practice should conform to the letter of the law. This should mean that at best the possibility of civil litigation is avoided or at worst an adequate defence is provided against any allegations of negligence that might be made.

Insurance

In some circumstances the law demands that compulsory insurance cover is obtained. These are situations that might result in accidents leading to court action. The purpose of the insurance is to ensure that funds are available to cover damages that might be awarded. The most important are:

- for users of motor vehicles, to cover third party accident claims
- for employers to cover claims arising from accidents to employees
- medical liability insurance for active GPs (now compulsory in accordance with regulations under the 1999 Act).

Although not compulsory, it is prudent for the owner of any business (including a medical practice) to have insurance cover for any claims that could be made by way of a tortious action. This insurance cover is frequently included as part of the buildings insurance.

See also Chapter 6 re insurance.

Contract law

Legal contracts

Practices enter into legal contracts with a number of non-NHS individuals and bodies (see the next section for the particular status of NHS contracts) as part of their day by day working. Legal contracts will exist between the partners and the suppliers of various goods, employees and in private dealings with patients.

Not all contracts are written down, but this does not make them any less binding in law. However, some contracts must be written, because the law says so, for example the deeds needed to buy and sell property.

The definition of a legal contract is an agreement between two or more people, or corporate bodies, which is legally binding.

A contract's conditions
The contract must fulfil certain conditions as illustrated in Figure 4.8.

- All the parties must have intended it to be legally binding at the time of agreement.
- If a breach of contract is taken to court, this intention will usually be assumed, unless there is evidence to the contrary.
- Parties must not make false statements or use tricks to induce the other party into the contract.
- All parties must be capable in the eyes of the law to enter into a contract. This contractual capacity means that:
  - no one under 18 or who is mentally incapable can normally become a contracting party

Figure 4.8   The basic conditions of a contract

- corporate bodies such as limited companies or NHS Trusts can be parties to contracts
- partnerships are not corporate bodies (see Chapter 5) and so individual partners must enter into a contract on behalf of all of the practice partners
- all parties must have entered into the contract of their own free will.
- At the time when the contract was made, it must have been possible to complete it.

The stages in making a contract
To make a contract there are three stages, as illustrated in Figure 4.9, that must be carried out:

- one party must *offer* something to the other
- the second party must *accept* the offer
- both parties must give something in return for what they receive: this is called *consideration*
- the consideration is usually money but other forms of benefits can be used.

Offer
- When an offer is made, the person making it (the *offeror*) may specify:
  - the date when the offer expires, and/or
  - the way in which the acceptance must be communicated.
- If the offeror changes his mind after having made the offer, he can withdraw it, providing it has not been accepted in the meantime. Offers and revocations of offers must be received by the person to whom they are made before they are effective in law.
- Note that an offer is not the same as an *invitation to treat*. An invitation to treat is when a person holds himself out as ready to receive offers. After the

Figure 4.9   The stages in making a contract

offer is made he might accept or reject it. An example is a shopkeeper putting goods on display and thus making an invitation to treat. An offer is then made by a customer who wants to buy the goods which the shopkeeper can accept or reject as he wishes.

- If a contractor gives a *quotation* for work at the surgery, this is a firm price being offered; it is therefore a legal offer which you might accept or reject. However, if the contractor gives you an *estimate* for the work, this is not the same thing at all. It is a guess how much the work will cost and it is not an offer in legal terms.

Acceptance

An offer can be accepted in several different ways, such as, face-to-face, on the telephone, by letter, by fax and so on. The only occasion the acceptor cannot choose the method to use is when the offeror has specified the acceptance method. Acceptance can be by post, by forms of instantaneous communication such as fax or e-mail, or by conduct.

- Acceptance by *post* is effective as soon as the letter is posted.
- The contract comes into effect at the time of posting, providing the letter has been correctly addressed.
- This is so even if the offeror never receives the letter of acceptance.
- *Instantaneous communication* means using systems like telephones, fax or electronic mail.
- Unlike postal acceptance, if any of these methods are used, the acceptance is only valid when the offeror has received it.
- Acceptance by *conduct* happens when, for example, you order goods from a catalogue. The catalogue company send the goods and this action is an acceptance of your offer (made by sending the order).

Except when an acceptance is made by post, the offeror must know that the acceptance has been made. This means that the offeror cannot claim that silence can be interpreted as an acceptance.

Consideration

For a simple contract to be valid, each party must give and receive a benefit. The legal points are as follows.

- Each party must give and receive consideration.
- The consideration must have some real value – even though that value could be trivial.
- The consideration must be greater than the existing public duty of the party. This means he must be committing himself to provide something new or extra under the contract.
- It must not be a past consideration. The consideration must normally be given after the contract has been made.
- The consideration itself might be a financial payment, an act, a promise to do something or a promise not to do something.

Breach of contract

This happens when a party to the contract either neglects, or refuses to honour his contractual obligation.

- When one party has breached the contract the other has a right of action and can sue.
- If the case is made out, the court will normally award damages. This means a sum of money will be awarded to the victim as compensation to put him in the same position as he would have been, had the contract not been broken.
- Rarely, the court might order *specific performance*; this means that an order is made for the contract breaker to carry out his contractual promise. This remedy is not normally used if damages will suffice.

As with other aspects of law, the law of contract is based upon a number of statutes and many cases that give particular precedents. All the points mentioned in these notes have been simplified to their basic features but all of them have been subject to legal interpretation.

This handbook gives you the basic outline of what a legal contract is. If you are involved in negotiating a major contract, or if there is some dispute about an existing contract, legal advice should be sought as soon as practicable.

NHS contracts

The National Health Service and Community Care Act 1990 introduced the principle of NHS contracts made between NHS bodies. The Act was amended to include Primary Care Trusts and the Commission for Health Improvement by the Health Act 1999.

The 1990 Act describes an NHS contract as an arrangement under which one health service body called the *acquirer* arranges for another health service body called the *provider* to provide goods or services that it needs for its functions. These contracts are used to control matters relating to patients, money, information and associated non-medical services throughout the Health Service.

The patterns and usage of NHS contracts are defined by statute. The statute also states that irrespective of whether or not an NHS contract would be a contract in law, it shall *not* be regarded as leading to contractual rights or liabilities that can be pursued through the courts.

If any dispute arises in an NHS contract concerning any matter as below listed either party can refer the matter to the Health Secretary for determination:

- if it is claimed that the proposed terms are unfair because the provider is seeking to take advantage of a monopoly or any other unequal bargaining position, or
- if any of the terms of the proposed arrangement cannot be agreed by the parties.

After determination by the Health Secretary he may:

- vary the terms of the NHS contract
- bring it to an end
- direct that the NHS contract be proceeded with and it will then be the duty of the parties to comply with his directions.

As National Health Service contracts are not enforceable through the courts they are not deemed to be part of contract law and their details are therefore outside the range of this handbook.

Part II
The Law and the Practice as a Business Undertaking

- Partnership law
- Workplace health and safety

Chapter 5
Partnership Law

General points of partnership law

Owning and running a medical general practice is as much a business as providing any other service for financial reward. Even though patients do not pay for the service at the point of delivery, but pay the doctor indirectly by way of their taxes does not alter this fact.

If a doctor sets up a general medical practice on his own account, he will be in legal terms, a *sole trader*. This means that he will have personal responsibility for the way in which his business is conducted, including the liability to pay all of its debts to the full extent of his personal assets. However, fewer than 10% of GP practices are singlehanded. Note that this 'business' responsibility is additional to the professional responsibilities he accepts as a doctor.

When several doctors work together, some or all of them may form a *partnership*, a legally recognised form of business unit. Partners in a business venture can elect to make a legally binding agreement between themselves called a deed of partnership or sometimes the articles of partnership. This document will provide the legal framework that would be used in a court of law to decide any matter concerning the relationship between the partners. It will also define the relationship between any or all the partners and anyone else. If a formal private arrangement has not been made, the legal rules that must be followed by any partnership are contained in the Partnership Act 1890.

Disputes can arise in any professional partnership but if it gets as far as the courts it usually means that the problem is one concerning money – who owes how much to whom.

Of the 90% or so practices that are run on a joint basis, the BMA estimates that at least half of them either have no formal written agreement or they are working to an old outdated agreement. This might not seem to be important, but it could cause legal problems for the partners. For example, without a deed of partnership covering the point, if one partner dies, or decides to leave, the partnership is automatically dissolved. This means that the assets must be divided and the leaving partner or the estate of the dead one must receive a suitable share (as laid down in the 1890 Act).

The General Medical Services Committee of the BMA and other bodies have published advice outlining suggested items that should be included in the deed of partnership and doctors are advised to consult these documents.

The legal framework of a partnership can be illustrated as in Figure 5.1

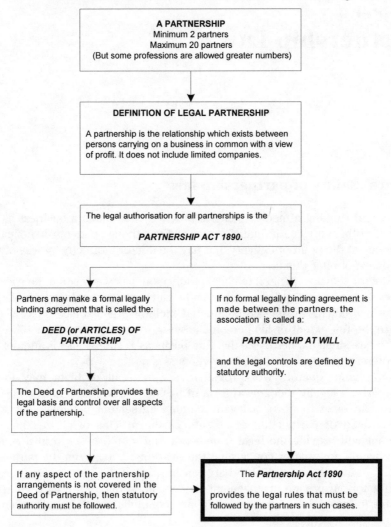

Figure 5.1 Partnership law

Any aspect of a partnership that cannot be settled by an examination of the deed of partnership, either because:

- the subject matter of the dispute is omitted from the deed, or
- the deed lacks clarity, or
- the deed can be open to different interpretations,

will be settled by reference to the 1890 Act.

Partnership principles

There are some general principles that can be said to apply to all partnerships, irrespective of whether they are founded by a deed of partnership or are partnerships at will under the 1890 Act.

In general these terms will be similar in most deeds of partnership, but the detailed wording might vary considerably.

- Each partner is expected to act towards his co-partners with the utmost good faith. This means that he will tell them of anything that can affect the partnership in any way.
- All partners shall be entitled to participate in the management of the organisation.
- All partners must agree to the acceptance of any new partners.
- A majority of the partners cannot expel a partner unless the action has legal authority in a deed of partnership. Without such power, the only alternative is to dissolve the existing partnership entirely.
- All partners must agree to any change in the business objectives.
- According to the 1890 Act other decisions should be made by a majority of the partners. However, a deed of partnership might require unanimous approval or different levels of majority for different forms of decision.
- Each partner is deemed in law to be a legal agent for the partnership as a whole. This means that one partner can sign contracts that will bind all the partners or incur debts that place financial liability on all partners (unless the deed of partnership states otherwise).
- A partner is not entitled to a salary unless it is expressly agreed by all.
- All partners are entitled to an equal share of the capital and profits and to contribute equally to losses (unless the deed of partnership states otherwise).
- Every partner has unlimited personal financial liability for all debts, including legal judgments, incurred by the partnership. A deed of partnership might allocate the proportion of liability incurred by each partner.
- New partners are not liable for debts or legal judgments involving matters prior to their becoming a partner.
- Ex partners will be liable for debts, etc. that occurred before they left the partnership. They might be liable for debts, etc. occurring after they left if the creditor believed that they were still a partner, unless the ex partner has taken appropriate legal steps to show that he is no longer a partner. (This includes publishing legal notices describing the changed situation and ensuring that all letterheads and other papers containing his name are no longer used by the practice.)
- If any partner commits a legal wrong during his work that results in loss or injury for which he is liable to a penalty then all partners will be jointly and severally liable for the wrongful act.

There are also a number of points relating to the winding up of the business if it becomes insolvent.

Suggested matters for inclusion in a deed of partnership

Figure 5.2, whilst it is not an exhaustive list, shows many details that should be considered when devising a deed of partnership.

The reason for using this, or any other comprehensive list of points for inclusion in a legal agreement is that it will provide a framework that can be

The Law and the Practice as a Business Undertaking

THE DEED OF PARTNERSHIP - MATTERS TO BE CONSIDERED

PARTNERSHIP DETAILS

» The name and address of the business.
» The nature of the business.
» The date of the commencement of the agreement.
» The duration of the agreement.
» The partners' obligations to each other.
» Any appropriate restrictive covenants.
» The mode of acceptance of new partners.
» The mode of retirement of existing partners.
» The mode of expulsion of existing partners.
» Actions in respect of the prolonged sickness or incapacity of a partner.
» Arrangements for dissolving the association.
» The procedures for resolving disputes between partners.
» The hours of work of each partner.
» The duration of holidays of the partners.
» Sick leave arrangements.
» Maternity leave arrangements.
» Study leave arrangements.
» Arrangements to cover for partners' absence.
» Compulsory liability insurance arrangements.

MANAGERIAL MATTERS

» The arrangements for taking decisions.
» The voting procedures for different decisions.
» The allocation of specific managerial duties to particular partners.
» The arrangements for managing employed staff, to include responsibilities for:
  · appointment
  · disciplinary procedures, including staff dismissal
  · grievance procedures
  · staff appraisals
  · staff training
  · any other personnel matters such as the legal duties under the health and safety at work legislation.

FINANCIAL MATTERS

» Investment in the business by the partners.
» The arrangements to be made for the practice premises.
» Arrangements for acquiring fixed assets.
» Systems and principles to be followed when valuing premises and other assets.
» Arrangements to be followed for paying the value of a share of assets to an outgoing partner.
» The banking arrangements.
» Designation of cheque signatories, and values that individuals can authorise.
» Designation of the practice accountants.
» Arrangements for circulating copies of the practice accounts to all partners.
» Agreed definition of what constitutes practice income and what is individual partner's income.
» Profit sharing arrangements, noting NHS rules
» Allowable expenses chargeable to the practice
» Taxation arrangements.
» Superannuation arrangements.

Figure 5.2 Details for a deed of partnership

consulted when some matter is disputed. Such clarification may settle the disputed point before any legal action arises.

If arrangements are made in a deed of partnership for appropriate procedures to be followed when a partner leaves the practice, for whatever reason, a deed of variation will allow the partnership to have legal continuity. This is cheaper and easier to do than having one partner leave thus causing the partnership to dissolve and calling for the making of a new partnership agreement.

Following are some cases that illustrate the sort of disputes that have arisen over partnership arrangements.

In the absence of a deed of partnership, when a partnership is dissolved all assets, capital and revenue must be divided equally between the erstwhile partners and not in proportion to their respective shares of the capital of the partnership at the time of dissolution.

Popat *v*. Shonchhatra (1997)

If parties to a marriage are also business partners and both the marriage and the business partnerships are to be dissolved, their financial worth as business partners has to be determined before there is a financial settlement in the divorce proceedings.

White *v*. White (1998)

If some members of a partnership want to change the allocation of the share of profits, this must be done explicitly. Changing the apportionment of shares in the partnership accounts alone is not sufficient to achieve this.

Joyce *v*. Morrissey and Others (1998)

On the dissolution of a partnership, the valuation of the assets must be in accordance with the deed of partnership. If the deed does not give explicit guidance, then the assets must be valued as at the date of dissolution and not in accordance with an historic value that is used in the partnership accounts.

White *v*. Minnis and Another (1999)

The name of the practice

The Business Names Act 1985 states that if the partnership does not use a name that consists of the true surnames of all of the owners, such as 'The Sunshine Medical Centre', a notice must be displayed in the practice premises giving the details of the names of all of the partners.

Additionally this Act requires that all orders, invoices, business letters must disclose the true names of all owners of the business.

The underlying reason for the requirement is to ensure that any person who has any financial dealings with the practice should know exactly who he is dealing with. As mentioned previously, it is important that any documents that include the names of any ex partners must not be used, and the names of new partners should be included as soon as practicable.

Chapter 6
Workplace Health and Safety

Background to health and safety law

The first law of this sort was the Factories Act of 1833 which was followed by many other statutes designed to improve occupational safety law. In 1974 the introduction of the Health and Safety at Work Act brought about radical changes as, instead of regulating work activities, it initiated measures designed to prevent accidents and ill health from occurring.

This was an enormous change in legal terms, and after the law was introduced many employers had to undertake expensive alterations designed to meet the preventative principles of the new requirements.

European Union laws

British law was in advance of most other countries but in the 1980s the lead in occupational health and safety moved to the European Union. The next major step occurred in 1989 when the Council of the European Community (now called the European Union) adopted a Directive intended to encourage improvements in the health and safety of workers at work. The Directive defines general principles for the:

- prevention of occupational risks
- protection of safety and health
- elimination of risk and accident factors
- informing, consulting and training of workers,

and provides general guidelines for the implementation of these principles.

The EU Directive laid down minimum standards of safety that had to be implemented in each country via its own laws to enforce the minimum standards defined in the EU Directive, or provide standards that are more favourable for workers. The British government accepted all of these standards and has been introducing them since 1992 by means of regulations issued under the authority of the Health and Safety at Work Act 1974.

In the United Kingdom in any one year there are about 350 people killed at work, about 1.5 million people suffer some sort of injury and a further 2 million workers will be suffering from work-related ill health at any one time. With figures like these it seems reasonable to assume that legislation in this area and its enforcement is likely to increase in importance rather than decline, hence the significance of conforming to the law as it currently exists.

An overview of the existing law is shown in Figure 6.1.

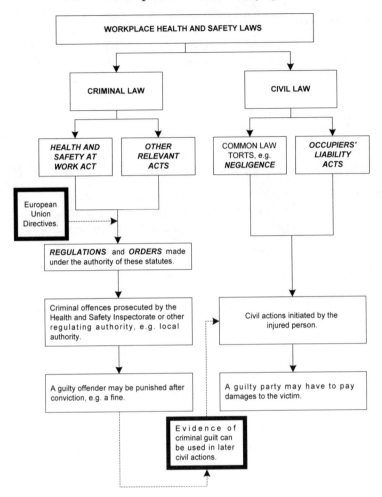

Figure 6.1 Health and safety laws

Criminal law

The most important statutes are:

- Fire Precautions Act 1971 (as amended)
- Health and Safety at Work etc. Act 1974
- Environmental Protection Act 1990

together with the regulations made under the authority of each Act of Parliament.

Information about these laws, avoiding the legal technicalities, is given on the following pages.

Fire Precautions Act 1971

The purpose of this Act is to ensure that the owners of certain designated premises undertake precautionary measures against the risk of fire. This is achieved by the issue of fire certificates by the local fire brigade.

Amongst the premises listed as requiring a fire certificate are premises

- used as an institution providing treatment or care
- that allow access by members of the public
- used as a place of work.

Premises that are classed as an office must obtain a fire certificate if

- at any one time there are 20 or more people on the premises
- if 10 or more employees work other than on the ground floor
- if explosives or highly flammable materials are used or stored.

The fire certificate will contain details of

- the use of the premises that the certificate covers
- the means of escape provided
- the ways in which the means of escape are kept safe and effective
- fire fighting appliances in the building
- the means of giving warning of fire to persons in the building
- if appropriate, where highly flammable materials may be stored.

Regulations amplify the basic terms of the Act which makes the rules very complex so advice should be sought from the local fire brigade whether or not a fire certificate is needed for your premises.

The Fire Precautions (Workplace) Regulations 1997; The Fire Precautions (Workplace)(Amendment) Regulations 1999

These Regulations extend the requirements of the 1971 Act to cover any 'workplace' which is defined as:

'Any premises, or part of premises, not domestic premises, used for any employer's purposes and made available to employees as a place of work.'

This definition will include virtually all practice premises, although a surgery that is part of a private house might not be included in it.

Employers must include an examination of any potential fire hazards as part of the risk assessment procedures required under the Management of Health and Safety at Work Regulations 1999.

These Regulations require employers to take steps to safeguard the safety of employees in case of fire by the provision of suitable fire precautions that will include:

- fire-fighting equipment, extinguishers, fire blankets, etc.
- installation of fire detectors and alarms
- designating safety routes to emergency exits that must be kept clear at all times
- emergency lighting if appropriate.

The detailed fire precautions needed in any one practice will depend upon such features as its size and layout, any specific fire hazards caused by either the structure or any flammable materials that are stored and any other relevant factor.

Any workplace can be inspected by a fire safety officer to ensure that the Regulations are being correctly complied with.

Any employee who works in the workplace may complain to the fire authority that his employer is in breach of the fire precautions legislation. If such a complaint is received, the fire prevention officer will inspect the workshop and order that action be taken to remedy any of the defects that he has found. In the event of an employer refusing to comply with the order, the Regulations lay down the legal procedures to be followed. It is an offence if:

(a) being under a requirement to do so, he [the employer] did fail to comply with any provision of the workplace fire precautions legislation, and

(b) that failure placed employees at serious risk of death or serious injury in case of fire; and

(c) the failure was intentional or due to recklessness whether he complied or not.

Fire Precautions Regulations 1997 (as amended) Regulation 11

See also regulations 7 and 8 of the Management of Health and Safety at Work Regulations 1999.

Health and Safety at Work Act 1974

This Act defines health and safety principles, the duties that are placed on employers and other people and it authorises the making of regulations which detail the rules concerning particular risks.

Health and safety duties

The following have duties under the Act that they must obey:

- employers
- persons in control of premises
- employees.

These duties are illustrated in Figures 6.2 to 6.4.

The responsibilities in respect of health and safety are extended beyond employees to any other person who might be affected. Such responsibility is not confined to people who might visit the premises, but also to anyone else who might be affected, such as passers-by, people in adjacent buildings, etc. This liability could be of particular relevance in a case where a building is occupied by more than one organisation.

The duties of an employer should not be lightly ignored, as shown in the following cases:

In the context of criminal proceedings the duties of an employer to ensure the safety of his employees are comprehensive and there is no need to refer to specific examples used in the legislation. The case was remitted for a full hearing.

Health and Safety Executive *v.* Spindle Select Ltd. (1996)

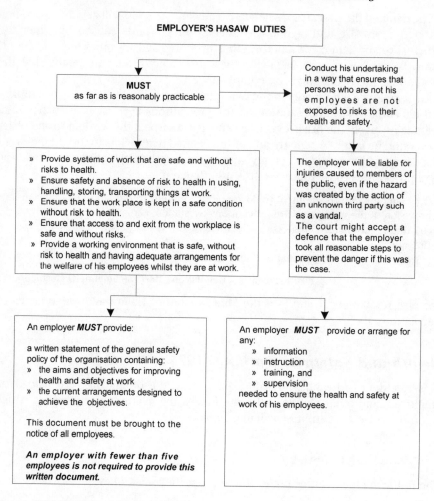

Figure 6.2 Employer's HASAW duties

An NHS Trust showed a blatant disregard for safety regulations. There was a lack of policy and training for manual workers, inadequacies in the laboratory handling arrangements for dangerous micro-organisms and poor ventilation in the mortuary. In consequence hospital patients and staff were put at risk. *The Trust was fined £4,000.*

Health and Safety Executive *v.* Swindon and Marlborough NHS Trust (1997)

A patient undergoing a cardiac angiography was mistakenly injected with air instead of radio opaque fluid which proved to be fatal.

The Trust was prosecuted and pleaded guilty to an offence under the Health and Safety at Work Act of 'failing to ensure the safe control of all procedures'. The judge said: 'This is an important case, raising issues not present in other cases concerning prosecutions of NHS trusts by the HSE. *The failure in this case was the absence of a safe system of work to protect patients and employees, which arose from the use of this equipment.*' The Trust was fined £38,000 plus £17,000 costs.

HSE *v.* Norfolk and Norwich Health Care Trust (1998)

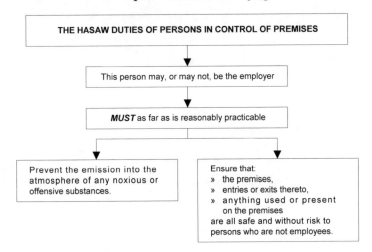

THE HASAW DUTIES OF PERSONS IN CONTROL OF PREMISES

This person may, or may not, be the employer

MUST as far as is reasonably practicable

Prevent the emission into the atmosphere of any noxious or offensive substances.

Ensure that:
» the premises,
» entries or exits thereto,
» anything used or present on the premises
are all safe and without risk to persons who are not employees.

Figure 6.3 HASAW duties of persons in control of premises

The HSE investigating officer said in respect of the foregoing case

'This case highlights the need for the health care sector to manage health and safety at work properly, just like any other employer. The investigation showed that it was not a failure of the equipment itself, but a failure of the management to implement a safe system of work to deliver a clinical judgement, which caused this tragic and avoidable death'.

It was also noted that between 1988 and 1998 there had been 38 prosecutions of NHS Trusts following the deaths or serious injury of patients of which 23 were in respect of patients being scalded or burned.

The importance of these cases is to emphasise that doctors have responsibilities for the health and safety of their patients as well as their staff.

The 1974 Act also places duties upon employees, as shown in Figure 6.4. See also page 67 in respect of further duties that fall on employees.

In addition to the employer's and employee's duties shown above, manufacturers, designers and suppliers of goods also have health and safety duties imposed on them. The details of these duties are not of direct concern in this handbook.

Consultation with employees

The 1974 Act was extended making it a duty for employers to consult with employees by giving them information about health and safety matters that affect them and subsequently taking note of workforce opinions before making any health and safety decisions.

Figure 6.5 shows the main points of the two sets of regulations that cover consultation matters. Safety and elected representatives are entitled to request and then receive any information concerning health and safety matters that they need to carry out their functions, except:

• if the disclosure would be against national security or contrary to law

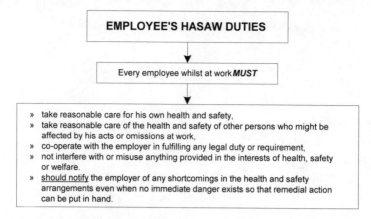

Figure 6.4   Employee's HASAW duties

- any information about an individual employee unless he consents to its disclosure,
- if the disclosure would, for other than health and safety reasons, damage the business
- if the information was obtained by the employer in connection with legal proceedings.

See also the appointment of competent persons, page 65.

Managing health and safety matters

In order to implement the requirements of various EU Directives the original 1974 Act has been supplemented with regulations that specifically detail how health and safety matters must be dealt with by employers.

Management of Health and Safety at Work Regulations 1999

These regulations came into force on 29 December 1999 and are designed to meet the most recent EU requirements. As the name implies, these regulations prescribe the procedures that an employer must follow when managing health and safety matters.

An overview of the coverage of the Regulations is shown in Figure 6.6. Each element is amplified as far as necessary for the manager's understanding.

Risk assessment (Reg. 3)

A risk assessment is a systematic analysis which will provide the information that an employer needs to fulfil his duty in respect of the provision of a health and

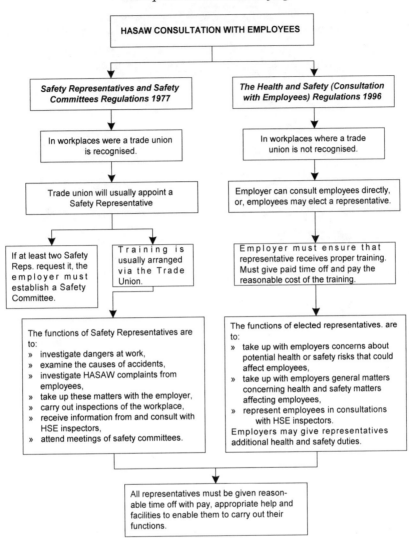

Figure 6.5   HASAW consultation

safety policy. The basic risk assessment requirements are illustrated in Figure 6.7.

Risk assessment re new and expectant mothers (Regs 16, 17 & 18)

The risk assessment must also include the identification of any potential risks that might specifically affect new or expectant mothers. These requirements are shown in Figure 6.8.

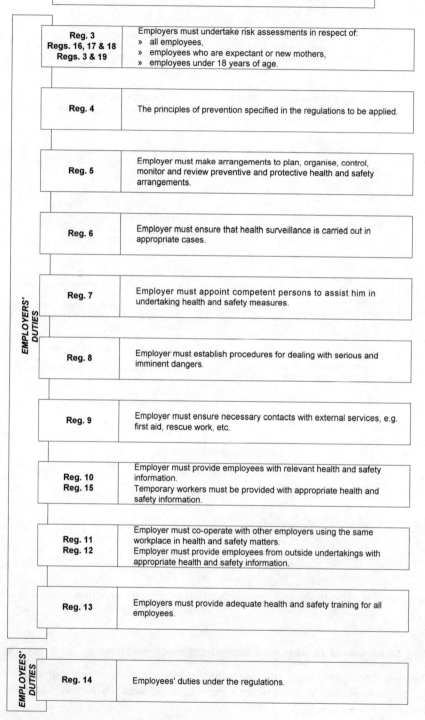

Figure 6.6   Management regulations

Risk assessment re young employees (Regs 3 & 19)

A young person is someone who is over compulsory school age (16) but has not reached the age of 18. The management regulations take special account of risks that might affect such young employees, the main points are illustrated in Figure 6.9.

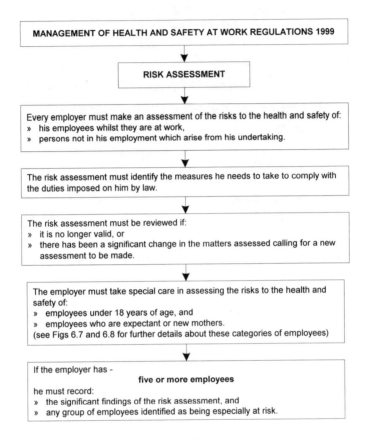

Figure 6.7 Risk assessment requirements 1

In a medical practice the single, greatest potential hazard for both pregnant women and young employees is probably posed by the handling of clinical specimens and clinical waste, see page 77.

Risk assessment miscellaneous points

The management regulations often overlap other regulations in their risk appraisal requirements, but this does not mean that tasks have to be duplicated. For instance a risk appraisal for the Control of Substance Hazardous to Health (COSHH) Regulations 1999 (see page 71) will also suffice for risk appraisals needed by the Management of Health and Safety at Work Regulations in that specific area of risk.

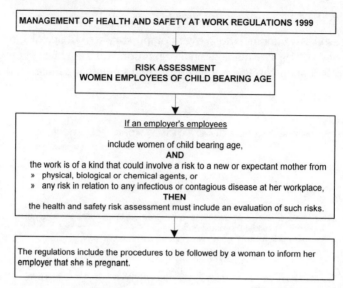

Figure 6.8   Risk assessment requirements 2

Readers will have noted on page 54 that a risk assessment must be made to ascertain potential fire hazards.

The principles of prevention (Reg. 4)

A risk assessment is the technique that is used to identify the preventive and protective measures that the employer must put in place in his undertaking.

The Regulations state that these measures must be implemented on the basis of the general principles of prevention set out in the relevant European Directive, they are as follows:

- avoiding risks
- evaluating the risks which cannot be avoided
- combating the risks at source
- adapting the work to the individual, especially as regards:
  - the design of workplaces
  - the choice of work equipment, and
  - the choice of working and production methods,
  with a view in particular to alleviating
  - monotonous work, and
  - work at a pre-determined work-rate, and
  reducing the bad effect of such work methods on health;
- adapting to technical progress
- replacing the dangerous by the non-dangerous or the less dangerous
- developing a coherent overall prevention policy which covers:
  - technology
  - the organisation of work

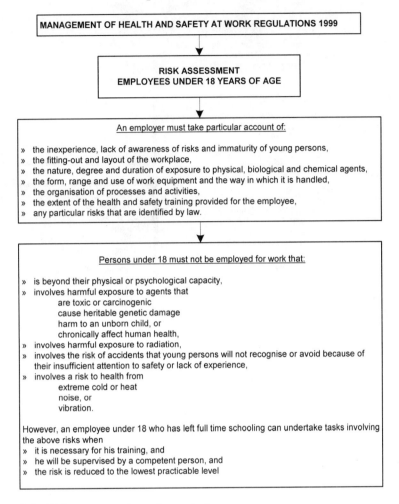

Figure 6.9   Risk assessment requirements 3

- ○ working conditions
- ○ social relationships, and
- ○ the influence of factors relating to the working environment;
- ● giving collective protective measures priority over individual protective measures, and
- ● giving appropriate instructions to employees.

Not all of these principles will be relevant in every general practice situation.

Health and Safety management (Reg 5)

Employers must have arrangements in place to cover health and safety; these arrangements must be made in consultation with employees, see pages 57 and 59. The system in place will depend on the size and nature of the activities of the

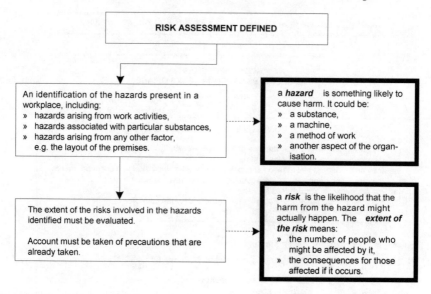

Figure 6.10   Risk assessment – defined

undertaking but generally will include the following elements that are typical of any other management function:

Planning
Managers should adopt a systematic approach that identifies priorities and sets objectives. Whenever possible, risks should be eliminated by the careful selection and design of facilities, equipment and processes or minimised by physical or control measures.

Organising
In every practice steps should be taken to put in place the necessary structure with the aim of ensuring that there is a progressive improvement in health and safety performance.

Controlling
It is a vital part of the manager's task to ensure that the decisions intended to establish and promote health and safety are being implemented as planned.

Monitoring and reviewing
This process should be adopted to achieve a progressive improvement in health and safety by constantly developing policies, and implementing the techniques of risk control.

Employers with five or more employees must record their arrangements for health and safety. This record, together with the risk assessment, could form part of the document containing the health and safety policy required by the Health and Safety at Work Act.

Health surveillance (Reg. 6)

Every employer must ensure that his employees are provided with such health surveillance as is appropriate having regard to the risks identified by the assessment. The risk assessment will identify any circumstances in which health surveillance is required by specific regulations (e.g. COSHH Regulations). Note also the requirement to provide health assessments for night workers, page 169.

Competent assistants (Reg. 7)

Every employer must appoint one or more competent persons to assist him in undertaking his legal obligations.

A person is regarded as competent in terms of the law when he has sufficient training, experience, knowledge and other qualities that enable him to undertake statutory health and safety responsibilities.

The Regulations specify details of the criteria for appointment to this role. These are mainly applicable to larger establishments, however, in the case of partnerships, if one of the partners has sufficient training and experience or knowledge and other qualities qualifying him properly to:

- undertake the measures needed to implement health and safety legislation, and
- assist his fellow partners in undertaking the measures needed,

that partner may be appointed to the statutory role of a competent person.

Procedures in the event of danger (Reg. 8)

The employer must establish appropriate procedures to be followed in the event of serious and imminent danger to his employees and nominate competent person(s) to implement procedures such as the evacuation of the building in case of emergency. (See also the requirements of the Fire Precautions legislation, page 54.)

Persons are regarded as competent when they have had sufficient training and experience or knowledge and other qualities to enable them to implement evacuation or other safety procedures.

Contacts with external services (Reg. 9)

This is a new requirement under the 1999 Regulations. The Regulation states that every employer must ensure that any necessary contacts with external services are arranged, particularly as regards first aid, emergency medical care and rescue work. This requirement will arise because of particular hazards that are identified in the risk assessment.

Information for employees (Regs 10 & 15)

All employees must be provided with information on:

- risks identified in the health and safety risk assessment
- the preventive and protection measures in place to deal with the risks

- the procedures to be followed in the event of serious and imminent danger
- the identity of anyone nominated to be a competent person for these procedures
- any risks notified by any other employer sharing the premises.

This information must be understandable to the employees receiving it and must take account of their level of training, knowledge and experience. Special consideration should be given to any employees with language difficulties or with disabilities that may impede their receipt of information. It can be provided in any suitable form so long as it is complies with the foregoing.

The requirement to provide information extends to temporary employees who must be given appropriate information on matters that will affect them in their post.

In addition, employees must be given some generalised information on health and safety matters, the appropriate regulations are:

The Health and Safety Information for Employees Regulations 1989
These Regulations require that the employer must ensure that either:

- the approved poster titled *Health and Safety Law – What you should know* is kept displayed in a readable condition,
  - at a place accessible to employees at work, and
  - in such a position that it can be easily seen and read, or that
- each employee is given an approved leaflet containing the same information.

When the approved poster or leaflet is revised, the employer must ensure that the revised edition of the poster is displayed, or revised leaflets are issued to employees. The latest revision of the poster and leaflets was published on 1 October 1999, and all employers must have this revised edition displayed on or before 1 July 2000.

Any safety signs used to convey information connected with health and safety matters, for example, fire exit signs, etc., must conform to the legal design standards.

The Health and Safety (Safety Signs and Signals) Regulations 1996
These Regulations apply to all premises where workers are employed. The most significant of the signs in a general practice will be those relating to fire alarms and fire safety signs such as fire exits and fire-fighting equipment.

Other signs may be needed to provide warning whenever there is an unavoidable risk present in the premises.

Cooperation with other employers (Regs 11 & 12)

If two or more employers share a workplace, each employer will cooperate with the other employers so far as is necessary to meet their legal obligations in health and safety matters.

Employers should agree to joint arrangements such as appointing a health and safety coordinator to oversee these matters.

Capabilities and training of staff (Reg. 13)

Every employer shall ensure that his employees are provided with adequate health and safety training:

- when they are recruited into the employer's undertaking
- when they are exposed to new or increased risks because of:
  - transfer or change of responsibilities
  - introduction of new work equipment, or changes to existing equipment
  - introduction of new technology
  - introduction of new systems of work.

The training must be:

- repeated periodically where appropriate
- adapted to take account of new or changed risks
- take place during working hours.

Special attention should be given to employees who occasionally deputise for others. Their skills are likely to be underdeveloped and they may need more frequent refresher training.

If it is necessary to arrange training outside an employee's normal hours, this should be treated as an extension of time at work.

If an employee suffers injury or ill health that is attributable to deficient training, the employer is liable to criminal prosecution.

> A woman suffered injury whilst operating a guillotine. The women operators were trained by each operator telling newcomers what they had to do and the woman's injury was a direct result of following her totally inadequate instructions. *The employer was fined for failing to provide proper training in breach of the requirements of the 1974 Act.*
>
> Health and Safety Executive *v.* Forbo Kingfisher (1993)

Training is particularly important for employees operating potentially dangerous equipment such as autoclaves.

Employees' duties (Reg. 14)

The 1974 Act placed responsibilities on individual employees, and they too have been amplified as follows:
Every employee shall use any

- machinery
- equipment
- dangerous substance
- transport equipment
- means of production or
- safety device

in accordance with

- any training received by him, and
- instructions provided by his employer relating to any legal provisions concerning the matter.

Every employee must inform his employer of

- any work situation which is reasonably considered to represent a serious and immediate danger to health and safety
- any matter which represents a shortcoming in the employer's health and safety protection arrangements.

The most important, but certainly not the only, hazards that are covered by the requirements to follow formal procedures will be the handling of clinical specimens and clinical waste.

Other regulations applicable in general practice

The regulations described on the following pages are those most likely to affect a general medical practice, all being made under the authority of the Health and Safety at Work Act. Not all regulations will affect all practices and in some cases, where a practice has unusual characteristics, some regulations not mentioned herein might be applicable.

Workplace (Health, Safety and Welfare) Regulations 1992

These regulations require every employer to ensure that every workplace controlled by him meets the stated minimum environmental standards defined by law. Following is an outline of the matters covered in the regulations, but the originals must be consulted for the detailed requirements.

Maintenance of workplace, equipment, devices and systems
The workplace, equipment, devices and systems shall be maintained, including being cleaned as appropriate, in an efficient state, good working order and repair.

Ventilation
Every enclosed workplace shall have provision for ventilation by a sufficient quantity of fresh or purified air.

Temperature indoors
During working hours, the temperature in all workplaces inside buildings shall be reasonable. This should normally be at least 16° Celsius unless the work involves severe physical effort in which case the temperature should be at least 13° Celsius.

There should be a sufficient number of thermometers provided so that persons can determine the temperature.

Lighting
Every workplace must have suitable and efficient lighting. As far as possible it should be natural light.

Emergency lighting shall also be provided in any room where persons at work could be specially exposed to danger in the event of a failure of the normal artificial lighting.

Cleanliness and waste materials

Every workplace and the furniture, furnishings and fittings in it must be kept sufficiently clean. As far as practicable, waste materials must not be allowed to accumulate in the workplace except in suitable receptacles.

Room dimensions and space

Every room where persons work shall have sufficient floor area, height and unoccupied space for purposes of health, safety and welfare. Details of measurements are contained in the Regulations.

Workstations and seating

Every workstation shall be so arranged that it is suitable both for any person likely to work there and for any task likely to be undertaken there.

The workstation should be capable of being vacated quickly in an emergency and must be arranged so that the occupier does not slip or fall.

A suitable seat must be provided for any person using the workstation for work that can be done sitting and a suitable footrest should also be provided where necessary.

Condition of floors and traffic routes

Every floor or traffic route should be of suitable construction. The floor or surface shall have no hole or slope, nor be uneven or slippery so as to expose any person to risk. Suitable handrails and guards should be fitted on staircases unless it would cause an obstruction.

As far as practicable every floor in the workplace and every traffic route surface must be kept free from any obstructions, articles or substances that could cause a person to slip, trip or fall. (Traffic routes mean routes for pedestrians, vehicles or both including stairs, doorways, ramps, etc.)

Falls or falling objects

Suitable and effective measures should be taken to prevent any person falling a distance likely to cause personal injury and to prevent any person being struck by a falling object likely to cause personal injury.

Windows, transparent/translucent doors, gates and walls

All windows and other transparent or translucent surfaces must be made of safety material and be appropriately marked to make them apparent.

Windows, skylights and ventilators

No window, skylights or ventilators which can be opened, closed or adjusted shall be likely to cause a risk in so doing.

Ability to clean windows, etc. safely

All windows and skylights in a workplace shall be constructed so that they can be cleaned safely.

Organisation, etc. of traffic routes

Every workplace shall be organised to ensure that pedestrians and vehicles can circulate in a safe manner.

Doors and gates

All doors and gates must be suitably constructed, including the fitting of any necessary safety devices. This will be of particular importance if toddlers have access to the gap between a door and its hinge side jamb.

Any sliding door or gate must have a device to prevent it coming off its track during use. Any upward opening door or gate must have a device to prevent it falling back. Any powered door or gate must have effective devices to prevent it causing injury or trapping anyone and it must be capable of being operated manually if the power fails.

Sanitary conveniences

There must be suitable and sufficient sanitary conveniences at readily accessible places. The rooms containing them must be adequately ventilated and lit and they must be kept in a clean and orderly condition.

Washing facilities

Suitable and sufficient washing facilities, including showers if required by the nature of the work or for health reasons shall be provided at readily accessible places.

Drinking water

An adequate supply of wholesome drinking water shall be provided for all persons at work in the workplace. It must be readily accessible at suitable places and be conspicuously marked by an appropriate sign where necessary for reasons of health and safety.

Accommodation for clothing

Suitable and sufficient accommodation shall be provided for the clothing of any person at work but which is not worn during working hours and for special clothing worn at work but not taken home.

Facilities for changing clothing

Suitable and sufficient facilities shall be provided for any person at work in the workplace to change clothing when that person has to wear special clothing for the purpose of the work and if that person cannot, for reasons of health or propriety, be expected to change in another room.

Facilities for rest and to eat meals

Suitable and sufficient rest facilities shall be provided at readily accessible places. They shall include facilities to eat meals where food eaten in the workplace would otherwise be likely to become contaminated.

The rest rooms and rest areas shall include suitable arrangements to protect non-smokers from discomfort caused by tobacco smoke.

Suitable facilities shall be provided for any worker who is a pregnant woman or nursing mother to rest.

Suitable and sufficient facilities shall be provided for persons at work to eat meals where meals are regularly eaten in the workplace.

Control of Substances Hazardous to Health Regulations 1999

The COSHH regulations require employers to consider the risks to the health and wellbeing of people who might be affected by hazardous substances used in the workplace. There is a wide range of such hazardous substances listed in the regulations. Employers must take defined steps to control any risks to health; these include the following:

- making a risk assessment of all activities that could expose people to hazardous substances
- identifying any potential exposure and taking measures to prevent or control the hazard
- specifying the means of control
- the control measures must be appropriate to the risk
- all personal protective equipment provided must be properly used and maintained in efficient order
- all personal protective clothing provided by an employer must conform to the appropriate legal standards
- if exposure to any substance could lead to an identifiable disease or other adverse health effect, the employees concerned must be kept under suitable health surveillance
- employees must be provided with adequate information and training on hazardous substances
- the special provisions in respect of biological agents must be followed.

The substances concerned

The Regulations apply to the following:

- products classified as toxic, very toxic, corrosive, harmful or irritant by the Chemicals (Hazard Information and Packaging for Supply) Regulations
- any substance assigned a maximum exposure limit (MEL) or occupational exposure standard (OES) by the Health and Safety Executive (HSE)
- a substantial airborne concentration of dust
- harmful micro-organisms
- any other comparable health hazards which may be created by any other substance.

When considering your own practice, remember that apart from substances connected to clinical activities, such things as the following, if they are present in sufficient quantities, will also come within the ambit of COSHH:

- some photocopier toners and developing fluids

- ozone generated from photocopiers and laser printers in small unventilated rooms
- domestic cleaning materials such as bleach, toilet cleaners and some floor cleaners
- pest control substances.

Reporting of Injuries, Diseases and Dangerous Occurrences Regulations 1995

The RIDDOR regulations set out the procedures to be followed in reporting accidents involving personal injuries, work related diseases and dangerous incidents in which no one was injured.

Under these regulations, the following must be reported:

- fatal accidents
- major injury accidents or conditions
- dangerous occurrences
- accidents causing more than three days' incapacity for work
- certain work-related diseases, these include:
  ○ poisoning by particular substances such as arsenic or lead
  ○ some skin diseases such as chrome ulceration, folliculitis or acne
  ○ some lung diseases such as pneumoconiosis
  ○ some infections such as leptospirosis, hepatitis
  ○ some other conditions such as malignant disease of the bones, cataract
  ○ certain gas incidents.

Reportable major injury accidents/conditions are as follows:

- skull, spine or pelvic fractures
- arm, wrist, leg or ankle fractures
- injuries resulting in the amputation of a hand or foot
- injuries resulting in the amputation of a finger, thumb or toe
- eye injuries
- loss of consciousness or injuries requiring immediate medical treatment as a result of an incident involving electricity
- unconsciousness resulting from a lack of oxygen
- decompression sickness needing immediate medical treatment (excluding work covered by the Diving Operations at Work Regulations 1981)
- any serious illness involving loss of consciousness resulting from the absorption of any substance by inhalation, ingestion or through the skin
- acute illness requiring medical treatment where it is believed that the cause is exposure to a pathogen or infected material
- any other injury which results in the person being admitted immediately into hospital for 24 hours or more.

Reportable dangerous occurrences are potentially dangerous incidents (e.g. the collapse of part of a building or scaffolding, accidental ignition of explosives and the release of large quantities of flammable liquid) which must be notified to the Health and Safety Executive (HSE) even if they do not, in fact, cause injury.

Reporting accidents

Fatal accidents, major injury accidents or conditions and dangerous occurrences must be reported immediately (normally by telephone) to the HSE and a written report on the appropriate form must be sent to the HSE within seven days.

Accidents causing more than three days' incapacity for work must be reported in writing on the appropriate form within seven days but the immediate telephone report is not required.

Written records

A record book must be kept of all fatalities, injuries and dangerous occurrences that are reported to the HSE. These are referred to as *reportable accidents*. The record should contain the following information:

- the date and time of the accident or occurrence
- the full name and occupation of the person affected
- the nature of the injury or condition
- the place where the accident or dangerous occurrence occurred
- a brief description of the circumstances.

In the case of reportable disease they should include:

- the date of diagnosis of the disease
- the occupation of the person affected
- the name or nature of the disease.

These records must be kept for at least three years from the date on which any entry is made and should be held on the practice premises.

Accident book

In addition to the requirements under RIDDOR, practices which employ 10 or more persons at any time must also keep an accident book on the premises and all injuries, no matter how trivial they seem to be, should be recorded in this book.

The accident book should be of a pattern approved by the DSS and it will contain the following information for each incident:

- the full name, address and occupation of injured person
- the date and time of accident
- the place where the accident happened
- the cause and nature of injury
- the name, address and occupation of person entering the details if other than the injured person.

Accident books should be kept for a period of three years from the date of the last entry.

Health and Safety (First Aid) Regulations 1981

These Regulations direct employers to provide adequate equipment and facilities appropriate to the circumstances for enabling first aid to be rendered to employees if they are injured or become ill at work. These arrangements include the requirement for suitable members of staff to be trained as qualified first aiders and the provision of suitable equipment and facilities to enable first aid to be rendered when required. The employer must inform employees of the arrangements that have been made in connection with the provision of first aid, including the location of equipment, facilities and personnel.

Electricity at Work Regulations 1989

The Regulations place a responsibility upon employers and employees to ensure that all electrically powered equipment is safe from electrical dangers.

To implement these Regulations it is necessary to have a plan of preventive maintenance. This plan will schedule regular checks of *all* electrical equipment used by employees, this will include such items as kettles and other domestic equipment used by staff as well as equipment used as part of the work undertaken.

The checks should be carried out by a competent person (not necessarily a qualified electrician) being followed by repair or replacement of any defective items or parts that are identified.

The Gas Safety (Installation and Use) Regulations 1998

These Regulations lay down the technical safety requirements for gas installations, they also require that any work on gas fittings must be carried out by a competent person.

The Regulations state that it is the duty of every employer to ensure that any gas appliance, installation pipework or flue installed at any place of work is maintained in a safe condition so as to prevent risk of injury to any person.

Provision and Use of Work Equipment Regulations 1998

These Regulations require equipment that is used at work to be safe. Examples of potential hazards include accidental contact with dangerous and/or moving parts of machines, risks of fire or explosion, contact with hot or cold surfaces and so on. The Regulations are mostly applicable to factories and workshops, however, the use of such things as autoclaves could be controlled by these regulations.

Ionising Radiations Regulations 1999

These Regulations cover any equipment that emits X-rays, gamma rays and particulate radiation such as radiography equipment. They also stipulate the qualifications needed by persons who operate the equipment.

Other non-ionising radiations, where present, should also be considered in the organisation's health and safety policy document. Examples could be:

- *Radio frequency and microwaves:* from some drying and heating equipment and possibly from communications equipment
- *Infra-red radiations:* from some laser equipment

- *Visible light:* from high intensity light sources such as laser equipment
- *Ultra violet radiation:* from mercury vapour lights, 'artificial sun' lights.

Health and Safety (Display Screen Equipment) Regulations 1992

These Regulations are for the protection of people who habitually use a VDU as a significant part of their normal work. The principal risks to health are musculo-skeletal problems, visual fatigue and mental stress. The regulations cover such matters as breaks in activity, eyesight testing and design requirements for the work environment.

Personal Protective Equipment at Work Regulations 1992

These Regulations cover all equipment which is intended to be worn or held by a person and which protects him against risks to his health or safety. Such equipment will include gloves, aprons, eye protectors, etc. that might be needed to protect a person from chemical or microbiological hazards.

Manual Handling Operations Regulations 1992

These Regulations provide guidelines for employers on the methods to be used by employees when lifting, carrying or otherwise manually handling weighty items.
See *Clark* v. *Commissioner of the Police for the Metropolis* (1999) page 80.

Employees' health and safety rights

The Employment Rights Act 1996 gives protection to employees against victimisation by the employer in many health and safety matters. The aggrieved employee or ex employee can take an employer to an employment tribunal for alleged breaches of parts of HASAW laws as shown in Figure 6.11 to seek redress.

Enforcement of health and safety law

Breaches of HASAW legislation including all of the regulations, are punishable in the criminal courts. Prosecutions are undertaken by the Health and Safety Executive's inspectorate. Many prosecutions follow accidents involving serious injury or situations that cause considerable danger, although the identification of health problems in employees and deficiencies revealed by inspections can also result in criminal proceedings.

The inspectors have wide powers to enter any workplace, to investigate breaches of the law, seize anything needed for evidence, examine books, documents etc. as part of their investigation and to require persons to answer questions and sign a declaration of the truth of those answers.

The number of health and safety inspectors is limited and regular visits to a small business are unlikely but if a complaint is made to the inspectorate by an aggrieved employee or a visitor to the premises there is likely to be an inspection

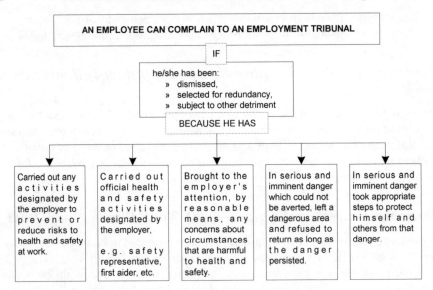

Figure 6.11 Health and safety rights

visit to see if there are any breaches of the law that justify official intervention.

It is the policy of the inspectorate to try to persuade employers to use good practices, and only if persuasion fails are more serious steps of enforcement taken. There have been instances were obstinate employers have not heeded the advice given, subsequently they have found all work on their particular site has been stopped by prohibition notices and they have subsequently been prosecuted for their disobedience of the law.

If, after due inspection, the inspector finds that he needs to take action, he can do one of four things.

(1) He can verbally explain the defects to the employer and tell him to remedy them within a certain time. Checks will later be made to ensure that matters have been corrected.

(2) He can serve an *improvement notice* requiring the employer to remedy faults within a certain time. If the improvements are not carried out by the end of the given time then the employer can be taken to court, unless there is a very good reason offered for failing to comply.

(3) He can serve a *prohibition notice* which prohibits the use of any process, machinery, equipment, etc. which he considers carries the risk of serious personal injury, until specified remedial action has been taken. He can also seize, render harmless or destroy any substance or article that he considers to be a cause of imminent danger or serious personal injury.

(4) He can institute a criminal prosecution alleging that the employer has committed an offence. This is normally only necessary in serious cases, or if the employer has deliberately flouted the law over a period of time.

In addition to the possible actions of the inspectorate, the owners of a business (the medical partners who own the practice) have civil liability. Any civil action instigated as a result of injury or damage to health is quite separate from, and nothing to do with, any criminal action that a safety inspector might institute. If an employer is guilty of a criminal act or omission under HASAW law it will greatly strengthen the litigant's claim for compensation when that case is heard in the civil courts.

Environmental protection law

The Environmental Protection Act 1990 is a framework document, somewhat similar to the Health and Safety at Work Act 1974 inasmuch as it defines basic principles which are amplified by regulations made under its authority.

The law sets out rules to prevent the pollution of the environment by commercial organisations, their associated companies and individuals who produce industrial waste as part of their processing. Further, it also controls such organisations as hospitals and scientific establishments whose waste products will include biological and irradiated materials. The points of the law that will affect general practices are as shown below.

The law regulates *controlled waste* which covers industrial and commercial waste. It is defined as follows.

- Any substance which constitutes
  - ○ scrap material
  - ○ an effluent
  - ○ another unwanted surplus substance
  arising from the application of any practice.
- Any substance or article which requires to be disposed of as being broken, worn out or otherwise spoilt.

The producer of the waste is responsible for

- storing it safely and securely
- ensuring that the person collecting and disposing of the waste is legally authorised to do so, and
- making a written description of the waste.

Many medical general practices make arrangements for disposal of their controlled waste by arrangements made with their health authority. This means that the practice's procedure should be based on the following principles.

- All waste is stored in appropriate containers.
- Precautions exist to prevent spillage or other 'escapes'.
- Ensuring that the waste collector is properly authorised (possibly done by HA).
- Ensuring that the waste collector disposes of the waste in an authorised fashion (possibly done by HA).
- Keeping accurate and up-to-date documentation concerning all waste disposal.
- Retaining all paperwork for at least two years.

The doctor's liability can extend to wrongful disposal of the waste as was seen in the following case:

> A doctor disposed of obsolete medicines by passing them on to a pharmacist. The pharmacist threw the medicines into a builder's skip where they were found by pollution inspectors. As a result *the doctor was subsequently prosecuted for an environmental protection offence.*
>
> Title unknown. Environmental case described in *Practice Manager.*

The Controlled Waste Regulations 1992

These Regulations define clinical waste as any waste which consists wholly or partly of the following which unless rendered safe may be hazardous to anyone coming into contact with it. It includes:

● human or animal tissue
● blood or other body fluids
● excretions
● drugs or other pharmaceutical products
● swabs or dressings
● syringes, needles or sharp instruments, or
● any other waste arising from medical, nursing or similar practice.

The Health and Safety Commission and Health Services Advisory Committee have stated that GPs must have in place a system that will ensure the identification, segregation and correct disposal of all clinical waste. This means that the duties under the COSHH Regulations 1999 (see page 71), particularly in respect of:

● risk assessment
● risk control
● using personal protective clothing
● appropriate training
● health surveillance and immunisation of those at risk

are properly undertaken in the practice.

Vicarious liability

If an employee offends against any health and safety or environmental protection law during the course of his work, the employer will probably have vicarious liability for the offence committed unless he can prove that the action was totally contrary to his instructions.

Civil law

The tort of negligence (See Chapter 4 re this topic.)

Deaths, injuries and ill health caused at a place of work will often lead to questions about responsibility and allegations of negligence. A brief summary of the factors involved in such negligence actions is shown in Figure 6.12.

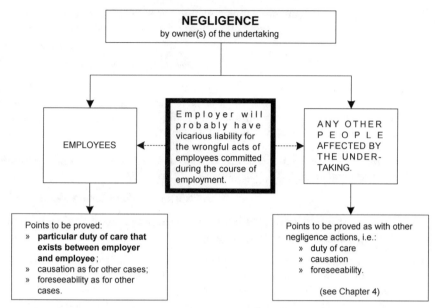

Figure 6.12 Negligence in the workplace

Employer's duty of care to employees

An employer has a duty of care towards his employees that goes beyond the reasonable objective standard of care that everyone owes his neighbour.

These are the common law standards that have been defined in cases over the years thus providing precedents that will be used in any civil claim. Each precedent relates to a specific aspect of the matter of negligence, the most significant of these points for a medical practice state that the employer must ensure that:

- competent staff are employed
- staff are trained to use any equipment in the correct manner
- proper equipment is provided that is safe to use
- all equipment must be inspected regularly and be properly maintained
- a safe working environment is provided for employees (In recent years there have been cases respecting people who can be classified as being at risk from contracting blood-borne diseases and in these cases a high level of risk control has been demanded from the employers.)
- safe work systems are provided (This means not only that safe systems must be devised, but also that the employer takes appropriate steps to ensure that these systems are used correctly by employees i.e. no dangerous short cuts are taken.)
- that reasonable care is taken to ensure the health and safety of all employees.

Examples of the employer's duties are seen in the following cases:

A part-time cleaner had to use detergents and cleansing products during her duties and she was supplied with gloves that she occasionally wore. She was not warned of the dangers of dermatitis from sustained exposure to the cleaning products. Subsequently the cleaner contracted acute dermatitis affecting her whole skin. It was held that *the employer had a duty to warn the cleaner of the dangers involved and they were in breach of that duty*.

Pape *v*. Cumbria County Council (1992)

A social services officer had a very heavy workload and suffered a nervous break-down. After he returned to work he was given little help and suffered a second breakdown, subsequently he was dismissed on the grounds of permanent ill health. The court held that the employer had a duty not to cause an employee psychiatric damage because of the volume of work. *After the first breakdown the employer should have seen that extra assistance was needed and in consequence was liable for the second breakdown*.

Walker *v*. Northumberland County Council (1995)

A recent case of interest clearly illustrates the importance of abiding by health and safety regulations, and of providing appropriate training:

A woman manager, in charge of four junior female staff, had to take on extra duties after a storeman left. These duties involved lifting boxes of photocopying paper and other stationery which had to be moved frequently from an outside yard to a third floor storeroom. No trolley or other assistance was provided for the task and she was given virtually no training. In consequence of the lifting and twisting she injured her back and was unable to work.

The judge held that *the employer had failed to carry out the health and safety requirements as no risk assessment had been undertaken to identify and take steps to reduce the risk of injury, nor had she been trained in lifting techniques* (see the Manual Handling Operations Regulations 1992). The employer was found liable and ordered to pay the injured woman £384,000 in compensation.

Clark *v*. Commissioner of the Police for the Metropolis (1999)

Breach of a statutory duty

In some circumstances, an employee might be able to sue for the tort of breach of a statutory duty. This could occur if a particular statute places a duty on the employer and he neglects to carry out that duty.

Some health and safety regulations respecting dangerous procedures clearly state that if an employer fails to carry out the duties laid down, he will be liable for the breach of the duty to any employee who suffers as a result of his omission. Not all health and safety regulations contain this particular caveat, for example, Regulation 22 of the Management Regulations states 'Breach of a duty imposed by these Regulations shall not confer a right of action in any civil proceedings'. The practicality is that the appropriate regulations must be examined in each individual case.

In the following case it was alleged that a statutory duty had been breached, but at the hearing the employer was able to show there had not been a breach. Nonetheless, it was shown that the employer was negligent as he had failed in his duty of care.

The employer had complied with a statutory duty to provide suitable safety goggles for the employee, however, *he had not insisted by way of instruction and appropriate supervision that the goggles be worn. The employers were liable at common law for negligence.*

Bux *v*. Slough Metals (1974)

Occupiers' Liability Acts 1957 and 1984

The occupier of premises has a duty of care towards all lawful visitors to the premises. There are also duties of care towards people who are trespassers.

Definitions

The 1957 Act defines 'occupier', 'premises' and 'visitor' as follows.

- An *occupier* is a person who has some control over the premises.
  - This person is not necessarily the owner of the premises.
  - There might be more than one occupier sometimes.
- *Premises* includes land, buildings, fixed or movable structures such as scaffolding and vehicles.
- *Visitors* are persons lawfully on the premises such as patients or others present with express or implied permission.

Note however, that even a burglar who trespasses in the premises at night is entitled to be treated with humanity, and if the trespasser is a child who is not old enough to know better then a reasonable standard of safety is demanded by the law. Figure 6.13 outlines the most important provisions of the Acts.

In helping to discharge the duty of care placed upon an occupier, he can place notices to warn people of particular hazards. In deciding whether this is adequate, the court will examine the surrounding circumstances, for example in the case of a young child or a blind person, a notice would be insufficient. Known dangers, such as wet floors, must always be clearly signed, a lack of warning may leave the occupier liable as in the following case.

> A policewoman went to a house in answer to a call that the house had been broken into. The occupier, wheelchair bound, had had a plywood ramp constructed from the french windows to the garden to facilitate his access. The policewoman went through the french windows without noticing the ramp, slipped on it, injured her back and arm and was rendered unconscious. *The occupier was held liable and was ordered to pay damages.*

Jones *v*. Smith (1995)

The special duty of care towards children, particularly in situations where they might be tempted to act in a way that an adult would not, was shown many years ago:

> A 7 year old boy entered a herb garden in Glasgow Botanic Gardens where he picked and ate the poisonous berries from a belladonna bush and subsequently died. The berries looked similar to blackberries and appeared tempting to the child. The bush was not fenced off, nor was there any warning that the berries were dangerous. *The owners of the Gardens were held to be liable.*

Glasgow Corporation *v*. Taylor (1922)

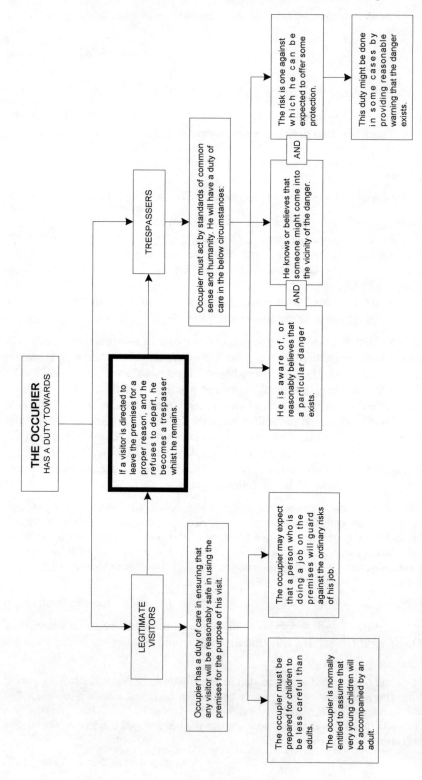

Figure 6.13 Occupiers' Liability Acts

In a recent appeal under the Occupiers' Liability Act 1957 it was said in the House of Lords:

> '... it [has] been repeatedly said in cases about children that their ingenuity in finding unexpected ways of doing mischief to themselves and others should never be under-estimated.'

Jolley v. Sutton LBC (2000)

This precedent becomes particularly important in the context of a medical practice where there will be many children visiting the premises. There will also be many things that could excite their attention if only through natural inquisitiveness.

The Disability Discrimination Act 1995

This Act places a duty on people who provide services to ensure that those services are properly available to disabled persons. A medical practice would probably be considered a 'provider of services' under section 21 of the Act. The main points of this section are illustrated in Figure 6.14.

Section 21 of the 1995 Act imposes duties only for the purpose of determining whether a provider of services has discriminated against a disabled person; and

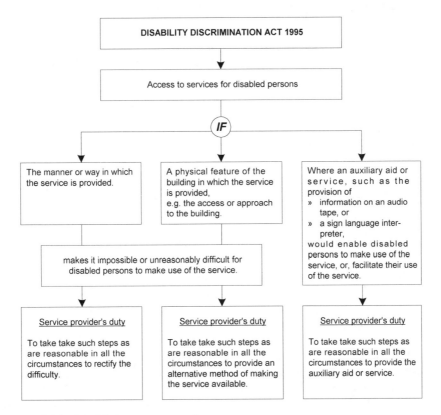

Figure 6.14 Disabled access to services

accordingly a breach of any of these duties is not actionable as such. See also page 196 re the Disability Discrimination Act

Insurance cover

Insurance cover for employees

Employers' Liability (Compulsory Insurance) Act 1969

Under the terms of this Act every employer carrying on a business *must* insure against the liability for bodily injury or disease sustained by his employees that arises out of their employment.

- The purpose of this insurance is to cover any successful civil claims that are made by injured or illness-affected employees.
- This insurance is normally obtained as part of the buildings insurance by the employer and *a valid certificate of insurance should be displayed in the premises* where it can be clearly seen by all employees.

The Employers Liability (Compulsory Insurance) Regulations 1998 came into force on 1st January 1999. These Regulations require that insurance cover under one or more policies must not be less that £5 million in respect of:

- a claim by an employee or employees arising out of any one occurrence
- any costs and expenses incurred in relation to such a claim, and
- all certificates of insurance issued on or after 1 January 1999 must be retained for a period of at least 40 years from the certificate's commencement or renewal date.

Although the 40 year requirement does not apply to certificates issued before 1999, it would be prudent for employers to retain them in a similar way.

In this form of insurance policy the insurance company is prohibited from imposing any condition that seeks to avoid its liability in the event of a claim.

Under this legislation an employer can be fined up to £2,500 per day for any day there is no suitable insurance cover in existence.

Employer's Liability (Defective Equipment) Act 1969

Although not strictly speaking an insurance requirement, this statute makes employers' liability insurance even more important.

If an employee suffers personal injury during his employment as a result of a defect in the equipment provided by his employer, the injury is deemed to be caused by the negligence of the employer for the purpose of civil proceedings, unless the employee was totally to blame for the accident.

The injured employee can, if the other elements of negligence are present, sue his employer for damages. The employer can subsequently sue the manufacturer or supplier of the faulty equipment to recover the damages paid together with any other costs he has incurred.

Property insurance

Although not compulsory, one would expect every practice to have adequate insurance cover for the building fabric and all equipment used in the practice against the risks of damage, theft, accident, etc.

Nowadays it is probably prudent to have insurance cover for computers to cover such things as damage to computer systems, corruption of records calling for reinstatement of data, etc.

Insurance cover: other persons

Public liability insurance to provide cover against claims made by other than employees is available from insurance companies. This is separate and quite distinct from medical indemnity insurance.

It will cover civil claims made by visitors who are injured in the practice premises or adjoining land, e.g. carparks. See also page 81 regarding liability in the case of trespassers.

This insurance is not compulsory by law, but it is wise to take out such insurance cover, particularly when, as with a medical practice, large numbers of people are continuously coming and going through the premises. This cover is sometimes allied to property insurance.

Product liability

This form of insurance covers the risk that some injury or other damage is caused by a service or goods provided by a doctor to another person. See page 222 on the Consumer Protection Act.

Repudiation of insurance cover

In other than the compulsory employers' liability insurance, if a business owner is found guilty of a criminal offence which, it is said, caused an injury, it is possible that the insurance company may try to repudiate liability for any subsequent civil claim brought by an injured person, e.g. a claim for negligence.

It is also important to note that if

- incorrect information is supplied
- details are omitted from the insurance proposal form, or
- known changes affecting the risk are not passed on,

the insurance company is likely to repudiate all or part of any subsequent claim.

Part III
The Law and Confidentiality

- Data protection
- Confidentiality
- The security of confidential information

Chapter 7
Personal Data – Protection and Access

Background to data protection

During the 1970s, following the increasing use of computers by commercial organisations and governments, many people became concerned about the enormous amount of personal information held by these organisations. The spectre of control exercised in a '1984' style of society caused much apprehension, especially when people realised that they had no way of knowing who held what records about them.

The first major step towards regulation occurred in 1981 with the publication of an international treaty document called *the Convention for the Protection of Individuals with Regard to Automatic Processing of Personal Data*. This Convention was associated with the European Convention on Human Rights and accordingly it was signed by the United Kingdom. Following the signing of the Convention the British Parliament enacted the Data Protection Act 1984 to cover the use of data processing on computers.

Meanwhile another body, the European Union, having been influenced by the Convention, examined the problem in detail. Eventually in 1990 the EU published a report on the protection of personal data and information security. This report had an advantage over the 1981 Convention having evidence on the efficacy of data control laws in several countries and better knowledge of the technological capacity of modern computers. Besides controlling computerised data the controls were extended to personal data held on written documents.

Subsequently, in 1995, the European Union issued a Directive to all Member States requiring them to meet defined minimum standards concerning the processing of all personal data. The consequence of this Directive was that the U.K. Parliament enacted the Data Protection Act 1998. The Act did not become operable immediately because there had to be consultation with interested parties about its application in particular circumstances. Eventually the Act came into force on 1 March 2000 together with about 20 sets of regulations and orders that specify the enforcement details of the Act's requirements.

It should be noted that the provisions of this Act are more wide ranging and more detailed than its 1984 predecessor, which has been completely repealed. Managers are therefore recommended to examine closely the requirements placed upon their particular practice, and to seek advice from the office of the Data Protection Commissioner (see Appendix B) in any matter that needs clarification.

The Data Protection Act 1998

The whole range of the Act and its subordinate legislation is too great to be included in a handbook of this size. Accordingly the information provided is restricted to those matters likely to be of most importance in the practice, and the points given are confined to their basic features.

The Act can be divided, roughly, into three elements (see Figure 7.1): the legal controls that are exerciseable, the duties laid on data controllers and the rights of data subjects.

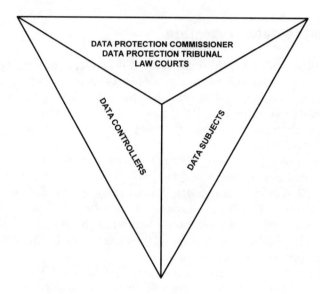

Figure 7.1   Elements of data protection

Glossary of definitions

The 1998 Act uses a number of words and phrases in very specific ways, and the legal definitions must be ascribed to those words when they are used in the legislation. Official pamphlets and forms will probably use the same words, so the most important of them are gathered here for easy reference.

Words or phrases in italics are further defined in this glossary. They are not in alphabetical order, but placed in an order that leads from one to another.

Data
Data is defined as any information that:

(1)   is automatically computer processed
(2)   is recorded for automatic computer processing
(3)   is recorded as part of a *relevant filing system*
(4)   forms part of an *accessible record*.

Note that the word 'data' is the plural form of 'datum', even though most of us tend to use data as a singular form in our ordinary speech.

Data controller

This is a person who alone, or jointly with others, decides the purpose and manner in which *personal data* are to be processed. In a medical general practice the 'data controllers' will be the practice partners.

Data processor

This means any person, who is *not* an employee of the *data controller*, who processes *personal data* on his behalf. In most practices the data will be input and processed by either the doctors or by employed staff, for whose actions the doctors will probably have vicarious liability. The use of a data processor, as defined, will not be usual.

Data subject

This term means any individual who is the subject of *personal data* that is recorded by a *data controller*. The most important group of data subjects will be the patients of the practice, but there will be others such as the employed staff who will have *personal data* recorded on their personnel records.

Personal data

Personal data is any data that relates to a *living individual* who can be identified:

- from that information, or
- from that information and other information in the possession of the *data controller*.

It will consist of such information as:

- names and addresses
- age
- marital status
- family details
- income/salary
- any other like details,

and includes any

- expression of opinion about the individual, and
- indication of the intentions of the *data controller* or other person regarding that individual.

Sensitive personal data

This comprises any personal information about the *data subject* regarding:

- his racial or ethnic origin
- his political opinions
- his religious beliefs or other beliefs of a similar nature
- whether he is a member of a trade union
- his physical or mental health or condition
- his sexual life
- the commission by him of any offence, or
- details of any criminal proceedings taken against him.

Any requirement of the Act concerning *sensitive personal data* must by definition be applicable to health records. Such records are covered in the Act by the specific authorisation to process sensitive personal data where the processing is necessary for medical purposes and it is undertaken by:

- a health professional, or
- a person who in the circumstances owes a duty of confidentiality that is equivalent to that of a health professional. (The Act does not say, but this presumably means employees directly supervised by the doctor.)

Note that the 1998 Act only covers information about living people, therefore health records of deceased patients are outside its scope (see the Access to Health Records Act on page 97).

In the practice, along with *health records*, the personal records of individual employees will contain items categorised as *sensitive personal data*.

Data for special purposes
This means data that are used for:

- the purposes of journalism
- artistic purposes, and
- literary purposes.

None of these cases are likely to affect medical general practice, but the definitions are given in case a manager comes across the phrase elsewhere.

Data processing
This phrase means:

- obtaining, recording or holding the information
- carrying out any operation on the information,

including:

- the organisation, adaptation or alteration of the information
- the retrieval, consultation or use of the information
- the disclosure of the information by making it available, or
- the blocking, erasure or destruction of the information.

In other words this means all the things that are done to, or with the aid of, records of data held in the practice.

Relevant filing system
A *relevant filing system* means any set of information relating to individuals to the extent that, although the information is not processed by means of a computer, it is structured in such a way that specific information relating to a particular individual is readily accessible.

This definition includes manual document files, card indexes, non-automated microfiche systems, etc. A relevant filing system will, by definition, include all of those health records that are not recorded on a computer system.

The definition is not totally clear and it seems likely that there will be many case decisions made before it is clarified in full. If in any doubt about whether or not a particular system used in the practice is covered by the terms of the Act, managers are strongly advised to seek advice from the DPC's office.

Accessible record

This definition lists a number of records relating to health, education, social services, housing, etc. to which the subject of the record has a statutory right of access. Amongst the records listed is an individual's health record.

The idea of accessibility was introduced into English law following a case heard before the European Court of Human Rights:

> The man concerned had been placed in care as a baby and remained in care until he was 18, passing through a large number of foster homes. He claimed that he had been ill-treated in some foster homes and applied to be given access to local authority documents about his time in care so that he could take legal action. He was given access to 65 of the 352 documents held, but access was refused to the remainder because either the contributors would not give consent or they could not be traced.
>
> *The Court of Human Rights ruled that everyone has a vital interest in receiving the information necessary to know and understand their childhood and early development. The former foster child was awarded compensation.*
>
> Gaskin *v.* United Kingdom (1990)

The judgment implied that a refusal to give a subject access to his personal records because a contributor is not available or improperly refuses consent to access is contrary to the Human Rights Convention. There must be very compelling reasons to justify refusal and disputes over disclosure should be referred to an independent tribunal set up to hear these matters.

The law was changed after the judgment, but still did not meet all the points raised by the Court of Human Rights. However, the new 1998 Act is designed to meet these requirements. Over the last few years several newspaper reports have recorded instances of hospitals and doctors not meeting their obligations to give patients access to their records. (See the case of *Hammond* on page xiv as an example.) The new Act, by specifying when a refusal is lawful, will for instance, make refusals designed to cover up incompetence more difficult to sustain.

Health record

This is any record which:

- consists of information relating to the physical or mental health or condition of an individual, and
- has been made by or on behalf of a *health professional* in connection with the care of that individual.

Health professional

This means any of the following

- *a registered medical practitioner*
- a registered dentist
- a registered optician
- a registered pharmaceutical chemist
- a registered nurse, midwife or health visitor

- a registered osteopath
- a registered chiropractor
- any person who is registered as a member of a profession to which the Professions Supplementary to Medicine Act 1960 for the time being extends
- a clinical psychologist, child psychotherapist or speech therapist
- a music therapist employed by a *health service body*, and
- a scientist employed by such a body as head of a department.

Registered medical practitioner

This includes any person who is provisionally registered under the Medical Act 1983 and is engaged in such employment as is mentioned in that Act.

Health service body

This means:

- a health authority
- a Special Health Authority
- a National Health Service Trust
- a Primary Care Trust.

Data Protection Commissioner (DPC)

The Commissioner is the new name for the old office of Registrar. The duties of the Commissioner have been extended to reflect the increasing influence of the European Union and to undertake responsibilities in disseminating best practice.

Data Protection Tribunal

This tribunal can hear appeals by persons aggrieved at decisions made by the *DPC*. It may uphold or dismiss an appeal, or it can substitute its own decision in place of that made by the *DPC*.

Data Protection Principles

These principles could well be called the centrepiece of the whole Act as they define how data can be collected and subsequently be processed and used. Any *data controller* who fails to comply with the principles is liable, at least, to receive directions from the *DPC* to take remedial action, and at worst to be the subject of legal proceedings.

There are eight principles covering similar ground to the principles contained in the 1984 Act, however, they have been extended to place new obligations on *data controllers* and to give new rights to *data subjects*.

The new principles are shown, in brief, in Figure 7.2.

The data controller

The data controller(s) in the practice is/are the doctor(s) who owns it. In the past, in some practices, because virtually all health records were documentary and little was stored on computer the implications of the Data Protection Act were not given great importance.

Times have now changed inasmuch as the 1998 Act places greater responsibilities on data controllers at the same time that computer use is increasing.

DATA PROTECTION ACT 1998
Section 4 and Schedule 1

THE DATA PROTECTION PRINCIPLES

PRINCIPLE 1	All personal data must be processed fairly and in accordance with the legal rules laid down in the Data Protection Act 1998.
PRINCIPLE 2	Personal data must only be obtained for a lawfully specified purpose and it must not be processed in a way that is incompatible with that purpose.
PRINCIPLE 3	Personal data must be adequate, relevant and not excessive in relation to the purpose for which they are to be processed.
PRINCIPLE 4	Personal data must be accurate and, where necessary, be kept up to date.
PRINCIPLE 5	Personal data that are processed for any purpose must not be kept for longer than is necessary for that purpose.
PRINCIPLE 6	Personal data must be processed in accordance with the rights of data subjects laid down in the Data Protection Act 1998.
PRINCIPLE 7	Appropriate technical and organisational measures must be taken to prevent: any unauthorised or unlawful processing of personal data **AND** any accidental loss, destruction or damage of personal data
PRINCIPLE 8	Personal data must not be transferred outside the European Union unless the receiving State ensures adequate protection for the data.

Figure 7.2 Data protection principles

Regulations make provision for partners to notify that they are joint data controllers.

It is not practicable in a handbook of this size to give a detailed list of the requirements of, for instance, the practical application of the data protection principles in all practices. Practice managers are strongly advised to seek information from the office of the DPC regarding the procedures that are used in their practice. The basic duties of the data controller are illustrated in Figure 7.3.

In the past there has been criticism that the terms of the old 1984 Act were not enforced strictly enough. However the new powers of the DPC and the more detailed controls of the 1998 Act are likely to lead to more robust enforcement.

In 1991 the Data Protection Registrar in conjunction with the BMA's General Medical Services Committee produced *A Code of Practice for General Medical Practitioners*. The Commissioner now has a statutory responsibility to encourage and then vet such codes so there is little doubt a new code will eventually be produced to cover the changed requirements. When published, it would be prudent for every practice to acquire a copy.

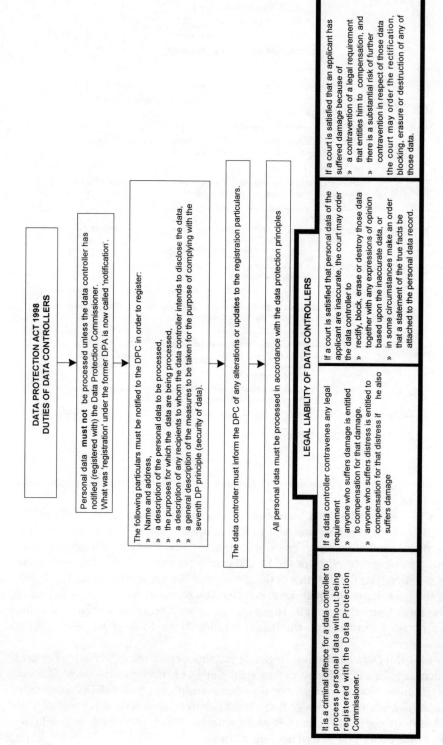

**DATA PROTECTION ACT 1998
DUTIES OF DATA CONTROLLERS**

Personal data **must not** be processed unless the data controller has notified (registered with) the Data Protection Commissioner. What was 'registration' under the former DPA is now called 'notification'.

The following particulars must be notified to the DPC in order to register:
» Name and address,
» a description of the personal data to be processed,
» the purposes for which the data are being processed,
» a description of any recipients to whom the data controller intends to disclose the data,
» a general description of the measures to be taken for the purpose of complying with the seventh DP principle (security of data).

The data controller must inform the DPC of any alterations or updates to the registration particulars.

All personal data must be processed in accordance with the data protection principles

LEGAL LIABILITY OF DATA CONTROLLERS

If a data controller contravenes any legal requirement
» anyone who suffers damage is entitled to compensation for that damage.
» anyone who suffers distress is entitled to compensation for that distress if he also suffers damage

If a court is satisfied that personal data of the applicant are inaccurate, the court may order the data controller to
» rectify, block, erase or destroy those data together with any expressions of opinion based upon the inaccurate data, or
» in some circumstances make an order that a statement of the true facts be attached to the personal data record.

If a court is satisfied that an applicant has suffered damage because of
» a contravention of a legal requirement that entitles him to compensation, and
» there is a substantial risk of further contravention in respect of those data the court may order the rectification, blocking, erasure or destruction of any of those data.

It is a criminal offence for a data controller to process personal data without being registered with the Data Protection Commissioner.

Figure 7.3 Data controller's duties

The data subject

In general, everyone is now entitled to see any personal information that is held about him, *unless* the information is specifically exempted by law. This right of access includes information that is held on a computer or on any other form of relevant filing system.

The basic details of the right to disclosure are shown in Figure 7.4. This right includes the right of access to health records, although there are further conditions on their disclosure (see below).

It should be noted that the main legal exception to the subject's right of access relates to the disclosure of information that will identify third parties.

In the practice the staff will have right of access to their personal records, but only if they are kept on either a computer or a relevant filing system. See page 160 regarding access to character references.

Health records – living patients

Health records are specifically mentioned in the 1998 Act, and the conditions of access to them are laid down in the Data Protection (Subject Access Modification)(Health) Order 2000. The provisions of these Regulations are shown in Figure 7.5. Those familiar with the old law will see that they are not a lot different from the original Access to Health Records Act. The one major change is that the Regulations recognise that in some cases the data controller holding the health record might not be a doctor. In such cases an appropriate medical professional must be consulted before a decision is made to grant or refuse access.

Health records – deceased patients

The Data Protection Act is quite specific in that it controls data of living persons although medical ethics extend confidentiality to the health records of deceased patients. To overcome what would be a shortcoming in the Act, the Access to Health Records Act 1990 has been amended to cover the disclosure of health records of those who have died. The Act only authorises the disclosure of records made after the Act came into force (1 November 1991), but doctors may supply earlier information if they wish to do so. It is very important to note that this Act now has no relevance to the health records of living patients.

The details of the Act are shown in Figure 7.6.

Medical reports

Another Act covering similar ground is the Access to Medical Reports Act 1988. This Act relates to reports that are supplied to employers about the health of employees or prospective employees or to insurance companies. The doctor supplying the information is usually the family GP.

This Act is unchanged apart from the references within it being altered to the 1998 Act and its main points are illustrated in Figure 7.7.

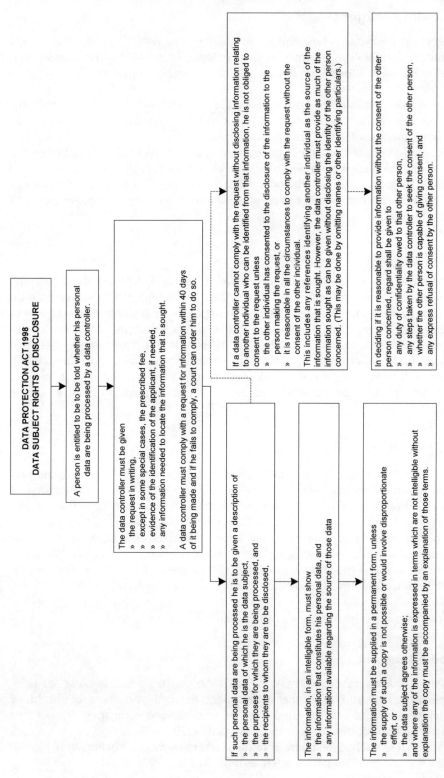

**DATA PROTECTION ACT 1998
DATA SUBJECT RIGHTS OF DISCLOSURE**

A person is entitled to be to be told whether his personal data are being processed by a data controller.

The data controller must be given
» the request in writing,
» except in some special cases, the prescribed fee,
» evidence of the identification of the applicant, if needed,
» any information needed to locate the information that is sought.

A data controller must comply with a request for information within 40 days of it being made and if he fails to comply, a court can order him to do so.

If such personal data are being processed he is to be given a description of
» the personal data of which he is the data subject,
» the purposes for which they are being processed, and
» the recipients to whom they are to be disclosed,

The information, in an intelligible form, must show
» the information that constitutes his personal data, and
» any information available regarding the source of those data

The information must be supplied in a permanent form, unless
» the supply of such a copy is not possible or would involve disproportionate effort, or
» the data subject agrees otherwise;
and where any of the information is expressed in terms which are not intelligible without explanation the copy must be accompanied by an explanation of those terms.

If a data controller cannot comply with the request without disclosing information relating to another individual who can be identified from that information, he is not obliged to comply with the request unless
» the other individual has consented to the disclosure of the information to the person making the request, or
» it is reasonable in all the circumstances to comply with the request without the consent of the other individual.
This includes any references identifying another individual as the source of the information that is sought. However, the data controller must provide as much of the information sought as can be given without disclosing the identity of the other person concerned. (This may be done by omitting names or other identifying particulars.)

In deciding if it is reasonable to provide information without the consent of the other person concerned, regard shall be given to
» any duty of confidentiality owed to that other person,
» any steps taken by the data controller to seek the consent of the other person,
» whether the other person is capable of giving consent, and
» any express refusal of consent by the other person.

Figure 7.4 Data subject's rights

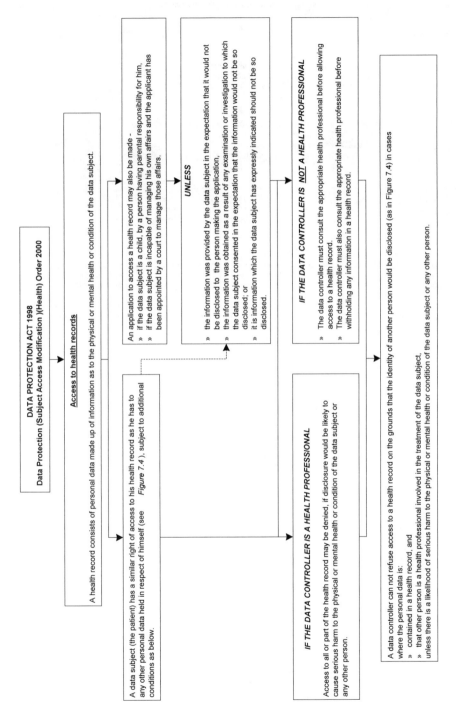

DATA PROTECTION ACT 1998
Data Protection (Subject Access Modification)(Health) Order 2000

Access to health records

A health record consists of personal data made up of information as to the physical or mental health or condition of the data subject.

A data subject (the patient) has a similar right of access to his health record as he has to any other personal data held in respect of himself (see *Figure 7.4*), subject to additional conditions as below.

An application to access a health record may also be made -
» if the data subject is a child, by a person having parental responsibility for him,
» if the data subject is incapable of managing his own affairs and the applicant has been appointed by a court to manage those affairs.

UNLESS

» the information was provided by the data subject in the expectation that it would not be disclosed to the person making the application,
» the information was obtained as a result of any examination or investigation to which the data subject consented in the expectation that the information would not be so disclosed; or
» it is information which the data subject has expressly indicated should not be so disclosed.

IF THE DATA CONTROLLER IS A HEALTH PROFESSIONAL

Access to all or part of the health record may be denied, if disclosure would be likely to cause serious harm to the physical or mental health or condition of the data subject or any other person.

IF THE DATA CONTROLLER IS NOT A HEALTH PROFESSIONAL

» The data controller must consult the appropriate health professional before allowing access to a health record.
» The data controller must also consult the appropriate health professional before withholding any information in a health record.

A data controller can not refuse access to a health record on the grounds that the identity of another person would be disclosed (as in Figure 7.4) in cases where the personal data is:
» contained in a health record, and
» that other person is a health professional involved in the treatment of the data subject,
unless there is a likelihood of serious harm to the physical or mental health or condition of the data subject or any other person.

Figure 7.5   Data subject's rights – health records

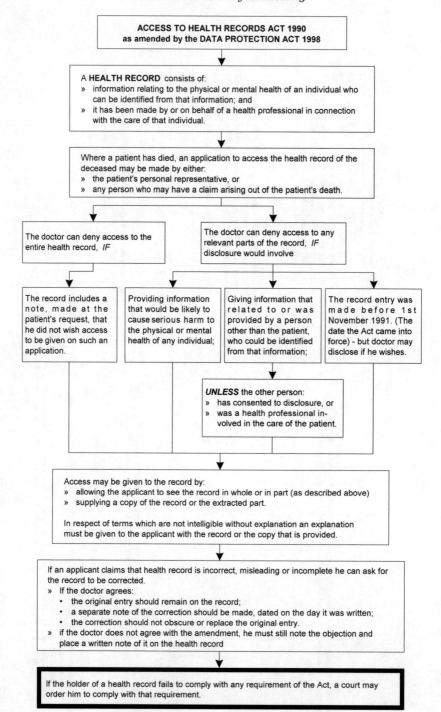

**ACCESS TO HEALTH RECORDS ACT 1990
as amended by the DATA PROTECTION ACT 1998**

A **HEALTH RECORD** consists of:
» information relating to the physical or mental health of an individual who can be identified from that information; and
» it has been made by or on behalf of a health professional in connection with the care of that individual.

Where a patient has died, an application to access the health record of the deceased may be made by either:
» the patient's personal representative, or
» any person who may have a claim arising out of the patient's death.

The doctor can deny access to the entire health record, *IF*

The doctor can deny access to any relevant parts of the record, *IF* disclosure would involve

The record includes a note, made at the patient's request, that he did not wish access to be given on such an application.

Providing information that would be likely to cause serious harm to the physical or mental health of any individual;

Giving information that related to or was provided by a person other than the patient, who could be identified from that information;

The record entry was made before 1st November 1991. (The date the Act came into force) - but doctor may disclose if he wishes.

UNLESS the other person:
» has consented to disclosure, or
» was a health professional involved in the care of the patient.

Access may be given to the record by:
» allowing the applicant to see the record in whole or in part (as described above)
» supplying a copy of the record or the extracted part.

In respect of terms which are not intelligible without explanation an explanation must be given to the applicant with the record or the copy that is provided.

If an applicant claims that health record is incorrect, misleading or incomplete he can ask for the record to be corrected.
» If the doctor agrees:
  • the original entry should remain on the record;
  • a separate note of the correction should be made, dated on the day it was written;
  • the correction should not obscure or replace the original entry.
» if the doctor does not agree with the amendment, he must still note the objection and place a written note of it on the health record

If the holder of a health record fails to comply with any requirement of the Act, a court may order him to comply with that requirement.

Figure 7.6 Access to Health Records Act

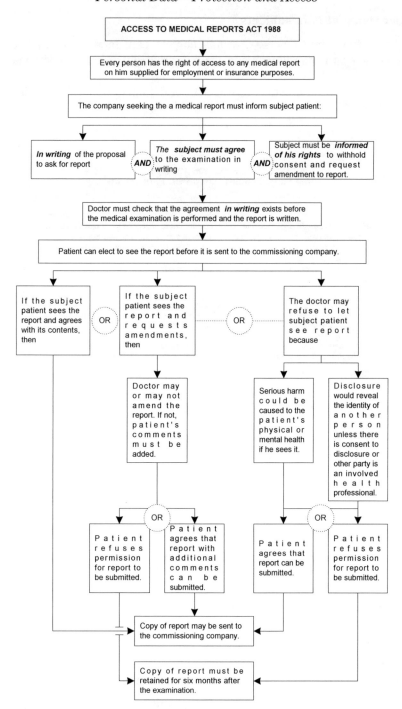

Figure 7.7 Access to Medical Reports Act

Further rights of data subjects

Along with the right of access, a data subject can, in some circumstances, demand that a data controller should cease or not begin processing personal data about him. It is unlikely that any data subject would try to use this right about the data held in a general practice, however brief details of this right are shown in Figure 7.8.

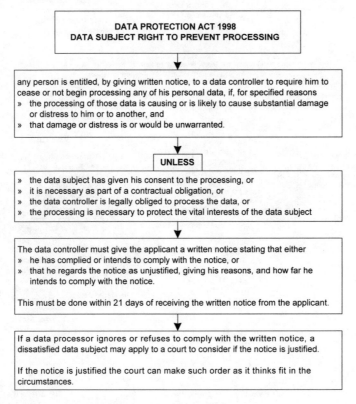

Figure 7.8 Right to prevent processing

Controls on data processing

Data Protection Commissioner

The office of Data Protection Commissioner replaces the older office of Data Protection Registrar. The Commissioner has the duties of:

- promoting the observance of the requirements of the 1998 Act by data controllers
- spreading information about the Act and how it works
- encouraging the development of Codes of Practice for guidance as to good practice in different professions and industries.

The DPC must keep a register recording the particulars of each registered data controller, and must make facilities available for members of the public to inspect such information on request.

The Commissioner has certain direct powers, which are shown in Figure 7.9.

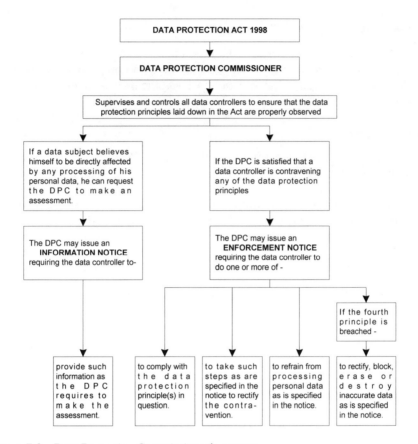

Figure 7.9 Data Protection Commissioner's powers

In any case in which the DPC's direct powers are insufficient to deal with a particular contravention he is empowered to institute appropriate criminal proceedings.

Data Protection Tribunal

Any data controller or data subject who is aggrieved by a decision of the DPC is entitled to take the matter to the Data Protection Tribunal. The tribunal will hear evidence from the appellant and from the DPC and will decide either to

- uphold the DPC's decision in whole or in part
- reject the DPC's decision, or
- substitute its own decision for that of the DPC.

The tribunal is a new body designed to meet the requirements first expressed in the *Gaskin* case. See page 93 for details. The decisions reached by the tribunal will eventually form a body of precedent that will be used to interpret the 1998 Act. Its procedures and jurisdiction are laid down in the Data Protection Tribunal (Enforcement Appeals) Rules 2000.

Criminal offences and civil wrongs

The Data Protection Act creates a large number of both criminal offences and civil rights that allow victims of wrongdoing to claim compensation. Following are the areas of liability that are of most significance to a medical general practice.

Criminal offences

- Processing personal data without notifying the DPC.
- Failing to notify the DPC of changes to the notification entry.
- Failing to comply with request from the DPC for particulars of processing.
- Failing to comply with an information notice or an enforcement notice.
- Making a false statement in answer to an information notice.
- Obtaining or disclosing personal data without the consent of the data controller.
- Procuring the disclosure to another person of personal data.

Further offences relate to the selling, etc. of personal data.

Civil actions

- *Damage:* any individual who suffers damage because a data controller contravenes any requirement of the Data Protection Act is entitled to compensation for that damage.
- *Distress:* any individual who suffers distress because a data controller contravenes any requirement of the Data Protection Act is entitled to compensation for that distress if the individual also suffers damage.

It can be seen that if a doctor provides a report for, say, employment or insurance purposes, all of that information must be totally accurate. Any inaccuracy could lead to a claim by the victim without the necessity of proving negligence.

Any civil action taken under the terms of the Act could be along with actions for such torts as negligence, breach of confidentiality, defamation, etc.

Liability

The main liability for contraventions of the Act lies upon the data controllers (the doctors).

The person responsible for breaking the law (either criminal or civil) will have personal liability as a principal in the matter. In the case of employees the employer(s) (the doctor(s)) will be vicariously liable for actions taken in the course of employment of the employee.

Chapter 8
Confidentiality and Privacy

Personal privacy

Unlike some other countries there is no specific law to guarantee personal privacy in Britain. Neither criminal laws nor civil laws provide any direct redress for a person who suffers an infringement of his privacy unless he can prove that he suffered a direct financial loss as a result. Even with such proof it would be difficult to prove the case.

In 1998 the government enacted the Human Rights Act 1998, which is intended to be in force by the end of the year 2000. This Act puts the main parts of the European Convention on Human Rights into British law. Importantly, from the aspect of this chapter, the following Convention Article is included:

'Everyone has the right to respect for his private and family life, his home and his correspondence.'

Article 8

There are legally permitted exceptions to the generality of this right, including 'as is necessary for the protection of health or morals'.

When the Act is fully implemented, case decisions will no doubt create precedents that will have the effect of increasing individual rights to privacy. Managers should keep an eye on any relevant press reports about matters that could concern the practice.

Some existing laws relate to particular aspects of confidential information that are associated with privacy. Figure 8.1 shows how these authorities overlap each other and how they may be breached in a practice situation.

Within the practice, for obvious reasons, the most sensitive information will be the medical records of individual patients and other documents associated with them. However there will also be many other records that will be considered to be of a confidential nature, for example:

- personnel records
- patient lists
- financial records
- contracts with other parties
- other documents concerning the business activities of the practice.

Every one of these records should be treated with the same regard for confidentiality. Any record containing personal data about a living person will come under the control of the Data Protection Act as has been described in Chapter 7.

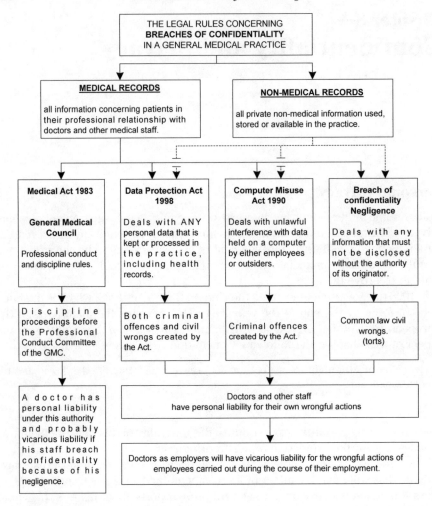

Figure 8.1   Breaches of confidentiality

The medical profession – rules of confidentiality

From ancient times it has been accepted that the relationship between the doctor and patient must be one of mutual trust if it is to be effective. To achieve and nurture this trust the doctor must treat everything that he learns from or about his patient with the strictest degree of confidentiality. The confidentiality extends to any information about a patient that has been obtained from sources other than the patient himself.

Nowadays the basic principles are laid down in the General Medical Council publication titled *Good Medical Practice*. Amplifying guidance details are contained in the publication *Confidentiality* published in October 1995.

The GMC principles of confidentiality

The principles of confidentiality that every doctor is expected to adhere to are, in brief:

- all confidential information is effectively protected against improper disclosure
- patients consenting to disclosure of information must understand what will be disclosed and the reasons for disclosure
- patients must be informed if information is to be disclosed to other health workers and be given the opportunity to withhold permission
- requests by patients that information should not be disclosed to third parties, save in exceptional circumstances must be respected
- if confidential information is disclosed only as much as is necessary for the purpose should be revealed
- health workers receiving disclosed information must understand the duty of confidentiality
- any doctor who decides to disclose confidential information must be prepared to explain and justify his decision.

These principles apply in all circumstances and aspects of a doctor's professional work.

The serious view taken by the GMC in any case of improper disclosure was shown in the following case:

> A GP was overheard talking in a pub about the fertility treatment that the landlord and landlady of the pub had received. *The GP was subsequently found guilty of serious professional misconduct* and it was recommended by the GMC that he be suspended from medical practice for three years.
>
> Re Shannon (1997)

The problem for GPs in maintaining confidentiality has increased in recent years, largely as a result of modern technology.

- New methods of treatment that require the collection of more detailed information together with the collection of biological samples leading to a variety of test results. This means not only that the medical 'dossier' of an individual patient will be large but also that it might not all be stored in the same location.
- Much patient information is now processed on computers and this has two effects.
  - As in any other 'computerised' organisation, the ease with which printed information can be generated encourages the production or more and more paper. Sometimes it can be difficult to keep track of all the paper.
  - Both stand alone computers and those linked by way of modems to wider area networks are vulnerable to unauthorised access that could result in improper disclosures.

It should be noted that even the death of a patient does not release a doctor from the obligation to maintain confidentiality. If the patient did not consent to disclosure during his lifetime, disclosures can only be made according to the rules governing the subject (see Figure 7.6).

Currently (May 2000) there is an application before the Court of Human Rights that relates to a deceased patient. The parents of a ten year old deceased patient are seeking disclosure of their son's record. Part of the claim alleges that it was altered post mortem. There is also a claim that a parent suffered psychiatric harm as a result of the failure of the doctors to provide relevant information. Apparently underlying the allegation is the inference that the assertion of confidentiality was made to avoid clinical negligence becoming known. After the case has been heard and the truth of the claims and counterclaims have been decided the court's decision might affect the rules of disclosure of a dead patient's record.

In February 1999 the GMC altered the ethical rules regarding consent. Amongst other things they say that doctors have a duty to keep their patients fully informed, in understandable language, throughout any course of treatment. If anything goes wrong they must also provide a full explanation.

Lawful disclosure by a doctor

If a doctor discloses any information imparted to him under the seal of professional confidence, then, unless there is a legal justification for the disclosure, he is in jeopardy of being disciplined by the GMC. Additionally, if the victim of the improper disclosure suffers any damage, financial loss or personal distress, then he can sue for a tort such as breach of confidentiality, negligence or defamation.

There are a number of circumstances under which a doctor, personally, can justifiably disclose confidential information about a patient to another person. Note that this is a personal decision that must be made by the individual doctor – an employee can not make the decision to disclose information. Figure 8.2 shows the various legal authorities that authorise disclosure by a doctor. If a doctor decides to disclose information he must ensure that his action comes exactly within the terms of the specific authority.

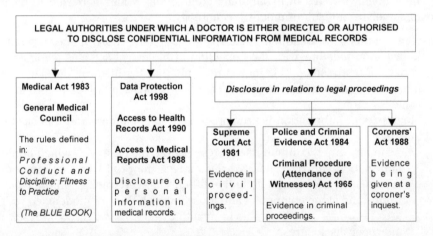

Figure 8.2   The laws governing disclosure of information

Disclosure authorised by the GMC

The following are the circumstances recognised by the GMC as justifying disclosure of confidential information by a doctor. Full details can be found in the GMC publication *Confidentiality* that is available on the GMC website (see Appendix B).

- **Disclosure of confidential information with the patient's consent**
  - ○ Confidential information may be disclosed in strict accordance with a patient's consent.
- **Disclosure within teams**
  - ○ To provide patients with the best possible care, it is often essential to pass confidential information between members of a medical team.
  - ○ It must be explained to a patient why and when information may be shared between team members as well as any circumstances in which team members providing non-medical care may be required to disclose information to third parties.
- **Disclosure to employers and insurance companies**
  - ○ If a patient is assessed by a doctor on behalf of a third party (e.g. an employer or insurance company) then he must be told of his rights. The assessment must only be made after the patient gives written consent.
  - ○ The Access to Medical Reports Act 1988 specifies the procedures to be followed. See page 97.

Disclosure of information without the patient's consent

- **Disclosure in the patient's medical interests**
  - ○ If a patient is incapable of giving consent to treatment because of immaturity, illness, or mental incapacity, and it is essential in the patient's medical interests, a doctor may disclose relevant information to an appropriate person or authority.
  - ○ The patient must be told before the disclosure of any information is made.
- **Disclosure after a patient's death**
  - ○ The obligation to keep information confidential after a patient's death remains in being.
  - ○ The Access to Health Records Act 1990 gives third parties right of access, in certain circumstances, to the medical records of a deceased patient (see page 97).

Disclosure for medical teaching, medical research, and medical audit

- **Research**
  - ○ Where, for the purposes of medical research there is a need to disclose information which it is not possible to anonymise effectively, every reasonable effort must be made to inform the patients concerned, or those who may properly give permission on their behalf, that they may, at any stage, withhold their consent to disclosure.
  - ○ Where consent cannot be obtained, this fact should be drawn to the attention of a research ethics committee which should decide whether the public interest in the research outweighs patients' right to confidentiality. Disclosures to a researcher may otherwise be improper, even if the researcher is a registered medical practitioner.
  - ○ Patients' consent to disclosure of information for teaching and audit must be obtained unless the data have been effectively anonymised.

- **Financial audit, etc.**
  (Note that this heading is not included in the GMC Confidentiality guidelines.)
  - ○ Doctors may allow access to patient records by health service financial auditors as part of the post-payment verification process.
  - ○ Originally each patient whose record was to be viewed was told individually about the purpose of the inspection but from May 1999 the GMC requirement was reduced to posters and leaflets in surgeries. Some doctors have expressed disquiet at this development.
- In a recent case examining the use of information contained on prescription forms, the objections of the Department of Health set out in a national circular were overruled by the court:

    The Court of Appeal held that *as long as a patient's identity is protected, it is not a breach of confidence for general practitioners and pharmacists to disclose to a third party, without the patient's consent, the information contained in the patient's prescription form for marketing research purposes.*

    R *v.* Department of Health, *ex parte* Source Informatics Ltd. (2000)

- **Disclosure in the interests of others**
  Disclosures may be made in the public interest if a failure to disclose information could expose the patient, or others, to risk of death or serious harm. In such circumstances the disclosure should be made promptly to an appropriate person or authority. Such disclosures could arise, for example, in the following situations.
  - ○ A patient continues to drive, against medical advice, when unfit to do so. In such circumstances the information should be disclosed to the Driver and Vehicle Licensing Agency without delay.
  - ○ If a colleague, who is also a patient, is placing patients at risk as a result of illness or another medical condition.
  - ○ If disclosure is necessary for the prevention or detection of a serious crime.
  An important case covering this matter was:

    The Court of Appeal held that where a patient had committed multiple killings and had been detained in a secure hospital, a doctor did not act in breach of his duty of confidence to the patient in disclosing a report to authorities responsible for the patient's care if it contained vital information relevant to decisions that might lead to the patient's release and the risk of consequent danger to the public, since, in those circumstances, *the public interest in protecting the public outweighed the public interest in maintaining confidences between a doctor and his patient.*

    W *v.* Edgell and others (1989)

- **Disclosure in connection with judicial or other statutory proceeding**
  Information may be disclosed in the following circumstances.
  - ○ To satisfy a specific statutory requirement, such as notification of a communicable disease or of attendance upon a person dependent upon certain controlled drugs.
  - ○ If a doctor is ordered to do so by a judge or presiding officer of a court, or a coroner. Without a court order, a request for disclosure by a third party, for example, a solicitor, police officer, or officer of a court, is not sufficient justification for disclosure without a patient's consent.

○ If a committee of the GMC investigating a doctor's fitness to practise has determined that the interests of justice require disclosure of confidential information, provided every reasonable effort has been made to seek the consent of the patients concerned. If consent is refused the patient's wishes must be respected.

- **Disclosure to inspectors of taxes**
  ○ A doctor who has a private practice, can disclose confidential information in response to a request from an inspector of taxes, provided every effort has been made to separate financial information from clinical records.

- **Media inquiries about patients** (November 1996)
  Doctors are sometimes approached by journalists for comments on medical issues. Where such comments include information about patients, doctors must respect patients' rights to privacy. Before releasing any information the doctor should:
  ○ remember that any information learnt in a professional capacity must be regarded as confidential, whether or not the information is also in the public domain
  ○ whenever possible, obtain explicit consent from patients before discussing matters relating to their care with journalists, whether or not the patients' names or other identifying information is to be revealed. Explicit consent must be obtained if patients will be identifiable from details disclosed.

Disclosure of medical records

The legal provisions of the Data Protection Act, the Access to Health Records Act and the Access to Medical Records Act are described in Chapter 7.

Disclosure in relation to legal proceedings

Civil cases

Supreme Court Act 1981

This Act requires a doctor to provide a patient's medical records to his (the patient's) legal or medical advisor when the information contained therein is required in the pursuance of legal proceedings. The procedure is illustrated in Figure 8.3.

Criminal cases

Police and Criminal Evidence Act 1984

Sometimes medical evidence is needed as part of the prosecution of an alleged offender. However, a police officer can not stroll into a surgery and demand information because he feels that it is necessary for his investigation.

Normally, the police would obtain a search warrant from a magistrate, but

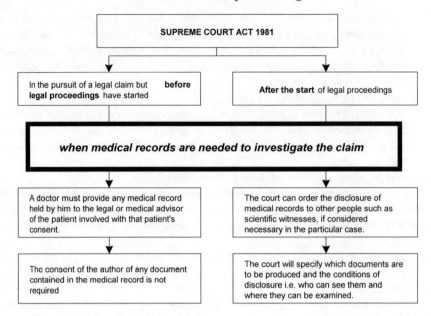

Figure 8.3   Supreme Court Act 1981

health records and clinical specimens are excluded from normal search warrants. In cases of 'excluded material' the police must make an application to a judge, and he, the judge, will decide if the application is reasonable. If it is reasonable a judicial order will be made and the doctor concerned will be required to produce the documents or other evidence required. The procedure is shown in Figure 8.4.

Note, as described on page 110, a doctor may act without the issue of a judicial order, if failure to disclose the information would expose either the patient or anyone else to the risk of death or other serious harm.

Criminal Procedure (Attendance of Witnesses) Act 1965

The law in this area of procedure has recently been amended to make information more readily available for defence purposes in criminal trials.

If a doctor refuses to provide information about a patient's health record, perhaps because the patient himself has refused consent to disclosure, or another third party likewise refuses consent, any party to the criminal proceedings may then seek a witness summons to compel disclosure. The basic points of the procedure are shown in Figure 8.5.

The important feature from the doctor's point of view is that he can, either personally or through legal representation, object to the disclosure before the trial itself occurs. The judge will listen to any oral representation and may examine any documents involved in the representation. He will then decide whether all, part or none of the information should be given at the trial.

If disclosure is ordered, the doctor must comply with the order.

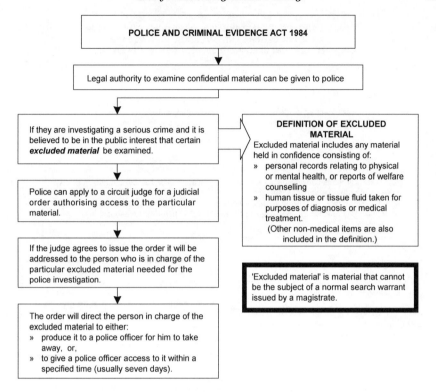

Figure 8.4   Police and Criminal Evidence Act 1984

Legal proceedings – a doctor's liability

If a doctor refuses to comply with a judicial order he will be called before the court to answer for his refusal. The court will listen to his reasons and if they are not considered acceptable he will probably be given another opportunity to produce the evidence required. However if he persists in his refusal he may be found in contempt of court. This will put him in jeopardy of a penalty that could be either a fine or imprisonment depending on the surrounding circumstances.

Coroners' Act 1988

The coroners' court is different to every other court in England and Wales. It is called an *inquisitorial court* which means that coroners themselves question witnesses and other people, including lawyers, can only question witnesses with the coroner's permission.

The coroner has extremely wide powers when holding an inquest in requiring witnesses to give evidence before him. He can call for almost any sort of evidence that he deems to be necessary to complete his inquiry into a death. See Chapter 12 for further information on the coroner.

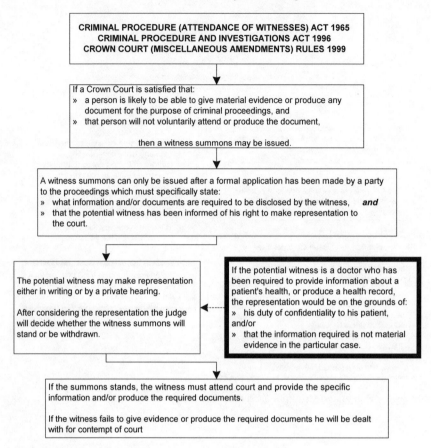

Figure 8.5   Witness in criminal proceedings

Breach of confidentiality

If an employee breaches confidentiality the legal situation is very complicated. Not only is the victim able to sue the employee, but the doctor, as his employer, will also be able to make out a case. Figure 8.6 shows the main points to be proved in these cases.

This is a complex area of legislation, but decided cases show that the points illustrated in Figure 8.6 must be proven if an action is to be successful. It can be seen that besides medical records any other information about the practice would come within the range of this tort.

In reality it is unlikely that a doctor would sue an employee for a breach of confidentiality because in every contract of employment confidentiality (based on this tort) is an implied term.

As all employees accept a duty *not* to disclose any confidential information, a breach of confidentiality is more likely to be dealt with by disciplinary action than by court action. A breach of confidentiality by an employee will be considered to be gross misconduct and the employer will be justified in dismissing the employee after he has satisfied himself that the infraction has occurred.

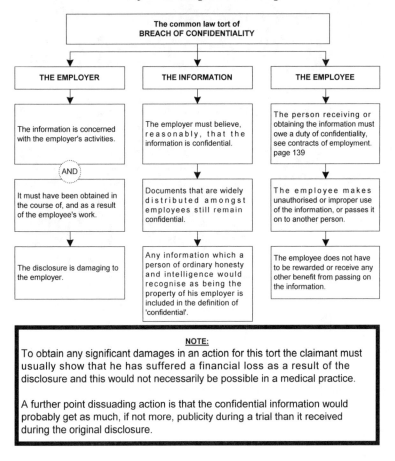

Figure 8.6 The tort of breach of confidentiality

The following statements have been made by tribunal chairmen when considering the duty of confidentiality:

Doctors receive sensitive information in confidence from patients and patients are reliant on confidentiality being maintained. *Staff must observe confidentiality when handling patients' notes and transferring information.* Should it become known that there are breaches of confidentiality, the public will cease to trust that practice, their confidence having been eroded, the GMC may become involved and *because of the doctrine of vicarious liability a doctor may be censured or even erased from the register.*

Unknown title, gross misconduct 1 quoted by BMA lecturer

...(the dismissal) for ... a relatively trivial breach of confidentiality might not be regarded as a reasonable penalty. On the other hand ... confidentiality is of the essence in any medical practice and any breach of confidentiality is not only most upsetting for the patient involved, but can have a devastating effect on a medical practice ... *even the*

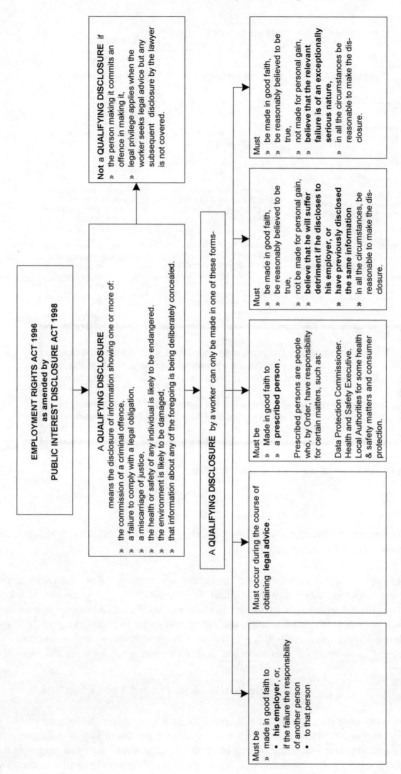

EMPLOYMENT RIGHTS ACT 1996
as amended by
PUBLIC INTEREST DISCLOSURE ACT 1998

A QUALIFYING DISCLOSURE
means the disclosure of information showing one or more of:

» the commission of a criminal offence,
» a failure to comply with a legal obligation,
» a miscarriage of justice,
» the health or safety of any individual is likely to be endangered.
» the environment is likely to be damaged,
» that information about any of the foregoing is being deliberately concealed.

Not a QUALIFYING DISCLOSURE if

» the person making it commits an offence in making it,
» legal privilege applies when the worker seeks legal advice but any subsequent disclosure by the lawyer is not covered.

A QUALIFYING DISCLOSURE by a worker can only be made in one of these forms-

Must be
» made in good faith to
  ▪ his employer, or,
  if the failure the responsibility of another person
  ▪ to that person

Must occur during the course of obtaining **legal advice**.

Must be
» Made in good faith to
» a **prescribed person**.

Prescribed persons are people who, by Order, have responsibility for certain matters, such as:

Data Protection Commissioner.
Health and Safety Executive.
Local Authorities for some health & safety matters and consumer protection.

Must
» be made in good faith,
» be reasonably believed to be true,
» not be made for personal gain, **believe that he will suffer detriment if he discloses to his employer, or have previously disclosed the same information**
» in all the circumstances, be reasonable to make the disclosure.

Must
» be made in good faith,
» be reasonably believed to be true,
» not made for personal gain, **believe that the relevant failure is of an exceptionally serious nature,**
» in all the circumstances be reasonable to make the disclosure.

Figure 8.7 Public interest – qualifying disclosures

slightest breach of confidentiality must be regarded most seriously and dismissal in such circumstances is appropriate.

Unknown title, gross misconduct 2 quoted by BMA lecturer

See Chapter 9 for more details on this topic.

Disclosure made in the public interest

Public Interest Disclosure Act 1998

This Act amended the Employment Rights Act 1996 and came into force on 2 July 1999. The press have referred to it as a 'whistleblower's charter' because it legitimises some disclosures of confidential material.

The Act provides protection for employees who disclose information from their work when it is in the public interest for them so to do. It describes what are termed 'qualifying disclosures' that are, in very general terms disclosures of matters or activities that are, or are likely to be, contrary to the law. Further details are shown in Figure 8.7.

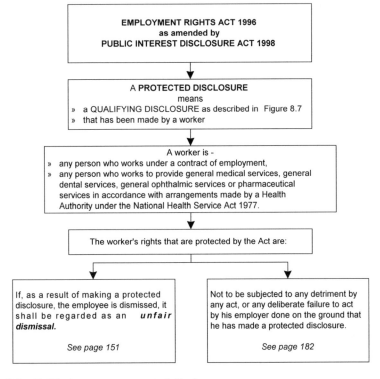

Figure 8.8 Public interest – protected disclosures

Besides defining the activity the Act also describes the manner in which the disclosures can be made, which are basically:

- to the worker's employer
- to a lawyer
- to a prescribed person,

and if none of these methods is appropriate to some other person not mentioned above, perhaps the press, providing the disclosure is of an exceptionally serious matter. In these circumstances, the worker must follow the very strict conditions that are laid down in the Act.

Protection

Protection is given to workers making qualifying disclosures if they meet the Act's definition of a worker which includes any employee working under a contract of employment. The Act also specifically includes in the definition of worker doctors and other health professionals who are working under a contract with a Health Authority. The protection provided (see Figure 8.8) is similar to the protection for other rights that are contained in the Employment Rights Act. This means that if the worker is dismissed the dismissal is automatically unfair and if the worker suffers detriment from the employer he can complain to an employment tribunal and seek compensation.

Chapter 9
The Security of Confidential Information

Practical problems involved

The seventh data principle is quite explicit about the need for data controllers to ensure that proper security measures are taken concerning any personal data that is held.

> Appropriate technical and organisational measures shall be taken against unauthorised or unlawful processing of personal data and against accidental loss or destruction of, or damage to, personal data.
>
> Having regard to the state of technological development and the cost of implementing any measures, the measures must ensure a level of security appropriate to
>
> (a)   the harm that might result from such unauthorised or unlawful processing or accidental loss, destruction or damage as are mentioned above, and
> (b)   the nature of the data to be protected.
>
> The data controller must take reasonable steps to ensure the reliability of any employees of his who have access to the personal data.
>
> Data Protection Act 1998

Security measures must cover:

- manual filing systems
- computer filing systems
- information known to individual employees.

Manual filing systems

Manual files seem to be such a mundane part of the practice that they are not worth much effort. For this reason less attention is often paid to the security of filed documents.

Some points that a manager might consider are listed below, although it is appreciated that not all are feasible in the smallest of practices:

- filing cabinets, drawers or suspended files should be locked when not under the supervision of an authorised person
- if practicable, the room containing the files should also be capable of being locked when not in use
- the windows of this room must be capable of being secured, and, if on the ground floor, should be screened to prevent files from being seen from outside

- only authorised members of staff should have access to confidential files, and authorisation might not extend to all confidential files
- any unauthorised person handling the files should be challenged immediately
- some form of tagging system should be used so that documents not in the system can quickly be traced to the person holding them
- the use of photocopiers should be controlled to prevent unauthorised copies of documents being made
- a systematic 'weeding' programme should be introduced to remove obsolete papers at regular intervals
- obsolete confidential papers, including yesterday's post-it notes, etc. that have personal data thereon should not be placed with other rubbish, but should go into a separate container marked 'confidential waste' to be disposed of properly
- a good quality paper shredder should be used to shred obsolete papers before their disposal – if not available, the papers should be burned to ash in an incinerator (not an open fire).

The last one of these items might seem to be a bit over the top, but not a year goes by without newspaper stories relating to obsolete confidential papers being found dumped in some public place. Both hospitals and general practices have offended in this way.

A security conscious ethos should be encouraged so that employees are continuously reminded of the importance of dealing with confidential papers. This is important both from an ethical point of view and for the avoidance of defending a legal action for the improper or careless handling of personal data.

Computer filing systems

Keeping and using data on a computer system causes special problems of security.

To see the nature of the problem, it is helpful to look at an illustrated summary of the factors involved, see Figure 9.1. The illustration shows the various aspects of the system that are vulnerable to interference, hence where security measures must be most efficient.

A person attempting to gain unauthorised access to confidential information can be either an employee or an outsider.

Depending on the circumstances a criminal offence might be committed in some cases, although a nosy patient peering at the monitor screen does not commit any offence even though the action is morally questionable.

The main law concerned with unlawful interference with computers is the Computer Misuse Act 1990 and the main elements in this Act are shown in Figure 9.2.

If an employee accesses or tries to access a part of the system that they are not entitled to access by, for example, using an unauthorised password, he would commit an offence under this Act. This was shown in the following case:

> The House of Lords held that *an employee commits an offence of securing unauthorised access to a computer contrary to the Computer Misuse Act where the employee, although authorised to use the computer for certain purposes, used it in a*

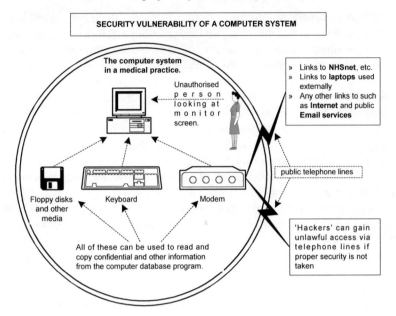

Figure 9.1   Computer system vulnerability

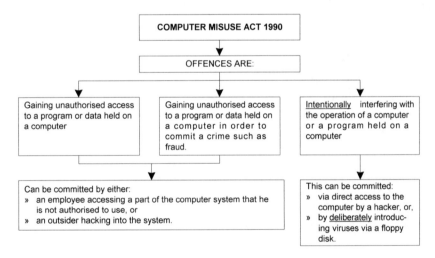

Figure 9.2   Computer Misuse Act 1990

way that exceeded his authorisation. These offences are not confined to 'hacking' by outsiders.

> R *v*. Bow Street Stipendiary Magistrate, *ex parte* Govt. of the USA(1999)

However, as seen in the case of *Denco Ltd.* v. *Joinson* (1992) on page 154 it would probably be more satisfactory in the majority of instances to discipline the employee for gross misconduct.

In the case of patients or others trying to read a monitor screen the reason is probably idle curiosity or seeking a titbit of gossip. Because nosiness is not a crime in itself there is nothing that can be done about it. Indeed to raise the issue could cause embarrassment for the doctor as he would then have to explain why such a person could be able to see confidential information.

Most hackers see unauthorised entry as an electronic challenge rather than as a deliberate interference with confidential data although this does not excuse their activities. Some might have more sinister motives that could involve altering or deleting data for whatever reason. If the hacker taps into a public telephone line as part of his hacking, he might also commit offences under the Interception of Communications Act 1985.

The prosecution of such offenders does not remove the civil liability of data controllers under the terms of the Data Protection Act.

Data controllers must always take their responsibilities seriously. Whilst there have not been any significant civil cases in this area in the UK courts up to now in other countries with similar laws there has been a steady increase in litigation. This tends to come about as people became more aware of their rights through the publicity of early cases.

There is no reason to suppose that the situation will be any different here, and a major case involving substantial compensation payments could result in many other people pursuing claims through the courts. It is noteworthy that the number, diversity and complexity of complaints made to the Data Protection Registrar increased annually between 1984 and 2000 when the DPC took over the post. In the year to 31 March 1999 3,653 complaints were received.

Caldicott Guardians

Following the Caldicott Committee's review of the non-clinical use of patient identifiable information, the NHS Executive issued guideline instructions to the Service. These are intended to ensure that a tighter control is kept over such confidential data.

One important requirement is that all NHS organisations must appoint a Caldicott Guardian who will have the responsibility of overseeing all access to patient identifiable information held by the organisation.

The Guardian must have both the seniority and authority to exercise influence on policy and strategic planning. It is suggested that in a Primary Care Group the Guardian should be a board member with clinical governance responsibilities.

Information coordinator

The NHS Executive advises that in each practice there should be nominated a lead person for confidentiality and security issues. This person should be answerable to the Group's Caldicott Guardian.

No doubt there will be formal guidance on the duties of such a person, but following the example of commercial organisations they could include those tasks listed below. All of these tasks must be carried out anyway so more work is not generated, further having one person responsible helps to reduce errors and their possible consequences.

The duties could include the following.

- Checking the procedures for physical security including checks on files, magnetic media (disks, etc.) and modem connections.
- Ensuring that computer backup procedures are adhered to at the correct times.
- Establishing and confirming that appropriate procedures are in place to meet the legal requirements of the Data Protection Act. This will include maintaining and pruning records no longer needed.
- Dealing with requests made under either the Data Protection Act or other legislation for access to stored information.
- Maintaining proper records of all requests for access to records, together with details of how the request was dealt with and any action taken following a request to amend or delete information from the records.
- Ensuring that printouts no longer needed are properly shredded.
- Ensuring that disks, tapes, etc. for disposal are physically destroyed.
- Ensuring that before the disposal of computers no longer needed, any data on the hard disks are thoroughly deleted and the disks reformatted.

Perhaps the following additional tasks could also become the responsibility of such a coordinator if deemed to be appropriate in the practice:

- ensuring the safety of data accessible through a computer network including virus checking and any anti-hacking procedures that are considered to be necessary
- overseeing the implementation of the requirements of the Health and Safety (Display Screen Equipment) Regulations 1992. See page 75.

Other advice on data security

The Audit Commission has said that most computer security problems are not caused by sophisticated manipulation of computer programs but by poor basic security by the data controllers.

The following is a checklist based on the advice given by the Audit Commission and other experts.

- Do a risk assessment of the system and identify where security could be breached.
- Assign responsibility for security to a named member of staff.
- Use passwords and personal identification.
- Make sure that passwords are secure, unobvious and changed regularly.
- Use screen saver software, especially on a reception desk computer.
- Make a regular check that the safeguards are working correctly.
- Forbid the use of unauthorised software.
- Use control software to inhibit the loading of unauthorised software.
- Use virus control software.
- Make frequent backups of data.
- Store backups in a safe location.
- Store original official disks safely and securely.
- Discourage staff from browsing through data that they do not need for their job.
- Ensure that staff are aware of the rules and the penalties for breaching them.

To the foregoing will be added the security rules defined for users of network links that must also be scrupulously followed.

Advice from the BMA

The General Medical Services Committee published *The Data Protection Act: A Code of Practice for General Medical Practitioners* that reviewed the 1984 Act and its application in a medical practice. It is now out of date, but when rewritten will be worth acquiring by every practice.

Information known to individual employees

It is a fact of life that people dealing with similar information tend to overlook the significance of that information, especially when they are busy with several different things at the same time.

   Thoughtlessness by employees is much more likely than a deliberate breach of confidentiality. Consider the following examples of thoughtless or careless behaviour that could involve confidentiality being breached to some degree.

- Discussing clinical matters within earshot of unauthorised people. Sometimes they may be out of sight behind a screen, but this does not make them deaf.
- Papers being left on desks where they can be read by unauthorised people. In reception these things might be needed near to where patients are dealt with, but people can easily read things that are upside-down. A shelf below the counter would be one solution.
- Computers located where unauthorised people can see the monitor screens. If possible turn the monitor round, in any event, the use of a screen saver program set to operate after a fairly short delay should be considered.
- Giving 'helpful' answers to telephone callers. Most staff want to be polite and helpful to callers but it should be impressed on them that they have no way of knowing that a caller is who he or she says they are.
- Asking a patient's spouse to pass on a message about, perhaps, an appointment time. Does she/he want the spouse to know about the visit to the doctor?
- Discarding papers, computer disks, etc. without proper destruction. It is surprising how often papers and discarded disks are merely thrown into the waste paper basket for disposal with the normal rubbish. Some of these may end up on an ordinary rubbish tip, and every tip has got scavengers.
- Giving staff unaccountable access to confidential information. Each member of staff should be quite clear regarding what documents and which part of the computer system he is authorised to access. Any disobedience to these rules should be swiftly dealt with under the disciplinary code.
- Failing to secure information stored on computer in a proper manner. Any computer containing confidential information should be properly secured when not in use so that unauthorised persons cannot access it. This might mean providing keyboard locks and certainly disconnection from any modem lines that are not secure.

- Leaving confidential materials in insecure positions. This can apply particularly to papers and laptop computers left in motor cars, especially in areas that suffer much auto crime.
- Using fax machines without knowing how secure the receiving machine is. The sender's efforts at confidentiality are totally without effect if the receiving fax is in an open office where anyone can see incoming faxes.
- Using portable phones to transmit confidential information. Analogue phones provide no practical protection at all and messages can be intercepted at will by those interested in such matters. Such models will be obsolete by the end of 2000. Digital phones are rather more secure, but the safest thing is to avoid saying anything on a portable telephone that has a high level of confidentiality.

Although the foregoing and similar actions would not necessarily breach the laws of confidentiality, without exception they would all justify the instigation of discipline proceedings against the thoughtless or inept member of staff concerned.

An important duty of any practice manager is to consider the procedures followed by staff when dealing with confidential material. The manager must also forecast the possible worst case situation that could arise from breaching a procedure, hopefully preventing difficulties at source.

Future NHS information systems

The proposed way ahead for information technology in the NHS was described in 1997 in the following terms:

New information technology – supporting quality and efficiency
A modern and dependable NHS needs to be supported by accurate and up-to-date information and information technology. In recent years, information technology in the NHS has been focused on supporting the transaction processes of the internal market. This has been at the expense of realising the potential of IT to support front-line staff in delivering benefits for patients. In 1998, the Government will publish a new Information Management and Technology Strategy for the NHS which will harness the enormous potential benefits of IT to support the drive for quality and efficiency in the NHS by:

- making patient records electronically available when they're needed
- using the NHSnet and the Internet to bring patients quicker test results
- on-line booking of appointments and up-to-date specialist advice
- enabling accurate information about finance and performance to be available promptly
- providing knowledge about health, illness and best treatment practice to the public through the Internet and emerging public access media (e.g. digital TV)
- developing telemedicine to ensure specialist skills are available to all parts of the country

There will be robust safeguards to protect patients' confidentiality and privacy. The aim will be to create a powerful alliance between knowledgeable patients advised by knowledgeable professionals as a means of improving health and healthcare.

The New NHS – Modern, Dependable (1997)

Following the above, in September 1998 the Health Secretary announced that a
£1 billion investment in new technology for the NHS was to be made. It is
intended that over a seven year period all health records will be put on a national
data base that will be constantly updated, and looseleaf manual records will be
phased out.

It is planned to phase in the new system from the year 2001 after which date all
GPs will have access to the NHSnet. The details of the proposals are contained in
the paper *Information for Health* published in September 1998.

This paper outlines the overall information strategy for the NHS from 1998 to
2005. The strategy is ambitious, far-reaching and will be extremely complex to
implement, as it envisages amongst other things:

- lifelong electronic health records for every person in the country
- 24 hour on-line access to records and information for all NHS clinicians
- seamless care for patients through GPs, hospitals and community services all
  sharing information.

As far as primary care is concerned, it is suggested that a national programme
will be needed to develop the new systems. The details are too complex for
inclusion in this handbook but interested managers may care to read the
Information for Health document that can be downloaded from the DoH website, see Appendix B.

Enormous problems will have to be overcome before the proposed new system becomes fully operable. Arguably the most difficult task facing small general
practices will be the transfer of information to the electronic health records
(EHR). At present there is no single pattern of filing system universally in use,
and health records might be kept:

- in EC5 and EC6 envelopes
- in A4 size folders

taking note of the Terms of Service requirement to retain paper records.

Other records may be kept on computer programs, keeping printouts as the
paper records, however, there are several commercial programs that are used
and they are not compatible with each other.

The whole system, when implemented, will have to meet the requirements of
the Data Protection Act as described in Chapter 7. There will also be the onerous
responsibility of ensuring the confidentiality of every record of every patient.

Many other organisations have computerised their records but invariably the
task has taken a long time. For instance, police computerisation of criminal
records requiring similar confidentiality constraints took several years to complete.

Use of e-mail

As the use of both NHS and other networks increase, it is appropriate to insert a
word of caution at this point.

Many people seem to regard e-mail, especially when sent by way of a dedicated
network as a vehicle for idle gossip. Such users are certainly not as careful as
they should be when making statements that might be defamatory. The dangers

are shown in two cases that alleged libel in e-mails that were transmitted over private networks.

> A policeman returned a piece of bad meat to Asda and demanded a refund. He subsequently found out that his description had been circulated on the Asda private network under the heading 'refund fraud'. *He sued Asda for libel who settled out of court for a five figure sum.*

Eggleton *v.* Asda plc (1995)

The second case involved idle gossip over a private network:

> Employees of an insurance company exchanged messages about the business standing of another company. Subsequently, *the employers of the message writers, having vicarious liability for the actions of the users of the e-mail system, were sued for libel.* In the event, the matter was settled out of court when the defendant company paid £450,000 in compensation.

Western Provident *v.* Norwich Union (1997)

Although neither of the cases went to court, the legal advice was apparently quite clear that the e-mails constituted publications of libel.

It was announced in July 1999 that, after the 1998 Act has been brought into force (March 2000), a Code of Practice governing the use of personal data regarding employees, by employers, will be introduced. This will cover such things as the interception of e-mail, monitoring telephone calls and the use of closed circuit television systems. The Code will set out the rules governing the personal privacy of employees in the workplace. It is probable that employees will have to be told either in their contract of employment or otherwise exactly what monitoring is taking place. Additionally specific information will be needed about how much private use can be made of the employer's communication systems.

Part IV
Relations between Employers and Employees

- Contracts
- Pay and conditions of work
- Discrimination
- Trade unions

Chapter 10
Contracts of Employment

Employment law

Employment law or labour law as it is sometimes called, is that part of English law that deals with the relationship between an employer and his employees and to any problems arising from employment.

Figure 10.1 shows the main topics in these laws that are likely to affect people working in medical general practices. Appropriate details are given in this part of the handbook:

EMPLOYMENT LAW

EMPLOYER provides the rules that regulate the relations between an employer and his employees in such matters as - **EMPLOYEES**

> CONTRACTS OF EMPLOYMENT
> TERMINATION OF CONTRACT
> UNFAIR DISMISSAL
> REDUNDANCY
> AUTHORISED TIME OFF WORK
> PAY
> WORKING TIME
> DISCRIMINATION
> DISCIPLINE & GRIEVANCES
> TRADE UNIONS
> OTHER ASSOCIATED TOPICS

Figure 10.1   Employment law

The main Act of Parliament that deals with employment law matters is the Employment Rights Act 1996, which is a long and complex statute. In this part of the handbook, for convenience, the Act is referred to simply as ERA. Matters are further complicated in that the 1996 Act is affected by and refers to several other statutes, the most important being:

- Equal Pay Act 1970
- Sex Discrimination Act 1975
- Race Relations Act 1976

- Trade Union and Labour Relations (Consolidation) Act 1992
- Disability Discrimination Act 1995
- Employment Tribunals Act 1996
- Employment Rights (Dispute Resolution) Act 1998
- Public Interest Disclosure Act 1998
- Teaching and Higher Education Act 1998 (re training)
- National Minimum Wage Act 1998
- Tax Credits Act 1999
- Employment Relations Act 1999

Additionally, there are many orders and regulations that detail how the statutory principles are implemented and finally there are court judgments that have interpreted particular aspects of these laws.

The reason for detailing the foregoing legal authorities is to emphasise the complexity of the law in this particular area. A few chapters in a handbook of this size can only be used to skip over the most important elements, thus giving the practice manager some background knowledge of the principles involved. Therefore, it cannot be stressed too strongly that if a dispute is likely to arise between an employee or ex employee and his employer, formal legal advice should be sought as soon as possible. The maximum compensation that can now be awarded by an employment tribunal for unfair dismissal is £50,000, so it could be expensive to ignore a problem and hope it will go away – it won't!

Employment tribunals

An employment tribunal (before 1 August 1998 they were called industrial tribunals) is a form of informal court that hears disputed matters concerned with employment. Most of the hearings relate to claims of unfair dismissal but complaints of breaches of any of the statutes listed above are also heard.

The law concerning the structure, functions and procedures of employment tribunals is to be found in the Employment Tribunals Act 1996 (previously titled the Industrial Tribunals Act 1996), and the Employment Rights (Dispute Resolution) Act 1998.

Many of the statutes listed give people rights to take particular complaints to an employment tribunal.

An employment tribunal consists of a legally qualified chairman and two 'lay' members, both of who are experts in industrial relations. One lay member will be drawn from the employers' side of industry the other from the trade union side. The lay members are expected to reach conclusions on the facts of a particular case and not show bias towards any party. Decisions are made on a majority basis, although it is said that in over 95% of cases the decisions are unanimous. See Figure 4.2 on page 33 for the relationship of these tribunals to civil courts.

There are strict time limits for some complaints, and if a complaint is outside the prescribed time limit, the tribunal is barred from hearing it. In consequence, it is important for any complainant to institute action as soon as practicable.

For claims that relate to loss of employment such as unfair dismissal and redundancy matters, the employee must have at least one year of continuous employment with the same employer. The definition of 'continuous employment' is complicated and anyone contemplating taking a complaint to an employment tribunal should have these matters clarified before pursuing it.

Precedent

Employment tribunals are bound to follow decisions made by the Employment Appeal Tribunal or by other superior courts. However, a tribunal is not bound to follow the a decision made by another tribunal or its own previous decisions. For this reason, any decision made by an employment tribunal that is described in this handbook or elsewhere can only be regarded as a guideline and not a definitive description of the law.

Procedure

Parties to these tribunals do not have to know the law nor do they have to be legally represented. The chairman is expected to fit the facts that are found by the tribunal into the law as it stands. If one side is not legally represented and seems to be having difficulty in presenting the case, the chairman will ask pertinent questions. These are intended to draw out the facts and thus ascertain the truth of the particular situation. The detailed procedures that the tribunal must follow are laid down in law.

The burden of proof lies upon the applicant to prove to the tribunal the particular facts needed to sustain his complaint. This means that the applicant must show prima facie (this means 'at first sight') that employment law has been breached. The burden of proof then switches to the employer who must produce evidence to refute the claim that has been made.

After both parties have put their case to the tribunal, the evidence is considered and a decision is reached on the balance of probabilities.

Hearsay evidence is almost completely barred from criminal courts but it is acceptable in civil courts, including employment tribunals. Hearsay is evidence

- that a witness learned from someone else
- who was not the other party to the proceedings
- in the absence of that party.

Many documents will come under the heading of hearsay if they are produced by a witness who did not originally compile them.

The significance of this point for a practice manager is that comprehensive records should be kept of all matters concerning employees *and* they should be updated at the time of each new event. If such records are correctly kept they may be producible as evidence at a tribunal hearing. Even though they are hearsay the tribunal might accept them as a contemporaneous record of disputed facts. A record is contemporaneous if it is made at or close to the time that the events recorded actually occurred.

Remedies

If an employment tribunal finds that a complaint is 'well founded', it will make a declaration to that effect, and then according to the rules covering the particular complaint might decide to make:

- a declaration on the legality of the particular situation
- an order for the payment of compensation to the wronged person by the employer (or ex employer)
- an order that one party should pay a given sum of money to another (not normal costs or allowances)
- an order for an employee to be reinstated (this means that the employee will be treated in all respects as though he had not been dismissed)
- an order for an employee to be re-engaged (this means the employee will be re-engaged on another job, with terms and conditions no less favourable than the original job).

Appeals

Appeals can be made from the decisions of these tribunals regarding points of law. The appeal will be made to the Employment Appeal Tribunal (EAT) and, subsequently, in some cases to the Court of Appeal. These long appeal procedures mean that some contentious issues take a very long time to resolve. In some very rare cases the appeals might go further to the House of Lords and/or European courts. See Figure 4.2 on page 33.

Settlements made outside tribunals

Not all complaints of breaches of employment law go to a full tribunal hearing. The law allows some disputes to be settled with the assistance of an Advisory, Conciliation and Arbitration Service (ACAS) conciliation officer. If the parties agree to this procedure, both are bound by the decision, and thus the time and expense of a full hearing are avoided. In some other cases the chairman of the tribunal is authorised to reach a decision with or without a hearing, providing the parties agree. As with conciliation this will lead to a quicker and cheaper resolution of the problem. At the time of writing (May 2000) the recently announced introduction of a full binding arbitration service to be provided by ACAS is still awaited.

Contracts of employment

A contract of employment exists if the employee agrees that he will provide his work and skill in the performance of some service and will receive in return wages or some other benefit.

The employee agrees that regarding the service provided the employer can decide:

- what is to be done
- the way it is to be done
- the means to be employed doing it
- the time it is to be done
- where it shall be done.

It is intended that the agreement constitutes a legal contract. Look in Chapter 4 at the details of a contract in law and you will see that an employment contract is:

- an *offer* by the employer
- an *acceptance* by the employee
- the employee receives *consideration* by way of wages
- the employer receives *consideration* by way of service rendered.

The elements of a contract of employment

As a matter of law, the actual contract of employment does not have to be written, apart from certain details mentioned below. However, as a matter of prudence it is wiser to have a written contract that has been accepted in writing rather than an oral arrangement.

The terms of a contract of employment are based upon a number of things and Figure 10.2 illustrates the main elements likely to affect an employee in a medical practice.

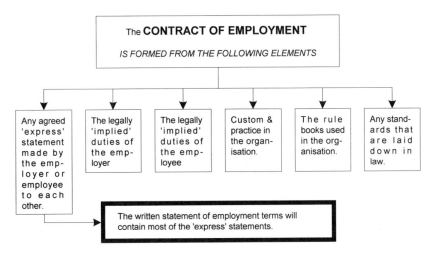

Figure 10.2 Elements of a contract of employment

If there is a dispute between an employer and employee, the terms of the contract of employment will be used by the court to decided which party has breached the conditions.

Express and implied statements and duties

The words *express* and *implied* are used in contract law when describing the details of a contract as shown in Figure 10.3.

Express words, statements, duties, etc. will have been communicated between the parties to the contract directly expressing or stating a particular idea.

Implied words, statements, duties, etc. are logically inherent in the express terms, even though they are not explained in detail. The law implies that some things will be done as a matter of course, even though they are not expressed in a contract. For example, it is implied that the employer will obey the terms of the

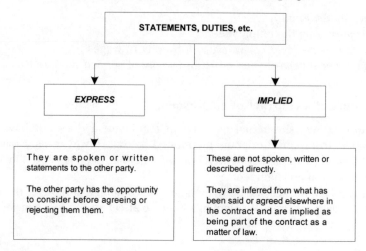

Figure 10.3   Express and implied statements

Health and Safety at Work Act, even though this might not be especially mentioned in the contract.

Express terms of a contract of employment

These terms will consist of all the written or oral terms that have been agreed between the parties. They will include such things as correspondence, agreements made during interviews and so on but will not include anything written in an advertisement because that is not a part of the contract.

By law some terms must be put into writing and be given to the new employee (see below). These written particulars are not, in legal terms, the contract of employment although the courts can use them as an aid in deciding the terms of a particular contract.

Void terms

Any illegal term in the contract is automatically void and cannot be enforced. An example would be a 'gagging' clause intended to stop a worker making a public interest disclosure. See page 117.

Written statement of particulars of employment

Every employer must give to each new employee a written statement of the particulars of his employment. This must be given to the employee within two months of the beginning of his employment. This statement can be given in instalments providing it is all received within the two month period.

The statement must be given to all employees, even those who leave the job before the two month period has passed.

The following information must be provided in a single document titled the Statement of initial particulars:

(1) the names of the employer and employee

(2) the date when the employment began

(3) the date on which the employee's period of continuous employment began (taking into account any employment with a previous employer that counts towards that period)

(4) the scale or rate of remuneration or the method of calculating remuneration

(5) the intervals at which remuneration is paid (that is, weekly, monthly or other specified intervals)

(6) any terms and conditions relating to hours of work (including any terms and conditions relating to normal working hours)

(7) any terms and conditions relating to any of the following

    (i) entitlement to holidays, including public holidays, and holiday pay; the particulars given must be sufficient to enable the employee's entitlement, including any entitlement to accrued holiday pay on the termination of employment, to be precisely calculated (For this the employee may be referred to another document that specifies the particulars. The employee must have reasonable opportunities of reading it or it is reasonably accessible some other way.)

    (ii) incapacity for work due to sickness or injury, including any provision for sick pay and

    (iii) pensions and pension schemes (For this the employee may be referred to another document that specifies the particulars. The employee must have reasonable opportunities of reading it or it is reasonably accessible some other way.)

(8) the length of notice which the employee is obliged to give and is entitled to receive to terminate his contract of employment

(9) the title of the job which the employee is employed to do or a brief description of the work for which he is employed

(10) where the employment is not intended to be permanent, the period for which it is expected to continue or, if it is for a fixed term, the date when it is to end

(11) either the place of work or, where the employee is required or permitted to work at various places, an indication of that and of the address of the employer

(12) any collective agreements which directly affect the terms and conditions of the employment including, where the employer is not a party, the persons by whom they were made.

The written statement must also include a note specifying

(13) any disciplinary rules applicable to the employee (For this the employee may be referred to another document that specifies the particulars. The employee must have reasonable opportunities of reading it or it is reasonably accessible some other way.)

(14) a person to whom the employee can apply if dissatisfied with any disciplinary decision relating to him (For this the employee may be referred to another document that specifies the particulars. The employee must have reasonable opportunities of reading it or it is reasonably accessible some other way.)

(15)   a person to whom the employee can apply for the purpose of seeking redress of any grievance relating to his employment, and the manner and procedures to be followed in such applications (For this the employee may be referred to another document that specifies the particulars. The employee must have reasonable opportunities of reading it or it is reasonably accessible some other way.)

(16)   information whether there is in force a pension scheme contracting-out certificate.

If the employer has fewer than 20 employees, he is not required to have written discipline procedures.

Casual employees are not entitled to written particulars of employment. See page 142.

Written statement not given

If an employee is not given a written statement, or it contains incorrect details, he may complain to an employment tribunal that can:

- with no written statement or an incomplete one – determine what the missing particulars are,
- with incorrect details – can confirm, amend or replace particulars in the statement.

It is also a criminal offence not to provide an employee with a written statement within the prescribed period.

Statement of changes

If there is a change in any of the particulars of the written statement the employee must be given details of any changes in writing. The statement of change must be given at the earliest opportunity and, in any event, not later than one month after the change in question. See also variation of contract on page 139.

Implied duties of the employer

The common law implies that certain duties will fall on an employer unless the contract of employment says otherwise. An employer has the following responsibilities towards each of his employees:

- to pay the employee the agreed wage or benefit
- to observe agreements in such matters as sick pay, holidays, hours of work
- to allow time off work for public duties
- to repay the employee any expense properly incurred on behalf of the employer
- to meet all legal safety requirements
- to provide details of an employee's service to a new employer
- to act in good faith and undertake any other duty imposed by law.

Implied duties of the employee

The common law implies that certain duties will fall on an employee unless the contract of employment says otherwise. The following are these implied duties of an employee towards his employer:

- to be ready and willing to work
- to use reasonable care and skill in the work
- to obey all proper orders
- to take care of the employer's property
- to act in good faith
- not to disclose any confidential information from the business. Note that maintaining confidentiality is a common law duty irrespective of whether it is made an express contractual term.

Custom and practice

If there are particular longstanding customs relating to matters such as work breaks, suspension and dismissal procedures, etc. in a particular organisation, then those customs will be considered to be part of the contract of employment, even though they are not written down.

Custom and practice, being unwritten, may be difficult to prove and employers and employees may have different ideas about what actually constitutes a particular custom.

Rule books

These are the written rules for running the organisation as determined by the owner(s) and they can be expressly or impliedly incorporated into an employee's contract of employment.

An employer can lawfully change these rules at any time. A refusal to obey the revised rules could be seen as a breach of contract by the employee that is to say failure to obey lawful and reasonable orders (but see Variation of contract below).

If the employee was disciplined and complained to an employment tribunal the changes in the rules would be examined to see if they were reasonable in the context of running the organisation.

Contract conditions laid down by law

Various statutes lay down particular conditions that must be included in the contract. An example of this is the Equal Pay Act. This Act directs that if a woman's contract of employment does not include an 'equality of pay' clause, then the law will consider that such a clause has been put into the contract. Other examples relate to health and safety at work rights.

Variation of contract

In law neither party to a contract can unilaterally change any of its terms or conditions as they can only be changed with the mutual agreement of all contracted parties. If a change is agreed between the parties, then a notice to vary the written statement of particulars of employment must be given by the employer.

If the employer wishes to change the contract unilaterally, in legal terms he is ending the original contract and offering the employee a new contract; the employee then has the options of:

- claiming that the employer is in breach of contract and claiming constructive dismissal (see details on page 155), or,
- affirming agreement to the new contract.

The agreement to a change in contractual conditions can be expressed in writing or it can be implied.

> *After the employer varied the contract, the employee carried on working as normal and he was deemed to have affirmed the new contract and to be bound by the new conditions.*
>
> Bliss *v.* SE Thames Regional Health Authority (1987)

If an employee states that he will work to the varied contract 'under protest', the extent of the implied acceptance can be examined in tribunal proceedings; however the employee must complain as soon as practicable.

Employers can offer the tribunal as a fair reason for changing contractual conditions that the situation was caused by sound business reasoning that justify any changes that had to be made.

The employer will have to show that he took some steps to consult his employees, listened to any objections that they put forward and sought to make compromises. If this has been done the changes will usually be acceptable, especially if the majority of employees have accepted them. In such circumstances the dismissal of an employee for refusing to work to revised conditions would probably not be unlawful.

These matters were shown in the following case:

> Two clerks were employed to work five days a week from 9.30 am to 5.30 pm The employer, seeking to achieve greater efficiency, proposed to introduce six day working divided into two shifts of 8.00 am to 3.00 pm, and 1.00 pm to 8.00 pm. Both clerks refused to change over to the new system of working, asserting that their contracts of employment had been unilaterally altered by the employer. They were both dismissed and claimed that the dismissal was unfair.
>
> It was said by the Court of Appeal that *an employee has a right to object if an order affects or alters his terms of employment, his pay, hours of work, or conditions of work. However, these factors must be balanced against the employer's needs to improve efficiency and in this case the dismissals were fair.* It was also held that the dismissal was not due to redundancy as the work remained the same it was 'the same job done to a different schedule'.
>
> Johnson *v.* Nottinghamshire Combined Police Authority (1974)

> A charity run hospital faced closure when funding was reduced. After consultation, the employer offered the staff new contracts which although less beneficial were accepted by most of the staff. One of the employees who refused to accept the new terms was dismissed and claimed that the dismissal was unfair. The Employment Appeal Tribunal held that *it was necessary to examine the surrounding events to see if the new terms*

were those that a reasonable employer would offer. It was also significant that most of the other employees had accepted the offer. There was a sound business reason for the reorganisation and therefore the dismissal was fair on the basis of some other substantial reason.

St John of God (Care Services) Ltd v. Brooks (1992)

New skills needed by employees

Employers sometimes need employees to acquire new skills to carry out the same work in a different way. Most notable in a practice would probably be a requirement to acquire specific computer skills. The following case examined this point:

> Taxmen refused to use computers for collecting PAYE. The court held that *whilst new skills were needed to operate the computers this did not go beyond the existing contract of employment. The consent of the employee was not needed as it can not be considered that to ask an employee to acquire basic skills is something unusual nowadays.*

Cresswell v. Board of Inland Revenue (1984)

Particular classes of employees

Probationary employees

A person can be employed with a condition that he serves a specified period of probation before the position is confirmed and the employer must confirm or terminate the employment within that period of time. The employee must be made aware of the conditions attaching to any period of probation (ACAS advice).

If a probationary employee completes one year of continuous employment and his services are then terminated he will be able to claim that the dismissal was unfair.

Fixed term contracts

The provision for a worker on a fixed term contract lasting for one year or more to sign a 'waiver' clause that he will not make a claim of unfair dismissal at the conclusion of the contract has been abolished.

It follows that if a fixed term contract is not renewed the employee is deemed to be dismissed. If the employee has one year of continuous employment he will be able to complain that he has been unfairly dismissed. The employer might claim the reason for the dismissal was some other substantial reason (see page 150).

If an employee employed under a fixed term contract of two years or more has agreed in writing that he will not claim redundancy payment at the expiry (without renewal) of the contract, that agreement holds good.

Replacement employees

An employer engaging a temporary replacement in place of an absent employee must inform the replacement in writing that his employment will be terminated on the resumption of work by the absent employee.

The relevant reasons for absence are:

- pregnancy or childbirth
- suspension of an employee on medical grounds
- suspension of an employee on maternity grounds.

Providing the written notice mentioned above was given to the replacement employee he can be dismissed to allow the absent employee to resume work. The reason for the dismissal will be some other substantial reason.

Part-time employees

In 1994 the House of Lords held that to require workers to work for at least 16 hours a week before they could claim unfair dismissal or redundancy payments indirectly discriminated against women. This was because nearly 90% of such employees were women (see also page 191). The Employment Protection (Part-time Employees) Regulations 1995 were enacted to remove this barrier and thus give part-timers some of the employment protection rights enjoyed by full-time workers.

The Employment Relations Act 1999 authorises the making of regulations to ensure that part-time employees are treated no less favourably than full-time employees. Consequently, the Part-time Employees (Prevention of Less Favourable Treatment) Regulations 2000 came into effect on 1 July 2000.

The points of significance for a general practice are that a part-time employee should:

- receive the same hourly rate of pay as a comparable full-time employee
- receive the same hourly rate for overtime work as a comparable full-time employee once they have exceeded the normal full-time hours
- not be excluded from training only because he is a part-timer
- have the same rights to
  - annual leave
  - maternity leave
  - parental leave

  on a proportionate basis, when compared with a corresponding full-time employee.

If a part-timer considers that his employer has treated him unfairly he can request a written statement giving reasons for the treatment, and this must be provided within 21 days. The written statement is admissible in evidence in any employment tribunal proceedings.

Most part-timers in general medical practices already have these benefits and it is unlikely that the new Regulations will have any significant effect on practices but if queries arise detailed information is available on the DTI employment relations website (*see* Appendix B).

Casual employees

Some practices have arrangements whereby a person agrees to provide cover during the absence of a regular member of staff. Employers should realise that casual employment that continues through a series of contracts lasting over a year, even with some gaps in continuity, might put the employee into a position of claiming rights under the ERA.

The status of such employees was examined by the House of Lords in the following case.

The House of Lords held that *if the employment is casual then the following relationship between the employer and the employee must exist.*

- The agreement between employer and employee must make it quite clear that the casual employee is under no obligation to accept any particular offer of work nor is the employer obliged to provide any work.
- The arrangement must contain no provisions regarding
  - when, how or the frequency of work to be offered
  - the termination of any employment
  - any benefits to be accorded to regular staff such as sickness and holiday pay, pension arrangements, discipline or grievance procedures.
- The status of a casual arrangement will be seen from:
  - any written agreement supplemented by verbal agreements, and
  - the parties subsequent conduct to infer what the parties believed their obligations to be.

Carmichael and Another *v.* National Power PLC (1999)

Casual employees should not be given a formal contract of employment and employers must be careful to ensure that any written documentation emphasises the lack of mutual obligations. It is also important that no action should be taken by the employer to alter the status by, for example, using disciplinary procedures against a casual employee who is late or absent from work.

Changing circumstances of employer

Insolvency

If an employer becomes insolvent, under certain circumstances former employees may be able to claim up to eight weeks' arrears of pay up to a maximum amount of £230 per week. Claims can also be made concerning any holiday pay that is owing to them.

Change of ownership

If the ownership of the organisation changes hands, then the new owner inherits the existing contracts of employment. The circumstances of each transfer of ownership will be unique and advice regarding the application of the Transfer of Undertakings (Protection of Employment) Regulations 1981, as later amended) should be sought by any affected employee. See *Lynch* v. *Martin* (1993) page 191.

Termination of a contract of employment

A contract of employment may be terminated by either the employer or the employee. In the vast majority of cases contracts are terminated in a lawful way by both parties. However, in a minority of instances either the employer or the employee does not act lawfully. Conflicts arise when an employer claims to have acted lawfully, but for some reason the employee makes a challenge that the dismissal was unfair. Figure 10.4 illustrates how the contract may be terminated.

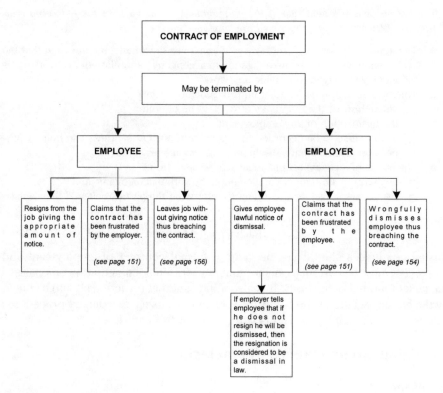

Figure 10.4　Termination of contract of employment

Minimum period of notice

The following are the minimum periods of notice required from either employee or employer to terminate contract, providing the employment has lasted for more than one month.

By the employer
The period specified in the employment contract, or if not specified

- Employed less than two years　　one week
- Employed two to twelve years　　one week for each year of service
- Employed twelve years plus　　not less than twelve weeks.

By the employee
The period specified in the employment contract, or if not specified, not less than one week.

Breach of contract
If the contract is breached by either party it is terminable without notice by the wronged party.

Fair dismissal

Every employee has the right not to be unfairly dismissed from his job and employers are expected to:

- have a fair, legal reason for dismissing an employee
- use fair, reasonable procedures during the process of dismissal.

The decision made regarding the fairness or unfairness of a dismissal will also depend upon whether, in the circumstances (including the size and resources of the undertaking), the employer acted reasonably in dismissing the employee.

The legal reasons for dismissal as defined in the ERA are shown in Figure 10.5.

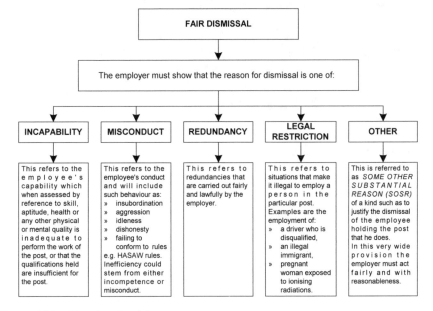

Figure 10.5   Fair dismissal 1

In terms of fairness, the procedure used to dismiss an employee is as important as the reason for dismissal. A tribunal might find a dismissal unfair for lack of or unfair procedures, even if the reason is justifiable. Accordingly it is essential for management to have due regard for this duty. The House of Lords explained these duties in the following terms:

An employer having grounds to dismiss will, in most cases not *act reasonably unless and until he has taken the 'procedural' steps that are necessary to justify that course of action.* Thus, for the employer to act reasonably, he must:

- in the case of incapability, give the employee fair warning, an opportunity to mend his ways and show that he can do the job

- in the case of misconduct, investigate the complaint of misconduct fully and fairly and hear whatever the employee wishes to say in his defence or in explanation or mitigation
- in the case of redundancy, warn and consult any employees affected or their representatives, adopt a fair basis on which to select for redundancy and take such steps as may be reasonable to avoid or minimise redundancy by redeployment within his own organisation.

Polkey *v.* A.E. Dayton Services Ltd. (1988)

The points of the *Polkey* judgement are summarised in Figure 10.6.

Figure 10.6   Fair dismissal 2

Unfair dismissal

Complaints of unfair dismissal may be pursued through an employment tribunal in the circumstances illustrated in Figure 10.7.

The aggrieved ex employee will have to prove that either the reason for the dismissal, or the procedure followed in dismissing him was unfair. Following are further details of the headings shown in Figure 10.6 above.

Incapability

The ERA defines capability as meaning the employee's capability assessed by reference to:

- skill
- aptitude
- health, or
- any other physical or mental quality.

Not being capable does not include laziness or carelessness by an employee who is in fact capable.

The skill may be assessed by means of qualifications of various sorts and, usually, these qualifications will be examined when the employee is recruited. If

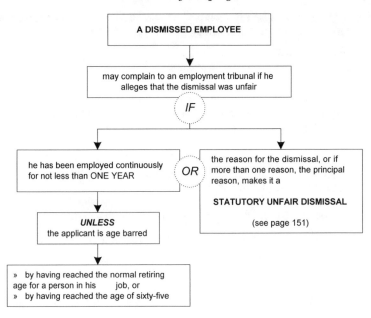

Figure 10.7   Complaints of unfair dismissal

an applicant claims to have qualifications that he does not possess, after due investigation, dismissal would almost certainly be fair.

In such cases it is possible that a criminal offence under the Theft Act 1968 of *obtaining a pecuniary advantage by deception* by dishonestly gaining remuneration in employment could arise. Numerous examples of this offence have come before the courts, some of which have related to unqualified people obtaining nursing posts dishonestly.

In a general practice, perhaps the most likely matter coming under the heading of incapacity will relate to the ill-health of a particular employee. The employer must be careful to ensure that his conduct is above reproach in such instances and the points raised in the following case must be considered.

> An employee suffered a stroke and was retired on the basis of a medical report that merely stated that he should be retired early but gave no medical details; he subsequently claimed unfair dismissal. It was held by the Employment Appeal Tribunal that the employer had not made a proper investigation of the facts as the report had been obtained without the knowledge or consent of the employee. *Neither consultation nor the proper medical position of the employee had been established therefore the dismissal was unfair.*

> East Lindsay District Council *v.* Daubney (1977)

See also *Notcutt* v. *Universal Equipment Co. (London) Ltd.* (1986) on page 152.

> An employee was absent from work for two months, and the company, with his permission, asked his GP how long it would be before he would be fit to return to work. The employer was told that it would be four to six weeks and in consequence the employee was dismissed. At the Employment Appeal Tribunal the question of ill health dismissals

was examined and it was said that employers should take into account the following factors before reaching a decision whether to dismiss or not:

- the nature of the illness
- the likely length of the continuing absence
- the work which the employee was engaged to do
- the urgency for the completion of that work, and
- other relevant circumstances such as the size and nature of the organisation and the availability of an alternative job within the employee's capability.

Further,

- there should always be proper consultation between the employer and the employee before any decision is taken
- points raised in the consultation should be properly considered
- a written notice might be given to the employee that dismissal is being considered.

In this particular case, the lengthy absence rendered the dismissal fair.

Spencer *v.* Paragon Wallpapers Ltd (1976)

See also frustration of contract on page 151.

The question of an employee's health is also affected by the terms of the Disability Discrimination Act 1995 see page 196.

Misconduct by the employee

This is improper conduct by the employee and it could include such things as rudeness to customers or deliberately making mistakes in work.

A TV repairman was grumpy and abrupt to customers and it was claimed that he frightened customers away; more than 100 complaints were received about his manner. Whilst he was on holiday he was dismissed for improper conduct. He later claimed unfair dismissal. It was held that *although the employer had received over 100 complaints about the employee he did not give him adequate warning about his behaviour or an opportunity to rectify it. As a result of this failure the dismissal was unfair for 'procedural' reasons.*

Sutton & Gates (Luton) Ltd *v.* Boxall (1979)

A medical receptionist was asked to type a letter referring a pregnant patient to a consultant for his opinion whether the patient should have an abortion. She refused to type the letter, claiming that section 4 of the Abortion Act, which says '...no person shall be under any duty ... to participate in any (abortion) treatment to which he has a conscientious objection' meant she was not under an obligation to type the letter. After due discipline procedures had been followed the receptionist was dismissed for refusing to obey proper instructions and she claimed unfair dismissal. The House of Lords held that *the dismissal was fair because the conscience clause refers to people who are required to take part in the actual termination procedures.*

R *v.* Salford Area Health Authority, *ex parte* Janaway (1988)

An office manager made use of the company's computer facilities to access the Internet to book her holidays. It was claimed that she had visited over 150 sites and lied when questioned about the matter. The employee had previously been given a written warning for not following company procedures. The tribunal ruled that *the employee was wrong to use company equipment to gather personal information and the dismissal was fair.*

Franxhi *v.* Focus Management Consultants (1999)

Redundancy

When the whole or the main reason for an employee's dismissal is that the employer has no, or less, need to do the particular sort of work where he was employed to do that work, then the employee is redundant.

- If possible the employee should be offered another job elsewhere in the company. If the employee accepts the job offer, even if the job has inferior conditions, pay or prospects for promotion, then he cannot claim to be redundant.
- If the employee is not offered another job or refuses the offer of an inferior job that is unsuitable to his skill or training or is located too far away from his home then he may be able to claim redundancy pay.
- To claim redundancy pay the employee must have been dismissed for reasons of redundancy and have at least two years' service.

The minimum amounts to be paid to redundant employees are laid down by law, but it is not uncommon for these amounts to be supplemented with additional payments by some employers.

A dismissal for redundancy can not be used as a subterfuge for a dismissal based on other reasons. The following case involved a prominent politician:

A woman was employed as a secretary in a political constituency office. Following personal difficulties the woman was absent for two months sick leave suffering from stress. The woman was declared redundant and given redundancy pay; however, the post was filled by two part-time secretaries on a job-sharing scheme. The tribunal ruled that *this was not a genuine redundancy as the post remained in existence and in consequence the dismissal was unfair.* The ex employer was ordered to pay compensation.

Easter *v.* Hain (1998)

Consultation regarding redundancy

Employers are required to consult with trade unions when it is proposed to make staff redundant, even if the person(s) to be made redundant are not members of the recognised trade union.

- The consultation must take place a specified period of time before the redundancies take place. The actual time varies depending upon the number of proposed redundancies.
- The employer must inform the trade union representative(s) of the reasons, numbers of employees concerned and the method of selection.
- If there is no consultation, the trade union can apply to an employment tribunal for the pay of the workers concerned to be protected for a time equal to the consultation period.
- If the employer and employee cannot agree details concerning redundancy, then the matter may be taken before an employment tribunal either for unfair dismissal or incorrect calculation of payment for judicial settlement.

Redundant employee – paid time off work

An employee made redundant is entitled to take reasonable time off work, with pay, to look for new employment or make arrangements for training for future employment.

Legal restrictions

This reason for dismissal applies if there is a legal restriction on employing certain people in particular circumstances. For example, it is unlawful to employ in any capacity an alien who does not hold a work permit. There are statutory minimum ages for some jobs, none of which are likely to affect a practice.

In some cases a person performing a particular job must hold a specific qualification or authority. For example, a driver must hold a current valid driving licence, and if an employed driver is disqualified by court order or for health reasons, then employment in that post must cease. The employer would be expected to consider if any alternative post is available before dismissing such an employee.

Some other substantial reason (SOSR)

The phrase used in the ERA is 'some other substantial reason of a kind such as to justify the dismissal of an employee holding the position he held'.

This heading covers a wide range of matters, probably the commonest being cases relating to company re-organisation (see cases *Johnson* v. *Nottinghamshire CPA* (1974) and *St. John of God (Care Services) Ltd.* v. *Brooks* (1992) on page 140) and the dismissal of replacement employees on page 141. Some case examples are:

> An employee was offered a job in Australia and told his employer that he was resigning at some future unspecified date to take up the new job. Three months later he told the employer that he wished to withdraw his resignation, but the employer refused to accept the withdrawal and treated the employment as terminated. The employee claimed unfair dismissal but it was held by the Court of Appeal that he had been dismissed (not resigned). *The reason for dismissal was the late change of mind by the employee that represented 'some other substantial reason of a kind such as to justify dismissal' and the dismissal was fair.*

> Ely *v.* YKK Fasteners Ltd (1994)

> The applicant, a supervisor, held strong views on some morality and sexual matters that distressed her younger subordinates although she could have avoided giving offence if she had wanted to. She was dismissed without the six weeks notice that she was entitled to receive. It was held in the High Court that *the dismissal for some other substantial reason was fair. Although there had been a breach of contract by the employer in failing to give due notice that was irrelevant as the applicant could recover the appropriate amount she was due from the county court.*

> Treganowan *v.* Robert Knee & Co. Ltd (1975)

> When applying for a job the applicant deliberately concealed that he had a history of mental illness. When the company learned of this they got further medical reports and he was dismissed on the basis of their contents for 'some other substantial reason'. *SOSR was based on the grounds that in his job he would have to go into private homes*

and speak to individuals and the company could not risk the possibility that unde-
sirable behaviour might occur. The High Court held that the dismissal was fair.

O'Brien *v.* Prudential Assurance Co. (1979)

Dismissals which are defined as unfair by statute

The ERA and other statutes define circumstances where the dismissal is stated to
be unfair as a matter of law.

This situation arises when the principal reason for dismissal can be found
under one of the following headings. In each case, further details will be found at
the reference given.

- race, sex or disability discrimination (see pages 188 and 196)
- pregnancy, unless the woman's condition makes it impossible for her to do
  her job (see page 177)
- maternity or parental leave (see pages 175 and 180)
- health and safety cases (see Figure 6.11)
- working time cases (see page 174)
- trustees of occupational pension schemes (see Figure 11.19)
- a workers' representative at redundancy or transfer consultations (see Figure
  11.19)
- public interest disclosure cases (see page 117)
- the assertion of a statutory employment right (see Chapter 11)
- national minimum wage cases (see page 163)
- tax credit cases (see page 165)
- unfair selection for redundancy (see page 149)
- trade union membership or activity, or, refusing to join a union (see Chapter
  13)
- transfer of ownership of the business (see page 143)
- cases involving unfavourable treatment of part-time workers (see page 142).

In all of these cases, once it has been proved that the principal reason for the
dismissal is one of the above, the aggrieved employee will be entitled to be given
redress by the tribunal.

An employee making a complaint under any of these headings need not have
completed the one year of continuous employment required for other unfair
dismissal cases, nor is there an age bar.

Frustration of contract

This means that the provisions of the contract cannot be performed for reasons
outside the control of either party. This will usually apply in cases of imprisonment, injury or long-term sickness. The rules are not clear cut, and each case
would have to be examined on its own facts. Following are some examples:

A sentence of 12 months' imprisonment was passed on an employee for an offence
outside his work. It was held by the Court of Appeal that *the sentence made it
impossible for him to carry out his part of the contract. In consequence, the contract
was ended on the grounds that it was frustrated.*

Hare *v.* Murphy Bros (1974)

Note that the frustration is caused, not by the nature of the offence, but by the length of time that the employee is unable to perform his duties. Thus, taking into account remission, a short absence might be no more significant than a holiday or mild illness, in terms of frustration.

Sickness or serious injury can be a frustrating event; the matters that will be considered by a court or tribunal in such instances will include the following:

> An employee with 26 years' service suffered a coronary and this prevented him from working again. In this case the Court of Appeal held that *the illness had frustrated the contract.*

Notcutt *v.* Universal Equipment Co. (London) Ltd. (1986)

See also *East Lindsay District Council* v. *Daubney* (1977) on page 147.

Matters relating to the duration of the sickness were considered in the following case.

> An employee was injured in an accident and was absent for four months. The employer appointed a replacement and refused to let the injured employee return to work.
>
> The Employment Appeal Tribunal said that it might be a long time before illness brings about the frustration of a contract. However, *the time might come when the employer considers that the prospects of future employment are so poor that the contract no longer subsists and frustration has occurred. In reaching this conclusion the following factors must be considered by an employment tribunal:*
>
> (1)   the length of previous employment
> (2)   how long it would be expected to continue
> (3)   the nature of the job involved
> (4)   the nature of the illness or injury and the prospect of recovery
> (5)   the need for the employer to get the work done and/or find a replacement
> (6)   the risk to the employer of getting further obligations for redundancy payments or unfair dismissal claims by the replacement employee
> (7)   whether wages are still being paid
> (8)   the actions of the employer in dismissing or not dismissing the employee
> (9)   whether, in the circumstances, a reasonable employer could be expected to wait any longer.

Egg Stores (Stamford Hill) Ltd *v.* Leibovici (1976)

To this judgment, two further factors were added by a later judgment.

- the terms of the contract in respect of sick pay
- a consideration of the prospects of recovery.

Williams *v.* Watsons Luxury Coaches Ltd. (1990)

Note also *Spencer* v. *Paragon Wallpapers Ltd* (1976) on page 147.

The question of an employee's health is also affected by the terms of the Disability Discrimination Act see page 196.

Summary dismissal

When an employee wilfully disregards some essential part of his contract of employment it can amount to breach of contract. This is called gross misconduct and in such cases the employee can be summarily dismissed, i.e. without the notice that he would normally be entitled to receive.

Gross misconduct is not defined in the ERA as it is a common law principle that involves the employee failing to abide by all the terms of his contract of employment. (See page 135)

A prudent employer will define the circumstances that justify summary dismissal for gross misconduct in the contract of employment so that employees will have no doubts about the matter. Examples of gross misconduct could include the following:

- insubordination (not just an isolated 'fit of temper')
- serious neglect of duties
- a breach of safety rules potentially involving serious injury
- abuse of alcohol or drugs in work time
- absence from work without having either permission or a good reason
- theft at work
- violence towards employer or other employees
- deliberate damage to employer's property
- breach of confidentiality
- any other conduct defined in the contract of employment as gross misconduct.

Even if an employer appears to be legally justified in summarily dismissing an employee, in a medical practice it will be wiser to undertake an investigation according to the disciplinary procedures. Then, if the allegation is proven, dismissal might follow in appropriate cases. Whilst the investigation is carried out providing the disciplinary procedures authorise it, the employee may be suspended from duty.

If the employee contends that summary dismissal is not justified in the particular circumstance he can make a complaint of wrongful dismissal, see page 154.

Examples of incidents of gross misconduct resulting in dismissal have been:

A receptionist went to a patient in the waiting room and said 'Well who's been a silly girl then? How many weeks are you?' The comments were overheard by another patient. *The receptionist was dismissed and at a subsequent tribunal hearing the dismissal was held to be fair.*

Unknown title, gross misconduct 1 quoted by BMA lecturer.

A receptionist telephoned a patient's home and, as the patient was out, left a message with her husband that the patient should call at the surgery to pick up her test results. *The receptionist was dismissed and at a subsequent tribunal hearing the dismissal was held to be fair.*

Unknown title, gross misconduct 2 quoted by BMA lecturer.

For further details on the above two cases see page 115.

A temporary employee was found looking through medical records of her boyfriend's ex girlfriend and her family. *She was immediately dismissed for gross misconduct.* This case did not go to a tribunal.

Unknown title, gross misconduct 3 quoted by BMA lecturer.

An employee gained unauthorised access to confidential information held on a computer. The Employment Appeal Tribunal held that *the deliberate use of an unauthorised password to gain access to computer information was gross misconduct, which, on the face of it, could attract summary dismissal.* It was also said that the action could be compared to dishonesty such as entering a manager's office, opening a filing cabinet, taking out a file and reading it when not authorised so to do.

Denco Ltd *v.* Joinson (1992)

See also the case *R* v. *Bow Street Stipendiary Magistrate, ex parte Government of the USA* (1999) described on page 120 and Chapter 8 re confidentiality issues.

A complaint was made that a practice receptionist had verbally abused a patient and threatened her with violence. The receptionist identified as being responsible was interviewed by two of the partners in the presence of the senior receptionist but her response was that she could not remember anything. She was suspended and the following day at a full partners' meeting the receptionist was again interviewed but said again that she could not remember anything. Following discussions she was dismissed for gross misconduct.

A claim for unfair dismissal was made and the tribunal upheld the claim saying that a proper investigation had not been carried out. There was no evidence who was on the reception desk at the time of the incident and the dismissal might have been an overreaction by the employers.

In this case, after the dismissal of the employee, the employers offered reinstatement with certain conditions regarding training, etc. but the ex employee rejected the offer. The industrial tribunal, knowing of the offer, doubted whether the action really was gross misconduct and thus questioned whether the punishment actually fitted the offence.

Crummey *v.* Hughes (1993)

Although not an example of gross misconduct the following case is described as a comparison with *Crummey* v. *Hughes.*

A receptionist was the subject of a number of complaints over an eighteen month period. The complaints from patients became worse and other members of staff refused to work with her because of her conduct. She was advised about her manner and sent on a course to improve her telephone technique. However, the complaints continued and after verbal and written warnings about her attitude she was finally dismissed on the grounds of misconduct. The employee claimed that she had been unfairly dismissed because she was pregnant at the time

The tribunal held that *she had been cautioned about her conduct and there was no evidence to suggest that the dismissal occurred because of her pregnancy. Therefore the tribunal held unanimously that the dismissal was fair.*

Wood *v.* Thimmegowda (1996)

Breach of contract by employer

Wrongful dismissal

Wrongful dismissal is a breach of the contract of employment by the employer that can occur in different ways, as for instance, dismissal:

- without notice, or being given less notice than the contract states
- without using the contractual disciplinary procedures

- prior to the expiry of a fixed term contract
- prior to the completion of a task that the contract covers
- by selecting for redundancy without following the contractual procedures.

Such cases might be dealt with as unfair dismissal via an employment tribunal or the aggrieved person might sue the employer for breach of contract, seeking compensation through the civil courts. The latter course might be more beneficial to the aggrieved employee than the normal complaint to an employment tribunal. Legal advice should be sought as to the preferable way of proceeding.

An example of such a case is:

Following an independent inquiry a social worker was found to be grossly negligent in the performance of her duties. The employer dismissed her without holding a disciplinary inquiry and she sued for wrongful dismissal. The Court of Appeal held that *she had been denied her contractual right to a pre-dismissal hearing at which she would have had the opportunity to explain her conduct and/or put forward any mitigating circumstances. Therefore, this was a wrongful dismissal.*

Dietman *v.* Brent London Borough Council (1988)

Constructive dismissal

This occurs when an employer's conduct is in breach of the contract of employment. It is important to note that the alleged breach might be of any element of the contract (as illustrated in Figure 10.2 on page 135). Breaches of the express terms such as reducing the employee's pay, demotion or transferring him to another work location not mentioned in the contract are claimed. Similarly breaches of the implied duty of trust and fidelity are not uncommon. The claim can be based on a single serious incident, or from several acts that, if taken together, breach the contract.

If the employee feels forced to resign because of the treatment that he has received, the tribunal can accept that the resignation was a constructive dismissal. If constructive dismissal is accepted then further evidence can be heard to support either unfair dismissal or redundancy payment claims.

There is a great range of claims under this heading, following are a small number of such cases to illustrate the kind of matters that might arise.

A female employee made a complaint that two supervisors had sexually assaulted her, but *the employers failed to carry out an adequate investigation and this undermined the confidence of female staff.* It was held by the Employment Appeal Tribunal that the complainant was entitled to leave and claim that *she had been constructively dismissed.*

Bracebridge Engineering Ltd. *v.* Darby (1990)

A personal secretary had an argument with the director to whom she worked. She later heard the director say to another employee 'She is an intolerable bitch on a Monday morning'. The employee left and claimed constructive dismissal on the grounds that *the director had breached the implied term of trust and confidence that should exist between employer and employee. The claim for constructive dismissal was upheld* by the Employment Appeal Tribunal.

Isle of Wight Tourist Board *v.* Coombes (1976)

The contract of employment permitted an employer to demote a member of staff who did not obtain a satisfactory level of performance. After a series of warnings regarding his administrative errors and failings, the employee left and claimed constructive dismissal. The Employment Appeal Tribunal held that *the employer had acted within the terms of the contract and therefore there had not been a constructive dismissal.*

Halstead *v.* Marshall of Wisbech Ltd. (1989)

A 'no smoking' policy had been in operation for many years, with areas set aside in which smoking was permitted; following consultation it was proposed to introduce a total prohibition on smoking. Arrangements were made to help staff to give up smoking. The employee took no action when told of the policy proposal and, after the policy was introduced she suffered considerable discomfort. After three days she resigned and claimed unfair constructive dismissal arguing that the introduction of the smoking ban breached the implied terms of her contract.

The Employment Appeal Tribunal held that *the rules banning smoking were not part of the contract. Where a rule is introduced for a legitimate purpose, because it bears hardly on a particular employee does not mean that the employer has repudiated that individual's contract. There was no constructive dismissal and therefore her action was a resignation.*

Dryden *v.* Greater Glasgow Health Board (1992)

An employee must act quickly after a breach of contract by the employer. If not, the law will assume by implication that he has affirmed the employer's action and is prepared to work under the changed conditions.

Similarly, at the time of leaving employment, the aggrieved employee must make it clear to his employer that his departure has been caused by a particular course of conduct.

An employee suffered severe and increasing stress that was caused by his employer's misconduct. He left his employment telling his employer that he was taking early retirement but this was a sham. The Employment Appeal Tribunal held that *as he did not make clear to his employer the real reason for leaving, he could not, in consequence, later claim that he had been constructively dismissed.*

Holland *v.* Glendale Industries Ltd. (1998)

Breach of contract by employee

If an employee does not fulfil his contractual obligations, he will be in breach of the contract. Most of the cases that are concerned with this type of breach consist of gross misconduct by the employee, see above under summary dismissal, page 152.

Other cases relate to trade union activity that breaches the contract. However, the details of such activities are outside the scope of this handbook.

If a breach of contract occurred, by, for example, an employee leaving his job without giving contractual notice and taking up work elsewhere, the employer would be entitled to sue that individual. If the employee happened to be a highly paid artiste or sportsperson, the action might be worthwhile but in the case of most employees in general practice the legal cost of taking such action would not be justified.

Suspension from work

Employees may be suspended from work in cases where it is necessary for their health and safety. These suspensions relate to circumstances where people working with dangerous substances are likely to have their health jeopardised because they have exceeded appropriate safety dose levels. In such cases the employee can be suspended for his own safety. The main points of the ERA concerning medical suspensions are shown in Figure 10.8.

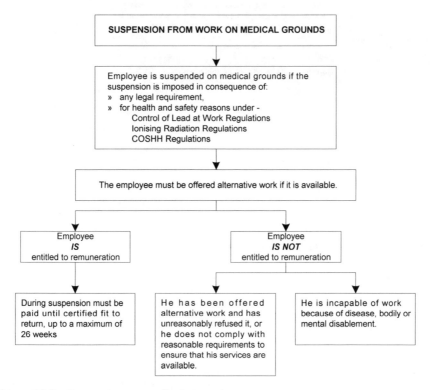

Figure 10.8 Suspension on medical grounds

There are other similar rules to look after the interests of women who are pregnant or have recently given birth. The ERA authorises suspension in those circumstances where either the mother or the child would be at risk. The legal points are illustrated in Figure 10.9.

Written statement of reasons for dismissal

An employee who is dismissed for any reason is entitled to receive a written statement giving the reasons for the dismissal. The legal requirements are illustrated in Figure 10.10. That the statement is admissible in evidence in any future proceedings makes it important to ensure that it is factually correct. A slipshod statement giving redundancy as the reason for dismissal when the real reason was incompetence cannot later be retracted and the tribunal will hear the claim

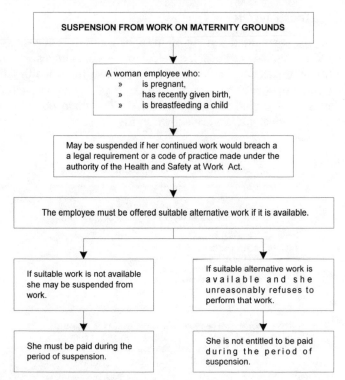

Figure 10.9   Suspension on maternity grounds

on the basis of redundancy, thus the employer's case will probably be lost before the hearing starts.

Character references

There is no duty on an employer to provide a character reference for a serving or ex employee. However the employer has an implied contractual duty to provide a record of service for an ex employee. This is of particular importance in those occupations where a post can only be taken up after the production of references. Note that a character reference is a matter of opinion, but a record of service merely records facts of the employee's service. If a character reference is to be provided for a person, it must be correct in its content, as was stated in the next case, where the Court of Appeal held if a reference is given:

- *there is a duty on the employer to ensure that references are true, accurate and fair in substance,*
- *there is no duty on the employer to make a full and comprehensive reference as this imposes too high a burden,*
- *an employer cannot break down a reference into individual sentences claiming each to be correct the reference must be looked at as a whole.*

Bartholomew *v.* London Borough of Hackney (1999)

If a reference is factually incorrect, being either too bad or too good, any of the following consequences could follow:

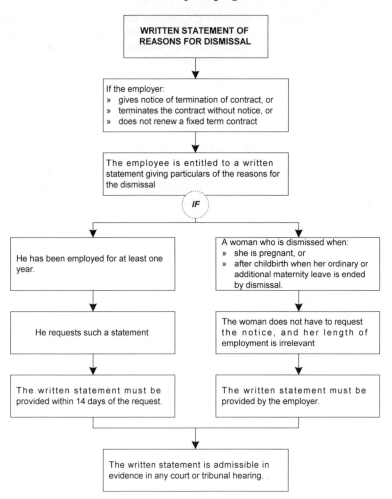

Figure 10.10 Written reasons for dismissal

'Too bad' a reference

If the ex employee disputes the information given in the reference he will be able to

- sue the employer for *defamation* or *malicious falsehood* when he will have to prove that the employer acted maliciously
- sue the employer for *negligence* when he will have to prove that the reference was not true, accurate or fair, taken as a whole and that he has suffered damage thereby.

The hazard of giving a bad reference without evidence to substantiate the statements was shown in the following:

A mature student at a polytechnic completed her course and applied for a job with a local authority but the job offer was withdrawn after receipt of a reference from the polytechnic. It took seven years before the complainant was able to see the damaging reference and she *instituted proceedings for negligent misstatement* by the polytechnic, claiming for loss of earnings caused by the inaccurate reference. In the event *the parties settled out of court, the defendants conceding liability and paying £25,000 in compensation.*

Brenton v. Mid-Glamorgan County Council (1996)

'Too good' a reference

In the converse case of 'too good' a reference:

- the new employer, if he relies on the reference in the appointment and subsequently finds that the employee is below the standards claimed, may sue the giver of the reference for negligent misstatement
- the ex employee may take the reference to an employment tribunal as evidence of unfair dismissal.

Note that the details given in a reference should not conflict with those given in the written statement for reasons of dismissal.

At a tribunal hearing a dismissed ex employee produced a reference from the employer that said, amongst other things 'he carried out his duties satisfactorily, often under difficult conditions' but it was stated in the written statement of reasons for dismissal that the employee was dismissed for incompetence. The tribunal *after considering the disagreement in the documents concluded that the dismissal had been unfair.*

Castledine v. Rothwell Engineering Ltd (1973)

Insofar as the new Data Protection Act is concerned, a character reference obviously consists of personal data. However, if a reference is given in confidence by a data controller for the purposes of:

- education
- training or employment
- prospective education, training or employment

of the data subject, then it is exempt from the obligation to disclose personal data.

This exemption only applies to a reference produced by a data controller and a reference prepared by another person is not exempted by this authority. Nevertheless, as disclosure would involve the identification of a third party if that party does not consent to the disclosure the data controller would not be obliged to show the data subject the reference. See Figure 7.4 on page 98.

A case of interest concerning references was:

A woman employed as a manager was dismissed because she became pregnant. Her erstwhile employer paid out of court compensation for the sexual discrimination that had been involved. After the birth of the baby she tried to get another job but her ex employer refused to provide her with a reference even though repeatedly asked.

The woman made a further claim that the refusal to supply a reference was another instance of sex discrimination. Her claim was rejected by the Employment Appeal Tribunal on the grounds that she was not an employee when this alleged discrimination occurred. The court agreed to submit the matter to the European Court of Justice for an authoritative decision.

The ECJ held that *even though the action had taken place after the employee ceased to serve it was still a discriminatory action under the law.* The matter was referred back to an employment tribunal for settlement but it was settled out of court for compensation of £195,000.

Coote *v.* Granada Hospitality Ltd. (2000)

Chapter 11
Pay and Conditions of Work

Wages law

Employers must pay employees the amount of wages or other financial benefits as set out in the contract of employment (see Written particulars of employment on page 136).

The written statement must include the following particulars that relate to pay and form a part of the contract of employment:

- the scale or rate of pay or the method of calculating pay
- the intervals at which wages, etc. are to be paid
- terms and conditions of
  - holiday pay
  - sickness and injury pay
  - pension contributions and payments.

Itemised pay statement

Employers must give all employees an individual itemised pay statement at or before the time that wages are paid. This statement must include details of:

- the gross wages or salary
- variable deductions showing detailed amounts and reasons for deductions
- fixed deductions showing either detailed amounts and reasons for them or, if a written statement is given in advance at least once a year the total sum of these deductions
- the net pay
- if different parts of the net amount are paid in different ways the amount and method of each part payment.

If an itemised pay statement is not provided, the aggrieved employee may take the matter to an employment tribunal.

Deductions from pay

It is illegal to make any deduction from an employee's pay that is not:

- required or authorised by law
- authorised by the employee's contract of employment e.g. pension contributions

unless the employee has given *written consent* agreeing to the deduction.

This point in the law was shown in the case:

> The employer of a lorry driver issued all staff with a new contract of employment. This contract included a clause that if the employee attended certain training and later resigned before a given time he would have to repay the cost of the training. The employee contended that this variation would amount to an unlawful deduction from his wages and therefore refused to sign the new contract. He was subsequently dismissed.
>
> The Employment Appeal Tribunal held that *the threat of dismissal by an employer to an employee who refused to agree to a variation in his contract of employment that negated his right not to suffer a deduction in wages without his freely given consent was unlawful.* Accordingly the action was an infringement of his right not to suffer detriment.
>
> Mennell *v.* Newell and Wright (Transport Contractors) Ltd. (1996)

Excepted deductions

The employer is authorised to make a deduction from an employee's wages for the purposes of:

- reimbursement of the employer
  - for an overpayment of wages
  - for an overpayment of expenses
- deductions made in consequence of lawful disciplinary proceedings
- deductions made in pursuance of a legal authority, i.e. PAYE, NIC, attachment of earnings orders, etc.
- deductions for employee's absence on strike or other industrial action.

If unauthorised deductions are made, the aggrieved employee may take the matter to an employment tribunal.

National minimum wage

The National Minimum Wage Act 1998 decrees that every worker must receive pay that is not less than the national minimum wage (NMW).The amount of the NMW is calculated at an hourly rate and fixed by regulation that will be altered from time to time as appropriate. From October 2000 the figure is set at £3.70 per hour with lesser amounts for workers under 22 years of age.

Employer's duties

Every employer must keep appropriate records of wages and these records must be retained for a minimum of three years after the period that they record.

If a worker believes that he has been paid less than the NMW, he can, following the procedures laid down in the Act (which includes the right to be accompanied by another person) require his employer to produce these records for his inspection.

If the employer refuses to produce the records the worker can complain to an employment tribunal. If the complaint is well founded the tribunal may award a sum equal to 80 times the NMW hourly rate to the aggrieved worker.

Enforcement

If a worker is paid less than the NMW he can act as shown in Figure 11.1.

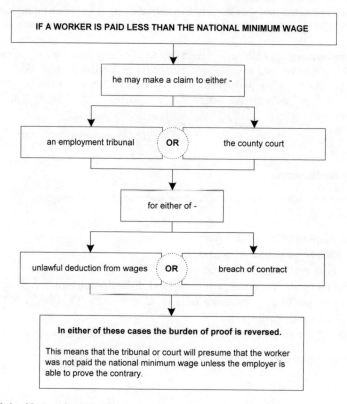

Figure 11.1　National minimum wage

The Act became law on 1 April 1999 and the first case was heard by an employment tribunal on 28 May 1999.

A qualified hairdresser in a hairdressing salon was paid £58 for a 38 hour week – just over £1.50 per hour. On the day that the new legislation came into force the worker was told that the employer could not afford to pay her the national minimum wage. As a consequence her working week was reduced to 20 hours. The worker left and complained that she had been constructively dismissed as the employer had breached the contract of employment.

The employment tribunal held that *there had been a constructive dismissal and the applicant was awarded compensation in respect of her loss of earnings and loss of statutory rights.*

Kaye *v.* Caldwell (1999)

Wages inspectors are authorised to inspect employer's records. If workers are not receiving the NMW the inspectors are empowered to enforce the terms of the Act including the institution of criminal proceedings.

Offences

The National Minimum Wage Act, section 31 creates a number of offences for which employers or their managers could be prosecuted:

- refusing or wilfully neglecting to pay at a rate that is at least equal to the national minimum wage rate
- failing to keep or preserve wage records
- making false wage records
- producing a record or information that is known to be false
- intentionally delaying or obstructing a wages inspector
- refusing or neglecting to answer any question, provide information or document when required to do so by a wages inspector.

Most employees in general practices are paid according to the Whitley Council pay scales that will doubtless exceed the national minimum wage. Any practice that does not use the Whitley Council grading system will have to ensure that minimum legal standards are maintained.

Tax credits

The Tax Credits Act 1999 introduced:

- Working Family Tax Credits, and
- Disabled Person's Tax Credits.

and from 6 April 2000 employers will be required to pay these tax credits to the employees concerned in their wage packets.

Employers will make the payments according to regulations made under the Act to:

- pay appropriate credits as officially notified
- verify the payments by means of suitable wage sheets and other documents
- give the affected employees information regarding the tax credits paid to them.

See also page 182 re the right of employee not to suffer detriment.

Equal pay

The Equal Pay Act 1970 applies equally to both men and women provided they are both performing like work, or the work is broadly similar in nature and any differences are not of practical importance.

The steps that an aggrieved employee needs to take to prove his complaint are complicated and proper advice should be taken when the employer is aware of the situation.

From an employer's point of view, an added difficulty will arise when a European Directive regarding the burden of proof in sex discrimination cases is embodied into English law. This should take place by 1 January 2001. This will mean that when an employee complains under the 1970 Act, the employer will have the responsibility of proving that the Act has not been breached.

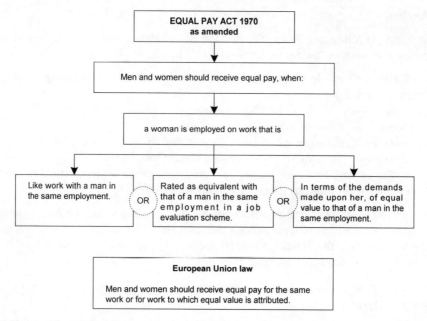

Figure 11.2   Equal pay legislation

Figure 11.2 shows the main points of the Act together with the EU definition regarding equal pay that overrides the English law in some appropriate cases.

Contract of employment

It is an implied condition of a contract of employment that any person (man or woman) must not have terms or conditions that are less favourable than those in a similar contract of a person of the opposite sex, purely on the grounds of gender.

Examples of equal pay decisions

If an employer rejects the claim, he will usually defend his position by claiming that there is a genuine material difference between the work of the aggrieved employee and the comparator that is used to justify the claim. Following are some cases that have examined issues of equal pay.

A woman 'warehouse operative' sought equal pay with a male 'checker warehouse operative'. She contended that her work was the same and of equal value to that of the comparator. Both men and women 'warehouse operatives' were paid at the same rate. This case was originally decided under English law and discrimination could not be proved because all 'warehouse operatives' received the same pay irrespective of sex. Eventually the case was decided in the House of Lords when EC principles were followed. It was held that *it was clear that as the woman's work was proven to be of equal value with that of the male 'checker warehouse operatives' she should receive equal pay to them.*

Pickstone and Others *v.* Freeman PLC (1988)

A council employed female nursery nurse sought to have her salary raised to the level enjoyed by male clerical staff employed by the same council. None of the men worked at the same place as the nursery nurse; they were paid more but also worked longer hours and were entitled to fewer holidays. It was held by the House of Lords that *it would be unrealistic to disregard different hours and holidays. The variation in pay was due to those factors and not the sex of the individual employees.*

Leverton *v.* Clwyd County Council (1989)

An NHS Board set up its own prosthetic fitting service. The rates of pay were decided, but it was necessary to offer higher pay to qualified persons from the private sector to attract them to the new service. The applicant went straight into the service from her training and subsequently sought equal pay with a man who had originally come from the private sector and therefore received higher pay. The House of Lords held that *all entrants (both male and female) from the private sector received the higher pay and all entrants from training (both male and female) received the standard pay. The reason for the difference in pay was unrelated to the sex of the employees concerned.*

Rainey *v.* Greater Glasgow Health Board (1987)

A man was employed as a stockroom manager. On his departure the post was left vacant for four months, when a woman was appointed to the post at a salary that was 16% lower than he had been paid. She claimed equal pay with her predecessor in the post. The Court of Appeal referred the case to the European Court of Justice. The ECJ held that the *comparator and the applicant did not have to be doing the equal work at the same time. Therefore, as the duties were similar she should receive equal pay for the same work as her predecessor.*

Macarthys Ltd *v.* Smith (1980)

A diocesan director of music was being paid £11,138 per annum when she resigned her post. Her successor was engaged at an annual salary of £20,000. The EAT directed that she should be allowed a rehearing by an industrial tribunal, based on its understanding of Article 119 of the Treaty of Rome, which states that *a woman should be paid the same as a man when they are consecutively engaged on like work.*

Diocese of Hallam Trustees *v.* Connaughton (1996)

Part-time employees

See page 142 for details on pay and conditions of part-time employees.

Equal Opportunities Commission guidelines

The Equal Opportunities Commission (EOC) has published guidelines that give examples of what are considered to be work of similar and dissimilar demands. They are based upon court and tribunal decisions.

Regulation of working time

In 1998 the Working Time Regulations 1998 were introduced to implement the EU Council Directive regarding the organisation of working time. These Regulations impose statutory minimum standards regarding the number of hours that can be worked and other associated matters. In the vast majority of medical general practices, the work conditions are better than these statutory minima so there will be no call to alter existing work practices. Nonetheless, the practice manager should be aware of the legal requirements for records to be maintained so that the law is not breached. Figure 11.3 shows the aspects of working time that are controlled by the Regulations.

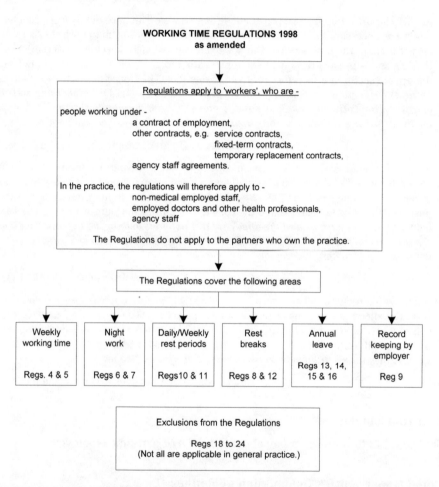

Figure 11.3   Working Time Regulations

Weekly working time

Briefly, the working week is restricted to 48 hours. Few of the non-medical staff are likely to approach that figure, although there could be some cases where employed medical professionals reach that total, especially when they are involved in night call-outs. See also the regulation of night work. Figure 11.4 illustrates the principal points of the Regulations. Note that time spent 'on call' is not regarded as working time in this context.

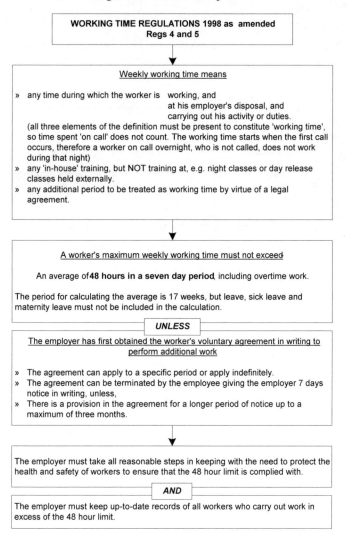

Figure 11.4   Weekly working time

Night time work

Night time work is more strictly regulated as there is greater concern over the health and safety implications for those so employed.

The relevant people included in night working in general practices could be such as employed doctors, community nurses, caretakers in larger practices and perhaps any employed staff in cooperative arrangements for providing out of hours services. The practice manager should pay particular attention to the health and safety requirements in the Regulations. Figure 11.5 provides the basic points of these regulations.

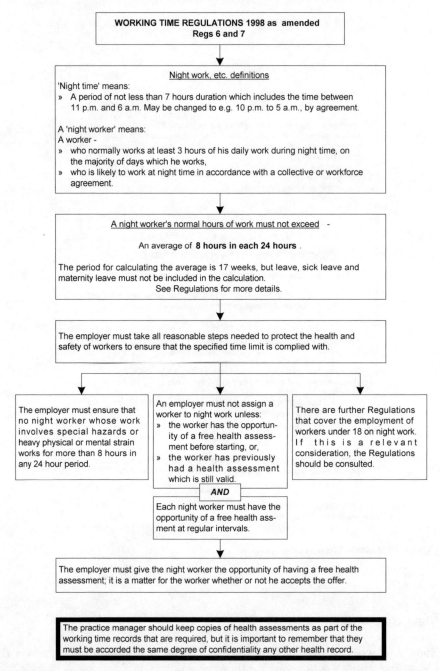

Figure 11.5 Night work

Rest periods

Rest periods refer to the time that a worker must have away from work. There are two measurements, the daily rest period that states the minimum number of hours the worker should *not* be at work in a day (11 hours), and the weekly rest period that defines the days of rest in a week (1 day).

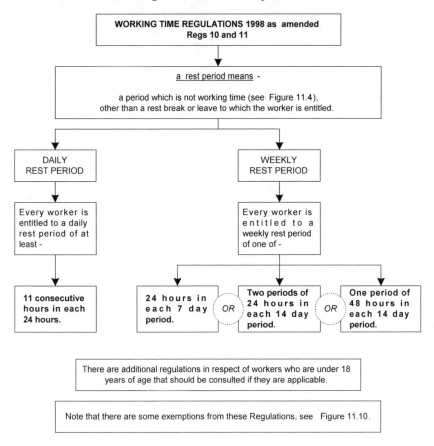

Figure 11.6   Rest periods

The details are shown in Figure 11.6 although it is unlikely that these minimum criteria will affect general practices.

Rest breaks

A *rest break* is a break in work activity during the working day. It is, by another name, a meal break. This is an area that could have an effect in general practices.

The Regulations are quite clear that workers must have a *minimum of 20 minutes uninterrupted time away from their work station*. To implement this requirement, even small practices should introduce properly organised break rotas and there should be a location to which the worker can retire. If a room is not available, then at the very least there should be a corner with a comfortable chair and table for the enjoyment of the rest break.

It is almost a fact of life in the public service that many people only have perfunctory breaks in the day. They often work through lunch time having coffee and a sandwich at their desk. Figure 11.7 illustrates the part of the Regulations that refers to rest breaks.

The practice manager will need to take steps to ensure that these Regulations are properly adhered to otherwise the practice could be in jeopardy of

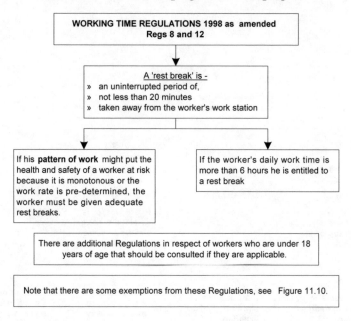

Figure 11.7   Rest breaks

prosecution by the Health and Safety Executive. (It is of interest to note that the TUC is currently lobbying the government to increase the penalties on employers for all breaches of health and safety legislation including these regulations.)

Annual paid leave

The Regulations give each worker a statutory right to receive the equivalent of four weeks paid holiday per year after he has been employed for 13 weeks.

If a worker is engaged for five days per week, then he is entitled to have paid leave of absence for 20 working days during the leave year. The leave year covers a period of 12 months starting on a date agreed in the practice. As shown in Figure 11.8, bank holidays that fall on any of a worker's normal working days may be included as part of the total. They are certainly not additional to the four weeks mentioned above.

The practice manager should note that if a replacement on a temporary contract is brought in to cover for annual leave, sickness, etc. a careful record must be kept of his working time. Once the 13 week threshold has been passed that worker is also entitled to receive annual paid leave on a *pro rata* basis.

Records

The Regulations state that records must be maintained by the employer to prove that the law is being properly observed. The form of the records is not specified, but it would not be prudent to ignore this requirement.

The records must show the weekly working time of individual workers, although each specific occurrence of a rest break, a rest period or a day of annual leave does not have to be recorded.

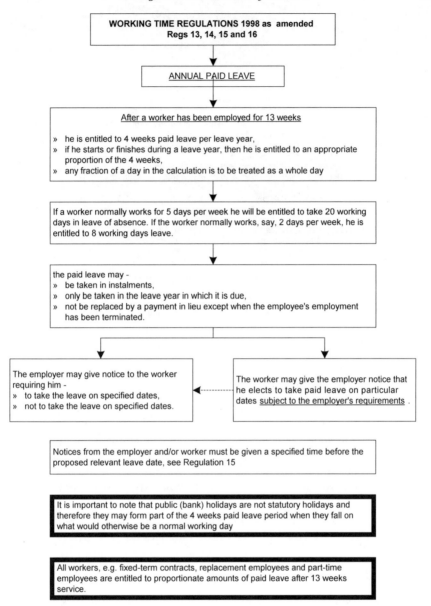

**WORKING TIME REGULATIONS 1998 as amended
Regs 13, 14, 15 and 16**

ANNUAL PAID LEAVE

After a worker has been employed for 13 weeks

» he is entitled to 4 weeks paid leave per leave year,
» if he starts or finishes during a leave year, then he is entitled to an appropriate proportion of the 4 weeks,
» any fraction of a day in the calculation is to be treated as a whole day

If a worker normally works for 5 days per week he will be entitled to take 20 working days in leave of absence. If the worker normally works, say, 2 days per week, he is entitled to 8 working days leave.

the paid leave may -
» be taken in instalments,
» only be taken in the leave year in which it is due,
» not be replaced by a payment in lieu except when the employee's employment has been terminated.

The employer may give notice to the worker requiring him -
» to take the leave on specified dates,
» not to take the leave on specified dates.

The worker may give the employer notice that he elects to take paid leave on particular dates subject to the employer's requirements .

Notices from the employer and/or worker must be given a specified time before the proposed relevant leave date, see Regulation 15

It is important to note that public (bank) holidays are not statutory holidays and therefore they may form part of the 4 weeks paid leave period when they fall on what would otherwise be a normal working day

All workers, e.g. fixed-term contracts, replacement employees and part-time employees are entitled to proportionate amounts of paid leave after 13 weeks service.

Figure 11.8   Annual leave

It might be necessary in some cases for weekly time sheets to be completed but in other cases that might not be necessary. No matter how they are kept the records should show quite clearly the procedures that are in place to ensure conformity with the law. They should show how each member of staff is affected in sufficient detail to satisfy an enquiry by either an inspector or an employment tribunal.

Figure 11.9 illustrates the legal requirements for working time records.

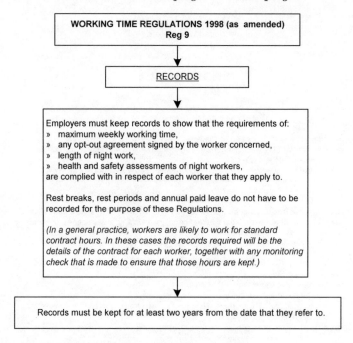

Figure 11.9   Working Time Regulations 1998 – records

Exceptions to the Regulations

There are a number of occupations that are specifically exempted from the Regulations but these details are outside the scope of this handbook.

In a practice the doctor partners are excepted from many of the rules. It is also appreciated that any organisation can experience circumstances when it would be quite impracticable to expect adherence to the letter of the law. Details of these exceptions are shown in Figure 11.10. When they arise a note should be made in the working time records that the exception provisions have been used. If this happens too frequently it could be interpreted that the provisions are being exploited to circumvent the purpose of the Regulations.

Employment tribunals

A worker can complain to an employment tribunal that his employer has refused to permit him to exercise his rights regarding:

- annual leave
- weekly rest periods
- daily rest periods
- rest breaks at work.

Criminal offences

It is a criminal offence for an employer to fail to comply with any requirement made by the Working Time Regulations 1998, as amended.

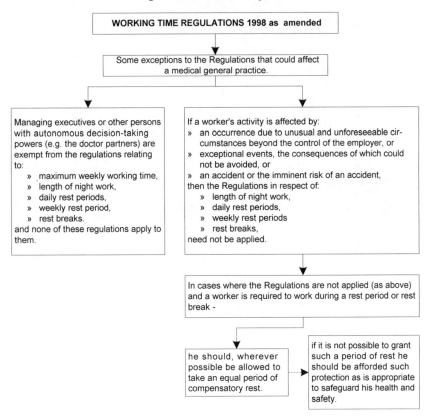

Figure 11.10   Exceptions to Working Time Regulations 1998

Maternity leave, etc.

Every employed pregnant woman has the right to take maternity leave. The rules are complex, but the main points are appropriately illustrated in the following pages. First, the basic time off and leave entitlements are shown in Figure 11.11.

Before starting maternity leave the employee must give her employer notice of matters concerning the pregnancy. The details are shown in Figure 11.12. These may seem to be just a piece of red tape but in some circumstances if the notices are not given correctly the employee might lose her right to maternity leave.

Similarly, at the end of her maternity leave, the employee must also provide information for the employer if she is to maintain her rights. The details of these notices are shown in Figure 11.13.

Cases concerning these notices of return are shown below.

The Court of Appeal considered two similar cases regarding return to work. It was held that an employee on extended maternity absence (now called 'additional maternity leave') from work *does not lose her statutory right to return to work if, as a result of a temporary illness, she is unable to return to work on the notified 'return to work date'.*

Crees *v.* Royal London Mutual Insurance Society Ltd. (1998)
Greaves *v.* Kwik Save Stores Ltd. (1998)

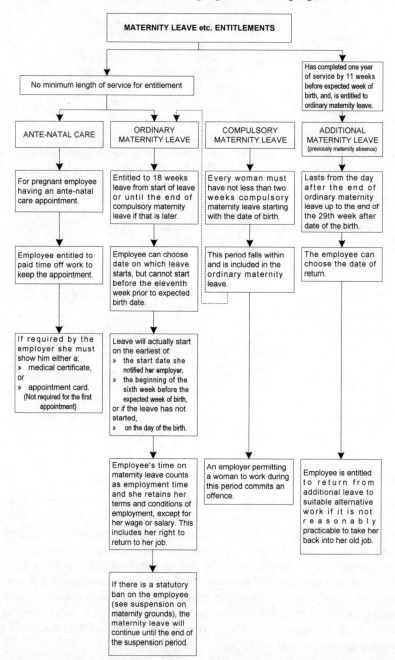

Figure 11.11 Maternity leave entitlement

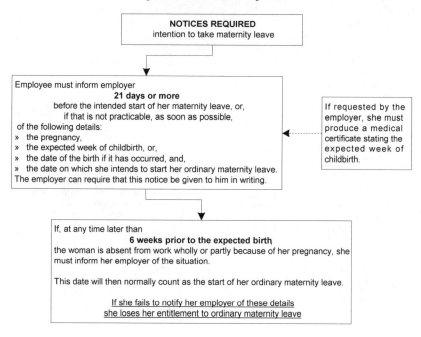

Figure 11.12 Notices re maternity leave

A woman fell ill whilst she was pregnant, the illness being related to the pregnancy. The woman was working under the terms of a contract of employment that stipulated that all employees were limited to a maximum absence of 26 weeks in a year. After the worker had been absent for 26 weeks she was dismissed – her child was born a month later. This case went through the English legal system and the House of Lords referred it to the European Court of Justice for a definitive statement of the law. The ECJ decided that *a dismissal during a woman's pregnancy was unlawful, irrespective of the terms of her contract of employment.*

Brown *v.* Rentokil Ltd. (1998)

In this case the information that the woman intended to return to work was given verbally at the same time as the notification of the birth. Subsequently, about two months later it was confirmed in writing. The employer refused to re-employ her. The Employment Appeal Tribunal held that *there is nothing in the statute that calls for this information to be provided in writing, therefore the employer's action amounted to unfair dismissal.*

King *v.* The Hundred of Hoo Nursery (1998)

The major right that such a woman has under the terms of the ERA is the right not to be unfairly dismissed whilst she is pregnant or has given birth. The details of this right are shown in Figure 11.14.

Following are some cases concerned with this matter.

A woman was engaged to act as a temporary replacement for a pregnant employee during the latter's maternity leave. Shortly after taking up the temporary post she found that she too was pregnant, with the expected date of birth occurring at about the same time as that of the woman she had replaced. The company dismissed her.

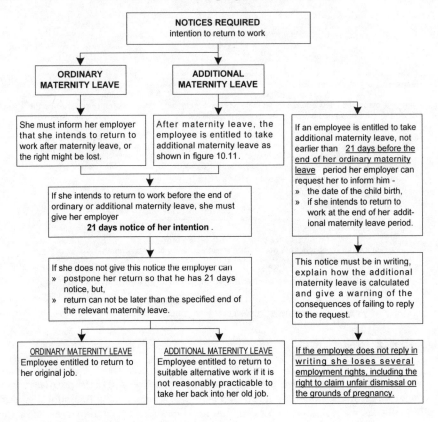

Figure 11.13   Notices re returning to work

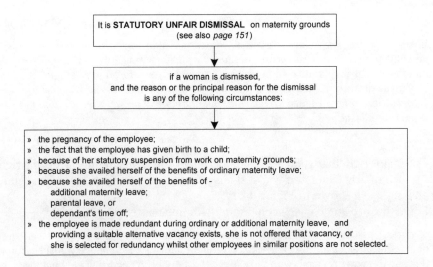

Figure 11.14   Dismissal on maternity grounds

This case went to the House of Lords, who in turn sought a ruling from the European Court of Justice. The ECJ held *that the dismissal constituted sexual discrimination and in consequence the House of Lords held that the dismissal was unfair* and the case was remitted to the tribunal to assess compensation.

Webb v. EMO Air Cargo (UK) Ltd. (No.2) (1995)

A pregnant woman applied for a job in place of another woman who had left work to have a baby. She did not disclose her pregnancy during the interview but did so after accepting the job whilst being shown around the premises. She then told the employer that she was five months pregnant. The employer stated that heavy lifting of gas bottles and caravan awnings was required and in consequence she was dismissed after 30 minutes employment. The woman claimed that she believed the job involved sitting behind a counter. *The tribunal decided that she had been unfairly dismissed and awarded compensation.*

Tomlinson v. Folding Caravan Centre (1998)

A woman who had returned to work after maternity leave was repeatedly absent through sickness, the origin of which lay with the childbirth and she was dismissed for these sickness absences. It was held by the European Court that *the dismissal was not discriminatory because men absent from work for similar reasons of other sickness causes would be dealt with in the same way.*

Handels-og KFD v. Dansk Arbeijdsgiverforening (1992)

This particular point has not been completely settled as shown in the next case.

A woman had been on maternity leave then took advantage of additional maternity leave. She gave notice of her intention to return to work. At the end of the leave period she was not able to return to work because of post-natal depression and she was therefore dismissed. The Court of Appeal held that *as she had given notice of return to work, from the day after her additional maternity leave she was employed under her contract of employment. Therefore, dismissal could only be justified if she was in breach of that contract. In this case, she had not exhausted her contractual entitlement to sick pay, consequently the dismissal was wrongful and she was entitled to damages.*

The employer was given leave to appeal to the House of Lords in this matter. The final decision is still awaited at the time of writing (May 2000).

Halfpenny v. IGE Medical Systems Ltd. (1999)

A woman was absent on maternity leave and another worker was employed as a replacement. The replacement worker was found to be more efficient than the original worker who was dismissed. *The employer claimed that the dismissal was based on grounds of efficiency. The Employment Appeal Tribunal held that this was irrelevant as the replacement would not have been employed but for the maternity leave. Therefore the dismissal was directly connected with the woman's pregnancy so the dismissal was unfair.*

Rees v. Apollo Watch Repairs plc (1996)

See also *Coote* v. *Granada Hospitality Ltd.* (2000) on page 160.

Pregnant applicants for jobs

It has been ruled in the European Court that if an employer refuses to accept a pregnant woman applicant because she is pregnant, irrespective of the surrounding circumstances, the action would be in breach of the principle of sex equality.

> A woman applied for a job where all the other applicants were also women but she alone was pregnant and she told the employer of this fact. She was the most suitable of the applicants but was not offered the position. This was because the employer's insurers would not pay her sickness benefit whilst she was absent on maternity leave because she was pregnant when appointed. The employer could not afford this cost himself. The European Court of Justice held that *as the applicant was refused employment because she was pregnant, and as only women can be pregnant, the refusal was discriminatory. The fact that the other applicants were all women was considered to be irrelevant.*

> Dekker *v.* VJV Centrum (1991)

See also *Lynch* v. *Martin* (1993) on page 191.

Pregnant workers, health and safety

As part of the health and safety risk assessment, employers are required to identify any risks that would be hazardous to an expectant mother or a new mother see page 59.

Additionally, suitable facilities for rest and to eat meals should be provided for the same employees see page 71.

Other leave and associated time off

Parental leave

Parental leave is an innovation in English employment law that was introduced to meet the requirements of a European Union Directive on the matter. It is available for both parents who have parental responsibility. The basic terms of the entitlement are shown in Figure 11.15.

The broad terms of the leave are that each parent is entitled to 13 weeks leave over a five year period (18 years in the case of disabled children).

The Regulations under the ERA include what are called the default provisions for parental leave entitlement. These default provisions will be followed in cases where either:

● an employee does not have a provision in his contract of employment regarding the care of children, or
● there is no written workforce agreement covering the matter.

The main points of the default provisions are illustrated in Figure 11.16 and it can be taken that these are the minimum acceptable standards.

Time off work for dependants

Another addition to the law requires employers to give unpaid time off work for employees to look after dependants when unexpected domestic incidents occur. The main details of these provisions are shown in Figure 11.17.

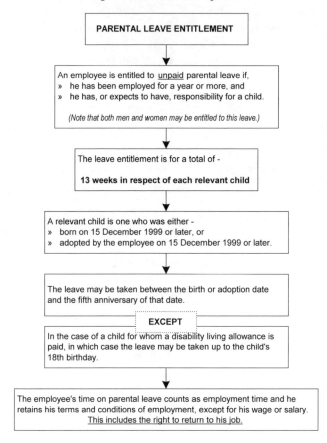

Figure 11.15 Parental leave entitlement

If an employer unreasonably refuses an employee permission to take time off under the circumstances above, the employee may complain to an employment tribunal.

Time off work for study

In furtherance of government policies designed to improve the educational standards of young people a requirement now exists for employers to give young people time for study or training that leads to a recognised qualification.

The legal authority is contained in the Teaching and Higher Education Act 1998 that amended the ERA. It is directed towards employed young people aged 16 or 17 who have not reached the minimum standard of 5 GCSE subjects graded A to C (or other equivalent qualifications). Details are shown in Figure 11.18.

Although unlikely, it is not impossible that a practice could employ a young person who could claim this right. If an employer refuses permission for the time off or refuses to pay the employee for this time a complaint may be made to an employment tribunal.

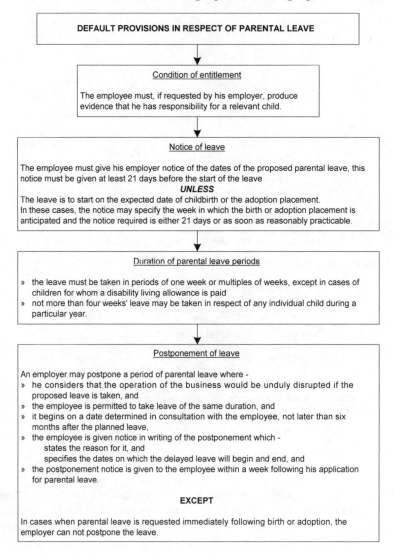

Figure 11.16 Parental leave default provisions

Authorised time off work

There are a number of circumstances defined in law when an employee has the right to claim time off work. Sometimes the right includes the right to receive pay when the time off is taken, in other cases it is unpaid.

Figure 11.19 shows rights to time off work which are enshrined in law and in appropriate cases the relevant page in this handbook is cross-referenced.

Victimisation or suffering detriment

The ERA gives employees the right not to be subjected to any detriment by way of:

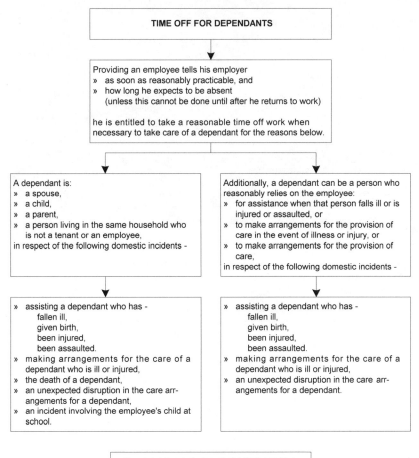

Figure 11.17 Time off for dependants

- any act, or
- any deliberate failure to act,

by his employer as a consequence of him availing or proposing to avail himself any of the statutory rights concerning:

- sex, racial or disability discrimination laws
- health and safety law
- the Working Time Regulations
- trustees of occupational pension schemes
- employee representatives at redundancy or transfer of undertakings discussions
- young employees taking time off for study or training
- making protected disclosures
- taking the time for
  - ○ ordinary maternity leave

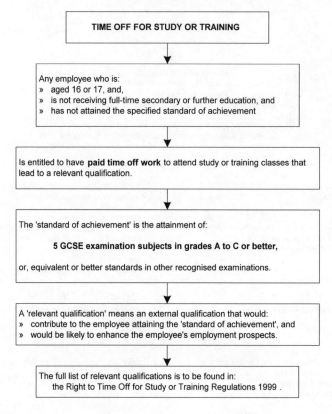

Figure 11.18   Time off for study or training

- ○ compulsory maternity leave
- ○ additional maternity leave
- ○ parental leave
- ○ dealing with dependants' domestic incidents
- ● trade union membership or non-membership
- ● involvement in authorised trade union activities
- ● any matter concerning the unfavourable treatment of part-time workers.

The detriment or victimisation includes any unlawful disciplinary action, bullying by supervisory staff, harassment, being passed over for promotion, denying opportunities for training, non-payment of bonuses, etc. The range of these actions can be shown in the following case.

> A member of a non-recognised independent trade union was denied a car park permit for that reason. The Employment Appeal Tribunal held that *this action constituted a form of penalisation that was unlawful. It was also said that the word 'penalising' could be taken to mean 'subjecting to a disadvantage'.*

Carlson v. Post Office (1981)

See also *Mennell* v. *Newell and Wright (Transport Contractors) Ltd.* (1996) on page 163.

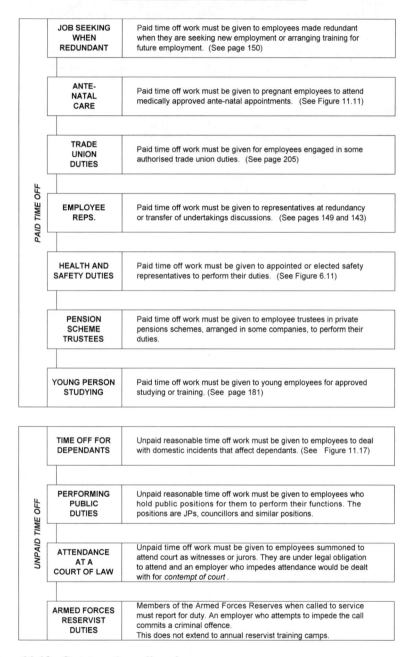

Figure 11.19   Statutory time off work

Any employee who is the victim of such detriment should seek advice as soon as practicable – in most cases a complaint must be made to an employment tribunal within three months of the alleged detriment. Note that the employee does not have to resign and claim constructive dismissal before complaining to the tribunal.

Employers found to be offending against these rules may be ordered to pay compensation and if after due warning the victimisation continues the penalties can be high.

Chapter 12
Discrimination in Employment

Discrimination – general

To 'discriminate' means:

> 'To identify a difference between, or to distinguish between different things, people, services, etc.'

Every time someone goes to a shop and buys a particular product he is discriminating and selecting some products in preference to others. The reasons for the discrimination are such things as quality, price, colour, taste, suitability for use and so on that are the results of his personal likes and dislikes.

Similarly, everyone's relations with other people are based on the individual's personal likes and dislikes. Sometimes employees are judged on their personality and appearance rather than on the basis of their skills and knowledge. Most of the qualities that are used to judge a person are common to everyone – being generous or mean, humorous or serious, exuberant or shy and so on. Sadly, other factors do intrude resulting in discrimination that might have serious adverse consequences for the victim and in such cases the law seeks to prevent that kind of discrimination. Figure 12.1 shows the overall coverage of discrimination issues that are subject to legal control.

It should be noted that some of these laws are not limited to discrimination in the workplace. They also extend to other commercial and social activities. In this handbook only the legal issues concerned with employment are considered.

Some words and phrases are defined so that the reader can identify the context in which they are used.

- *Ethnic* means: 'A human group having racial, religious, linguistic and other traits in common.' Everyone has ethnic origins and ethnic prejudice means a bias against someone from a different ethnic background.
- *Gender* means: 'Of or belonging to one sex.'
- *Gender reassignment* means: 'A process that is undertaken under medical supervision to reassign a person's sex by changing physiological or other characteristics of sex.'

It is of interest to note that English law does not make it an offence to discriminate on the grounds of religion, political or other opinion. These elements are included in Article 14 of the European Convention Human Rights and the Human Rights Act 1998 which will come into force during the year 2000,

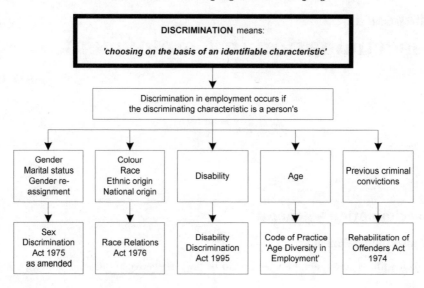

Figure 12.1   Discrimination subject to legal control

includes Article 14. Further changes in discrimination law may well follow in due course.

Sex and race discrimination

Although there are differences between the sex and race discrimination laws, the parts relating to employment are sufficiently alike for them to be treated together in this handbook. Statutory sex or racial discrimination is defined in law as: treating the person discriminated against less favourably than he/she would otherwise be treated on the grounds of colour, race, ethnic or national origin, sex or marital status (*direct discrimination*), or, imposing such conditions that would exclude persons from employment on the grounds of colour, race, ethnic or national origin, sex or marital status (*indirect discrimination*).

The main points are shown in Figure 12.2.

Direct discrimination

In the context of employment, the most common areas of complaints about discrimination are:

- job advertising
- terms of employment
- selection for
  - appointment
  - promotion
  - training
  - dismissal
  - compulsory retirement, etc.

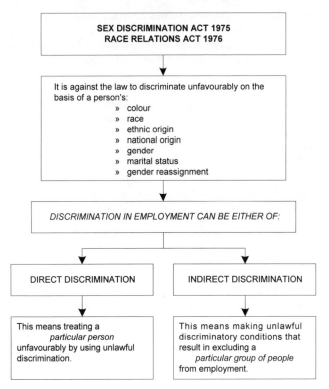

Figure 12.2   Sex and race discrimination

Most examples of direct discrimination are quite obvious to an objective observer, but some cases seem to trivialise this serious matter:

> A nurse objected to wearing a uniform cap because she thought that it was demeaning and undignified. Male nurses, wearing a different uniform did not have to wear head-gear. The tribunal held that *where there are uniform requirements imposed on employees, the fact that they are different for males and females does not make them discriminatory. The nurse had not been less favourably treated than a male employee and the fact that she thought she had been was irrelevant.*

> Burrett *v.* West Birmingham Health Authority (1994)

It is important to note that

- people can be guilty of unlawful discrimination against others of their own sex or racial origin
- men can be victims of sex discrimination just as much as women.

A well publicised case involving a female bank manager and a male clerk illustrated the latter:

> The woman bank manager was rude and patronising towards the victim, the only male employee at the branch. Several of the women employees were the victim's closest supporters and some of them advised him to keep a diary of the treatment afforded to him by the manager. The tribunal said that *the manager perceived the male clerk as a*

threat to her authority and in consequence he was treated less favourably than the female employees at the branch.

Although the female manager had personal liability for her discrimination, the employing bank was vicariously liable and had to pay compensation. The bank was also criticised by the tribunal chairman in the following terms:

... the bank spoke in its literature of the steps that it took to prevent discrimination but 'no matter how pious and well intended those sentiments are, the employer must also take practical and active steps to ensure they are implemented – I can say quite emphatically we do not regard the conduct of the bank as indicative of taking such steps as were reasonably practical to avoid discrimination'.

Gilbert *v.* Midland Bank Ltd. (1998)

A case in which the employee claimed sex discrimination and breach of her contract of employment (constructive dismissal) was:

A woman employed as a senior secretary claimed that she was degraded and humiliated when she was required to perform waitress duties during boardroom meetings. She had been put on a rota to prepare and subsequently clear away food, etc. She protested that no male staff had been put on the rota and then left the job. After hearing evidence, the tribunal held that *the job was reasonable because it was an extension of the applicant's normal 'meet and greet' duties.* It was added that *it was reasonable to expect senior secretaries to attend board meetings because they could be trusted in confidentiality matters and their secretarial skills might be needed. Further, all the secretaries involved were females, therefore there had not been any discrimination.*

Toon *v.* Jersey European Airlines (1999)

See further relevant cases described under Maternity leave, etc. page 175 *et seq.* and also under Harassment page 193 *et seq.*

As a result of a judgment in the European Court of Justice, the law of discrimination was extended by the Sex Discrimination (Gender Reassignment) Regulations 1999. As the title implies, the Sex Discrimination Act has now been amended to cover acts of discrimination made to the detriment of people who are undergoing gender reassignment treatment.

Sexual orientation of employee

The question of discrimination against a homosexual man or woman was considered as follows:

A homosexual man complained that he had been the victim of homophobic abuse from a fellow female employee. It was said by the Court of Appeal that although discrimination on the ground of sexual orientation was not sex discrimination under the 1975 Act, a male homosexual who claimed he had been discriminated against specifically *on the ground that he was a gay man might have a claim under the Act if he could show that a gay woman would have been treated differently. It was irrelevant to consider the sexual orientation of the victim. In the case of a male victim the question was whether he was treated in the way he was because he was a male not because he was a male with a particular sexual inclination.*

Smith *v.* Gardner Merchant Ltd. (1998)

Discrimination at job interviews

Difficulties are sometimes met with when interviewing applicants for jobs as interviewers are uncertain about what they can and cannot ask the applicant.

The following points should give a reasonably balanced approach to this matter.

- Questions that are sexually or racially stereotyped which, in consequence will tend to undermine the interviewee's confidence, will certainly be discriminatory.
- Interviewers can reasonably discuss any potential job difficulties when it is necessary to find out whether or not an applicant will be able to deal with them.
- Only questions that are relevant to the post, irrespective of either the gender or ethnic origin of the applicant should be asked and essentially the same questions should then be put to all interviewees.

A case involving a general practice was:

> A GP partnership was dissolved, a new practice set up in its place and the practice nurse expected to be reappointed (see Change of ownership, page 143). The GP did not reappoint her, claiming that he had offered the job to another person. The GP claimed that his action had nothing to do with the fact that she was pregnant, but allegedly said to her 'Mothers are like mammals in the animal kingdom. They should stay with their young until they are a certain age.' The employment tribunal held that *the nurse had been unfairly dismissed and the defendant was ordered to pay compensation for loss of earnings together with £1,000 for injury to her feelings.*
>
> Lynch *v.* Martin (1993)

Indirect discrimination

Indirect discrimination is also unlawful occurring in the circumstances shown in Figure 12.3. A silly example of indirect discrimination would be to claim to be an equal opportunities employer and to advertise for a filing clerk with a requirement that he or she must be over six feet in height and have a moustache. Per-

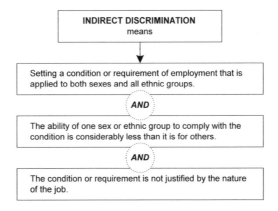

Figure 12.3   Indirect discrimination

haps there are women who could fill these requirements but they must be very rare, and there could be no justification for the requirements by the nature of the job. Therefore such an advertisement would be indirect discrimination, because in spite of claims to equality, this employer obviously wants to employ a man.

A recent case has illustrated the interpretation of indirect discrimination.

A woman, who was a single parent with a young child, was employed as a London tube train driver. Her normal working time was from 8.00 a.m. to 4.00 p.m. A new rota system was introduced that required her to start work at 4.45 a.m. but because of her domestic commitments she could not comply with these new times. *It was shown in court that there were 2,023 male train operators, all of who could comply with the new rota (100%). Of the 21 female operators, although only one could not comply, this meant that only 95.2% of the women could comply. The Court of Appeal held that the considerably smaller proportion of women than the men that could comply meant that there was indirect discrimination of any woman affected by the change.*

London Underground Ltd. *v.* Edwards (1998)

Here is another example that illustrates the principle of indirect discrimination.

A college sought to overcome cash shortages by charging overseas students at an increased rate unless they had been resident in the UK or another EU country for at least three years. The House of Lords held that *this requirement indirectly discriminated against non-British and non-EU students as many fewer could comply with the condition.* Further, although the reason for the discriminating condition was economic it could not be justified in other than racial terms. The college could have dealt with its economic problems by increasing all student fees or in some other way that had no regard to the nationality of the student applicants.

Orphanos *v.* Queen Mary College (1985)

Exceptions to the discrimination Acts

There are some limited and specific exceptions to the discrimination laws called genuine occupational qualifications (GOQs). Each case would have to be examined on its own merits but the following are examples that are acceptable in law.

Sex discrimination
If the post requires a person of one sex:

- for physiological reasons, (modelling, acting, etc.)
- to preserve decency or privacy (toilet attendant, security searching, etc.)
- if the post holder has to live on the premises but no separate sleeping and sanitary facilities are available (single sex establishments)
- in establishments for persons requiring special care or attention (single sex nursing homes, etc.)
- in the provision of personal welfare, etc. when it is most effectively done by one gender (counselling victims of sexual crime, some social work)
- when the job is one of two to be held by a married couple
- for employment in a private household which involves close personal contact if there could be objection to the employment of one sex
- for employment in a post sited mainly outside UK.

Note also the authority to suspend women from work on maternity grounds, page 157.

Racial discrimination

If the post requires:

- a person of a particular ethnic origin for physiological reasons (someone of a particular race for acting or authenticity such as a Chinese waiter in a Chinese restaurant)
- the provision of personal welfare services to persons of a particular racial group if those services can be most effectively provided by a person of that racial group (The services must involve direct contact between the parties, the discrimination would be unlawful if the contact was indirect.)
- employment mainly outside UK.

The operation of GOQs was shown in the following case.

> The employer had a policy of maintaining an ethnic balance amongst the staff of a preschool day care centre. After an Afro-Caribbean worker left, the post was advertised specifying the same ethnic origin. The applicant was rejected because of his ethnic origin. The Employment Appeal Tribunal held that *in this case Afro-Caribbean origin was a genuine occupational qualification for a nursery worker who would be required to talk and read to the children in dialect.*
>
> Tottenham Green Under Fives Centre *v.* Marshall (1989)

In contrast, the next decision differed for the reasons shown.

> An employer advertised posts in the housing department for applicants of Afro-Caribbean or Asian origin; GOQs were claimed because over half of the tenants had such ethnic origins. The Court of Appeal held that *the services being provided by the post holders were not of a 'personal' nature within the ordinary meaning of the word. The jobs were essentially managerial in character and therefore the mode of recruitment was discriminatory and unlawful.*
>
> London Borough of Lambeth *v.* Commission for Racial Equality (1990)

Harassment

There is no statutory definition of the term 'harassment' but the dictionary definition of the verb 'to harass' is 'to trouble and annoy continually or repeatedly'. This seems to be a reasonable definition as a starting point.

Racial harassment

With regard to racial harassment the CRE Code of Practice recommends that:

> 'Individual employees should refrain from harassment or intimidation of other employees on racial grounds. Such action may be unlawful if it is taken by employees against those who are subject to their authority.'

Although allegations of racial harassment can be dealt with under the 1976 Act it is not always easy to prove that particular conduct lies within the terms of that Act.

See cases of *Burton and Another* v. *De Vere Hotels* (1996) and *Jones* v. *Tower Boot Co. Ltd.* (1996) below.

Sexual harassment

There is no statutory definition of sexual harassment, but over the years a body of case law has evolved making the identification of what constitutes harassment less difficult.

The first significant sex harassment case was as follows.

A worker at a school was the victim of what the court described as 'a policy of vindictive unpleasantness'. This included her tormentors making suggestive remarks and obliging her to brush against them in order to pass by. It was their intention to force her to transfer to another school. She claimed discrimination on the basis that she had suffered 'detriment' as defined in the law. The Court of Session held that *any treatment of a woman that contained a significant sexual element was to be regarded as being on the grounds of her sex. It was said that the case showed the use of a particular kind of weapon, based upon the sex of the victim, which . . . would not have been used against an equally disliked man.*

Strathclyde Regional Council v. Porcelli (1986)

The evidence that can be called in these cases was examined:

A woman complained of sexual harassment and was *cross-examined about her sexual attitudes and behaviour in the workplace to ascertain if she had suffered detriment.* The Employment Appeal Tribunal held that *such evidence was valid to ascertain the sensitivity and extent of the hurt feelings of the complainant.* It was also noted that tribunals could hear such evidence in private.

Snowball v. Gardner Merchant Ltd. (1987)

There does not seem to be an objective standard of sexual harassment and individual complaints have to be treated on their own merits. Accordingly, a practice manager receiving a complaint of sexual harassment should investigate the following points:

- *frequency of the conduct:* the more often it occurs, the more harassing it becomes
- *severity of the harassment:* physical contact is worse than vulgar language
- *explicitness of the harassment:* the more sexually explicit the behaviour the worse it becomes
- *status of the harasser:* if the alleged harasser has a position of authority the situation will be worsened
- *location of the harassment:* public incidents may be more distressing than those in private
- *the age of the victim:* a teenager may find it more difficult to cope with harassment than an older woman who has the experience of life to help her in dealing with embarrassing situations.

Note also the points made regarding dealing with complaints of crime, page 27.

Liability in sex and race discrimination matters

Individuals have liability as principals for their own discriminatory actions. Additionally, employers have absolute vicarious liability for the actions of their employees in respect of discriminatory actions committed during the course of employment. This applies irrespective of whether or not it was done with the employer's knowledge or approval.

Employers have a legal defence if they can prove that reasonable steps were taken to prevent any employee from engaging in discriminatory behaviour. A case relating to this point was:

> *The employer had taken all reasonable steps to foresee or prevent harassment but before complaints were made no one in authority had known about the problem.* Staff had in general been properly supervised and knew of the equal opportunities policy. In this case *the employer was held by the Employment Appeal Tribunal to be not directly liable for the harassment.*
>
> Balgobin *v.* Tower Hamlets London Borough Council (1987)

However, contrast the following case.

> The Court of Appeal held that an employer's vicarious liability in race relations cases was not as restricted as that in tort (see page 6). It was not necessary to prove that the employee's racially abusive actions were performed 'during the course of his employment' so as to make the employer liable. In this case, *the victim had suffered both physical and verbal abuse from fellow employees that, after a few weeks caused him to leave his job. The employer had vicarious liability for not taking steps to control the racial harassment.*
>
> Jones *v.* Tower Boot Co. Ltd. (1996)

See also *Gilbert* v. *Midland Bank Ltd.* (1998) on page 189.

The vicarious liability can extend from the actions of fellow employees to the actions of other people, as:

> Two young Afro-Caribbean women were employed as casual waitresses at a function where Bernard Manning was a speaker. Mr. Manning both sexually and racially abused the women by making them the butt of offensive jokes. The employers had not themselves subjected the women to racial harassment. The Employment Appeal Tribunal held that *if an employer allowed a third party to racially abuse his staff in circumstances over which he had control and where he could have prevented or reduced the extent of the abuse, then he, the employer, was guilty of subjecting them to the harassment.*
>
> Burton and Another *v.* De Vere Hotels (1996)

Complaints of sexual or racial discrimination

Following are some brief points regarding the making of complaints about sexual or racial discrimination.

Equal Opportunities Commission (EOC)

The EOC has the duty to try to eliminate discrimination and encourage equal opportunities between the sexes.

Commission for Racial Equality (CRE)

The CRE has the duty to try and eliminate discrimination and encourage equal opportunities for all racial groups.

Both the EOC and the CRE issue codes of practice setting out the steps that should be taken to eliminate discrimination in employment. They can also

- investigate relevant matters
- start legal proceedings if the discrimination is persistent
- help individual complainants
- serve discrimination notices on an employer who has disobeyed a legal requirement requiring that the practice be stopped.

Both of the above bodies have Internet web sites that contain much useful information (see Appendix B).

Apart from approaching the EOC or the CRE, an individual can complain to an employment tribunal about alleged discrimination. After such a complaint a conciliation officer may be appointed to try and settle the matter but if this is unsuccessful the tribunal will hear the case, and if it is proved, may award:

- an order declaring the rights of both parties
- damages against the employer, or
- make a recommendation that the employer undertakes a particular course of action within a specified time.

Disabled persons

This is a relatively new piece of legislation and legal decisions are still needed to clarify some parts of the Act.

Definitions under the Disability Discrimination Act 1995 are:

- *Disability:* a physical or mental impairment that has a substantial and long-term adverse effect on the individual's ability to carry out normal day-to-day activities.
- A *disabled person:* a person who has a disability.
- *Small business:* this means an employer who has fewer than 15 employees. Such a business is exempt from the provisions of the Act dealing with employment.

The main points of the Act are shown in Figure 12.4. Some cases concerning disability discrimination are summarised below.

A job applicant suffered from photosensitive epilepsy but the condition was controlled by drugs. The interviewer was aware of the applicant's condition. At the interview the applicant wore sunglasses around her neck and explained that she might be affected by the lighting that consisted of fluorescent lighting, venetian blinds on the windows and light coloured walls. During the interview she did not use the glasses nor did she complain that she was either unwell or feeling disadvantaged.

She was not selected for the post and subsequently claimed discrimination because the employer had failed to make reasonable adjustments to the physical environment for the interview. The employer believed that the woman's condition was controlled by medication and said that if she had complained alternative arrangements would have been made.

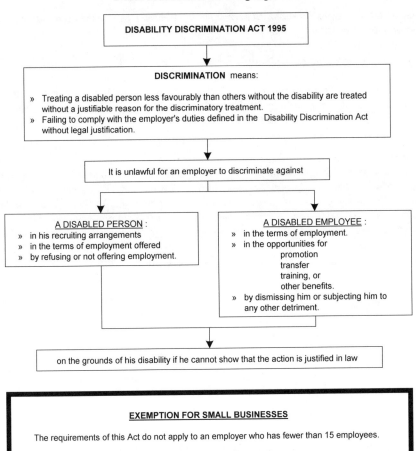

Figure 12.4 Disability discrimination

The Employment Appeal Tribunal held that she had not been discriminated against. *Disabled people do not have a duty to give detailed explanations of the effects of their condition. Similarly, employers are not required to ask a number of questions about whether a disabled person feels disadvantaged merely to protect themselves from liability.*

Ridout *v.* TC Group (1998)

A disabled employee was absent from work and did not submit a sick note as required. She was therefore dismissed. At the time of the dismissal the employer was not aware that the employee suffered from ME chronic fatigue syndrome. The Employment Appeal Tribunal held that *as the employer was not aware of her condition, there could not be any discrimination under the 1995 Act and as a result the dismissal was fair.*

O'Neil *v.* Symm and Co. Ltd. (1998)

The Employment Appeal Tribunal held that the correct comparator with an employee who was dismissed because he would be absent from work for a year owing to a disability was someone who could have been off work for the same time but for a non-disablement reason. *The disabled person should expect to be treated in the same way as a non-disabled person.*

Clark *v.* Novacold Ltd. (1998)

A worker suffered a back injury and was on sick leave for six months. It was held by the tribunal that *this was not a disability as defined by the Act as the worker had not suffered physical impairment that had substantial and long-term adverse effects upon his ability to carry out normal day-to-day activities.*

Rowley *v.* Walkers Nonsuch Ltd. (1997)

A worker with club foot found it progressively more difficult to stand for any length of time. She worked on a production line, and her output deteriorated as a result of her disability. *Although her employer consulted a doctor and the Shaw Trust (a body established to assist in such cases) and arranged a trial of a special seat for her, her performance continued to deteriorate and she was eventually dismissed. A tribunal awarded her £1200 for injured feelings and recommended her reinstatement, and that the employer should make further efforts to arrive at an 'appropriate adjustment' to permit her to continue to work.*

Tarling *v.* Wisdom Toothbrushes (1997)

The duties of an employer

The Act defines the duties of an employer as shown in Figure 12.5.

The Act provides examples of the steps that an employer might have to take to meet his responsibilities:

- making adjustments to premises
- allocating some of the disabled person's duties to another person
- transferring him to fill an existing vacancy
- altering his working hours

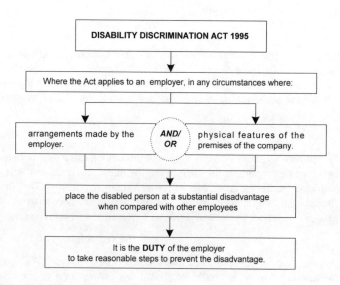

Figure 12.5   Disability discrimination – duties of employer

- assigning him to a different place of work
- allowing him to be absent during working hours for rehabilitation, assessment or treatment
- giving him, or arranging for him to be given, training
- acquiring or modifying equipment
- modifying instructions or reference manuals
- providing a reader or interpreter
- providing supervision.

In determining what is reasonable for an employer to do, regard shall be had to:

- the extent to which the step would prevent the disadvantage of the disabled person
- the extent to which it is practicable for the employer to take the step
- the financial and other costs which would be incurred by the employer
- the extent to which the employer's activities would be disrupted
- the extent of the employer's financial and other resources
- the availability to the employer of financial or other assistance.

These duties do not apply to an employer until a disabled person is employed or applies for a job as no 'anticipatory' action is required. Even prior to the act, some insight into the attitude of tribunals in such cases is provided by the case of *Tarling* v. *Wisdom Toothbrushes* (1997), see above.

In one of the first cases to be considered under this legislation, the rules for considering discrimination and unfair dismissal cases by tribunals were set out.

This case concerned a road worker who, following a road accident injury was disabled. For financial reasons the employer had to reduce the workforce to a smaller more flexible number. Those retained were required to hold driving licences but the appellant because of his disability did not, and was therefore made redundant. He claimed disability discrimination and unfair dismissal by his employer.

The Employment Appeal Tribunal stated that *a tribunal must go through a number of sequential steps when considering a complaint of discrimination under the Act.*

- Is a duty imposed on the employer in the particular case?
- If the duty is imposed, has the employer taken such steps as are reasonable in the circumstances to prevent the disabled person being placed at a substantial disadvantage?
- Could the employer have reasonably taken such steps (as listed in the Act)?
- At the same time the tribunal must have regard to the factors (as listed in the Act) that could affect the employer in the implementation of these steps.
- If, but only if, the tribunal found that an employer had failed to comply with a duty, did consideration have to be given as to whether the failure was justified?
- *If the employer showed that no reasonable adjustment to the working conditions would have avoided the dismissal there was probably no failure by the employer to perform a duty under the Act.*

It was held in this case that the employer had not failed to comply with his duty therefore there was no discrimination under the Act.

Morse *v.* Wiltshire County Council (1998)

Another case further defined the duties placed upon an employer.

A man suffering from cerebral palsy applied for a computer post. He was interviewed and offered the post subject to the employer being able to make appropriate arrangements for his needs that involved him receiving considerable assistance when going to the toilet. The employer asked for volunteers to assist in this matter but that was not successful. It was not possible for security reasons for the applicant to work from his home. An application for government funding for a part-time carer was made, but there would be a long delay before a decision could be made. In the meantime the employer considered that filling the post had become an urgent matter and the job offer was withdrawn.

The Employment Appeal Tribunal held that *the Act does not require employers to provide carers for the personal needs of disabled employees and there had been no discrimination in this case.*

Kenny *v.* Hampshire Constabulary (1998)

The employer will also have vicarious liability for any harassment by fellow employees that amounts to disability discrimination.

A dyslexic worker was bullied and subjected to verbal abuse because he could not read. He complained to the management but they failed to investigate or take any steps to stop the bullying. After 18 months he left his job and subsequently claimed constructive dismissal.

The employment tribunal held that the applicant had suffered discrimination because of his disability and that he had been constructively dismissed. He was awarded substantial compensation.

The chairman of the tribunal described the applicant as the factory 'punch bag'. He said 'We emphasise this is a rather extreme case of barbarous treatment which, though at one time accepted in the workplace, has now been outlawed. Employees as well as employers would be well advised to note this fact.'

Harling *v.* CL Plastics (2000)

Complaints of disability discrimination

Following are some brief points regarding the making of complaints about disability discrimination.

Disability Rights Commission (DRC)
The DRC has the duty to

- work towards the elimination of discrimination against disabled people
- promote equalisation of opportunities for disabled people with those of non-disabled people
- promote good practice, and
- advise the government on disability discrimination legislation.

The DRC also has the duty of issuing codes of practice setting out the steps that should be taken to eliminate all aspects of disability discrimination. A Code of Practice exists which gives advice to employers in these matters.

The DRC can:

- undertake formal investigations for any purpose connected with its duties
- provide conciliation in cases of dispute
- help individual disabled people with advice, information, and when needed, arrange for legal advice.

Employment tribunals

An aggrieved person can apply to an employment tribunal, and if successful can be awarded any of the following remedies:

- a declaration as to the rights of the parties
- compensation (including for injury to feelings)
- a recommendation that the employer undertakes actions within a specified time to ameliorate the cause of the complaint.

Discrimination because of age

There is no legal requirement that an employer should not discriminate by age. At the beginning of 1998 the Employment Minister said that the enactment of specific legislation in this area was fraught with difficulty and therefore a voluntary code of practice would be introduced. In June 1999 the Government published *Age Diversity in Employment: A Code of Practice* to deal with the problems of 'ageism'.

The Code covers good practice in six aspects of the employment cycle, namely:

- recruitment
- selection
- promotion
- training and development
- redundancy
- retirement.

The Code is advisory and carries no legal sanctions, although employment tribunal chairmen are being asked to consider taking on the enforcement of the Code.

In the two years from June 1999 employers will be monitored by way of surveys to gauge the effectiveness of the Code. After that, in 2001, the need for legislation will be reconsidered.

Part-time employees

Part-time employees must not be discriminated against and suffer less favourable treatment than comparable full-time employees. See Part-time employees page 142.

Convicted persons

The Rehabilitation of Offenders Act 1974, states that if persons convicted of certain offences do not commit any further offences over a given time they become rehabilitated.

Definitions

A 'spent conviction' is one that does not have to be disclosed in normal circumstances, whereas a 'live conviction' is one that normally has to be disclosed (it is not spent).

When a person applies for a job, if the employer requires information about past convictions the applicant must disclose any live convictions. Failure to disclose live convictions could result in prosecution for 'obtaining a pecuniary advantage by dishonestly gaining remuneration in employment' see page 147 for further details. The employer would probably be justified in dismissing the employee depending on all the surrounding circumstances.

Insofar as spent convictions are concerned the applicant does not have to disclose them to the employer. If, subsequently, the employer learns of these convictions and dismisses the employee then the dismissal will almost certainly be unfair if their existence is the only reason for the dismissal.

The rules that define when convictions are spent are complex, but put simply the following are the basic criteria.

- For a conviction that may become spent the date upon which the court awarded the penalty defines the start of the 'live' time.
- The duration of the 'live' time is shown in the table below.

Penalty awarded	*When spent*
absolute discharge	after six months
conditional discharge, binding over	after one year
probation, fine or community service order	after five years
imprisonment or detention in a young offenders institution up to 6 months	after seven years
imprisonment or detention in a young offenders institution between 6 and 30 months	after 10 years
more than 30 months imprisonment or detention in a young offenders institution	never spent.

Special occupations

There are certain professions and jobs that are exempted from the provisions of this Act and in these cases the employer can request details of both live and spent convictions. The applicant is required to give details of all convictions in such circumstances. The most important of these occupations from your point of view as a practice manager are:

- doctors
- dentists
- nurses
- police officers
- teachers
- social workers
- probation officers.

There are many other occupations also exempted from the terms of the Act but none of them are of direct concern to a practice manager.

Chapter 13
Trade Unions, Disciplinary and Grievance Procedures

Trade unions and their recognition

The main statute in trade union matters is the Trade Union and Labour Relations (Consolidation) Act 1992 and this Act was extensively amended by the Employment Relations Act 1999.

General points

A trade union is an organisation made up mainly of workers, whose main purpose is to act on behalf of its members in the regulation of relations between the workers and the employers.

Until 1999 a trade union had no 'right' to be recognised by an employer for consultation purposes but unions now have a right to request recognition in organisations that employ 21 or more people. The procedures leading to union recognition are long and detailed and they must be carried out punctiliously. Figure 13.1 shows the basic requirements of the recognition procedures. It is anticipated that this part of the Act will be brought into force during the year 2000.

Few lay employees in medical general practice belong to trade unions although the doctors belong to the BMA and nurses will belong to one of the professional nursing organisations. It has been noted over the last few years that UNISON which already represents many NHS workers has been trying to recruit more members from a wider working base including employees in general practice. It will be surprising if UNISON or another trade union does not attempt to recruit members in some of the bigger practices with a view to gaining recognition

Legal rights of employees

Employees have a number of legal rights regarding trade union membership and activities as follows:

- every employee has the right to belong to a trade union if he wishes to do so
- every employee has the right *not* to belong to a trade union if he does not wish so to do.

In either of these cases it would be wrong for the employer to dismiss or otherwise punish an employee for pursuing his legal rights. Any employee suf-

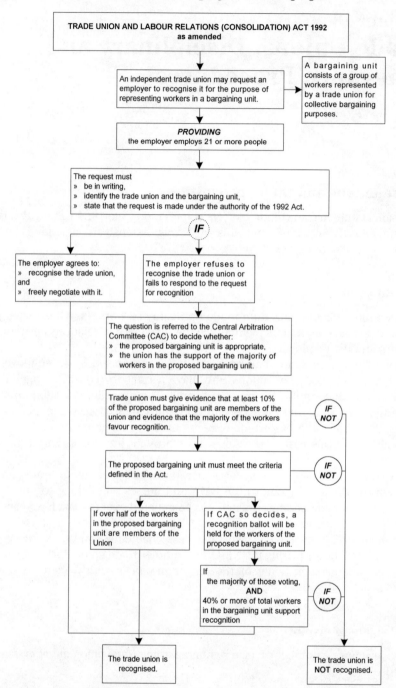

TRADE UNION AND LABOUR RELATIONS (CONSOLIDATION) ACT 1992
as amended

An independent trade union may request an employer to recognise it for the purpose of representing workers in a bargaining unit.

A bargaining unit consists of a group of workers represented by a trade union for collective bargaining purposes.

PROVIDING
the employer employs 21 or more people

The request must
» be in writing,
» identify the trade union and the bargaining unit,
» state that the request is made under the authority of the 1992 Act.

IF

The employer agrees to:
» recognise the trade union, and
» freely negotiate with it.

The employer refuses to recognise the trade union or fails to respond to the request for recognition

The question is referred to the Central Arbitration Committee (CAC) to decide whether:
» the proposed bargaining unit is appropriate,
» the union has the support of the majority of workers in the proposed bargaining unit.

Trade union must give evidence that at least 10% of the proposed bargaining unit are members of the union and evidence that the majority of the workers favour recognition.

IF NOT

The proposed bargaining unit must meet the criteria defined in the Act.

IF NOT

If over half of the workers in the proposed bargaining unit are members of the Union

If CAC so decides, a recognition ballot will be held for the workers of the proposed bargaining unit.

If
the majority of those voting,
AND
40% or more of total workers in the bargaining unit support recognition

IF NOT

The trade union is recognised.

The trade union is **NOT** recognised.

Figure 13.1   Trade union recognition

fering detriment as a result of belonging or not belonging to a trade union can complain to an employment tribunal. If the detriment extends to dismissal it will be automatically unfair, see page 151.

Once a trade union has been 'recognised' by an employer for consultation purposes there are additional rights involved.

- Employees have the right to take part in union activities at an appropriate time (not necessarily with pay):
  - o the appropriate time may be either inside working hours if an arrangement has been made and consent given, otherwise the activity must be outside working hours.
  - o industrial action is expressly excluded from the above.
- A trade union official should be allowed reasonable time off work with pay during working hours to enable him to carry out duties concerned with industrial relations (see page 185).

If the union has been recognised and the employer fails to allow time off for trade union activities as described above, then the employee concerned may complain to an employment tribunal within three months. If the complaint is sustained, the tribunal may award compensation and make a declaration regarding the legal rights of both parties.

> An employer refused to continue recognising an employee as a union shop steward because of the way he conducted himself. His terms of employment were not affected, and the only result of the employer's action was to deprive him of his status as a shop steward and his ability to represent his fellow workers. The Court of Appeal held that *to be derecognised as a shop steward could be extremely damaging to the employee as it would be a serious reflection on his character. In consequence the employee had suffered detrimental treatment from his employer.*
>
> F.W. Farnsworth Ltd. *v.* McCoid (1999)

Information booklets on this topic are available from ACAS (see Appendix B for website details).

Some terms used in respect of trade unions

The following are some terms and phrases used about trade unions; they need to be noted to understand the law in these matters.

Trade union branch
This is the basic unit of union organisation, and may have just a few members or several thousands. It will be based upon either the workplace, or in the case of scattered workers, upon a geographical area. The trade union official most closely concerned with the branch is the *shop steward*. He is usually elected to the position by the membership of the branch. Often this person is called the union representative.

The duties of the union representative will vary widely, but will usually include the following:

- recruiting new members
- explaining union activities to new members

- maintaining union branch records
- keeping union interest 'alive' with the membership
- arranging the collection of subscriptions
- acting as a channel of communication between the membership, paid union officials and the management.

See page 59 regarding trade union rights concerning HASAW safety representatives.

Collective bargaining

When workers negotiate with their employers as a group rather than as individuals this is usually done by way of trade union representatives. A *bargaining unit* is a group of workers who are represented by a trade union for collective bargaining purposes.

Consultation

Consultation takes place over certain matters which are still subject to managerial control such as redundancies or pension scheme administration. After having sought the opinions of the workforce, management will remain solely responsible for subsequent decisions affecting the workforce.

Negotiation

Negotiation takes place over matters that are jointly controlled by all the parties to the negotiation process. At the conclusion of negotiations an agreement will usually be drawn up by the parties, indicating the agreed responsibilities of each party. However, such a negotiated agreement is not usually legally binding on the parties.

Conciliation

A conciliator is a person who brings together the two sides involved in a dispute and helps them to resolve their differences. He is merely an adviser without personal authority using his expertise in industrial relations to help the parties to agree.

Arbitration

An arbitrator is a sort of judge who hears the case put forward by both sides in a dispute. On the evidence presented to him, he will make a decision which then becomes legally binding on both sides.

In a state of free collective bargaining, both sides must agree that the dispute can go to arbitration and that they will be bound by the arbitrator's findings.

Disciplinary matters

The Employment Rights Act 1996 states that the written statement of particulars of employment (see page 136) shall include a note specifying:

- any disciplinary rules applicable to the employee
- a person to whom the employee can apply if dissatisfied with any disciplinary decision relating to him

- a person to whom the employee can apply to seek redress concerning any grievance relating to his employment
- the manner in which such applications should be made.

Note that an employer employing fewer than 20 people does not need to have written disciplinary procedures.

Natural justice

If an employee takes a complaint to an employment tribunal, one factor that will be scrutinised will be the fairness of the discipline and grievance systems. The rules of the legal principles of 'natural justice' should be followed in any discipline system, the main points of which are illustrated in Figure 13.2.

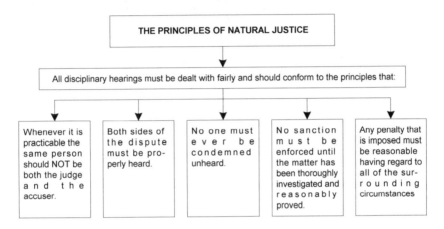

Figure 13.2 Natural justice

Prudent small employers should have formal disciplinary and grievance systems in place to ensure that discipline is carried out fairly. Without such procedures an employer might find it difficult to refute any allegation of procedural unfairness made to an employment tribunal as described in *Polkey* v. *A.E. Dayton Services Ltd.* (1988) on page 145. Dismissals must be 'procedurally' correct and employment tribunals have to be satisfied that the principles of natural justice were followed throughout the disciplinary proceedings otherwise the dismissal will be 'procedurally' unfair.

> The Employment Appeal Tribunal held that *an employee must be given the chance to both state his own case and challenge any allegations made against him.*
>
> Khanun v. Mid-Glamorgan Health Authority (1979)

> At the Court of Appeal it was said that *if an employee was denied the opportunity to state his case the tribunal would examine the facts. The tribunal would look to see if there were any real or substantial chance that the applicant could make any further observations that might alter the employer's final decision.*
>
> R v. Chief Constable of Thames Valley Police, *ex parte* Cotton (1990)

In addition, the Employment Relations Act 1999 provides employees with another new right in these matters. This is the right to be accompanied at any discipline or grievance proceedings by either a trade union official or another employee. The main points of this right are shown in Figure 13.3 and it is expected to be in force by the middle of 2000.

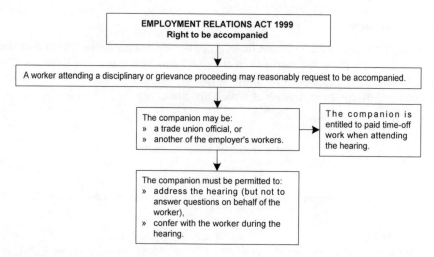

Figure 13.3   Right to be accompanied

All practice managers are strongly advised to have formal disciplinary procedures devised. They might never be needed, but it is both prudent and a matter of good practice to have them.

The disciplinary code

Organisational rules are necessary to ensure

- efficient performance of work
- safe performance of work
- maintenance of satisfactory relationships between employees and the management.

As well as controlling misconduct the rules should be drafted in such a way that when an employee displays a consistently poor standard of work there is a formal means of showing him that remedial action is needed. All employees should be aware of the rules that govern their conduct. Rules should not be so generalised that their lack of specificity renders them unenforceable or they will cease to have any effect.

Based on ACAS recommendations the discipline code should:

- be in writing
- specify to whom it applies
- allow matters to be dealt with speedily
- define the disciplinary actions that can be taken

- specify the authority possessed by each level of management
- ensure that individuals are told about complaints against them and they are given an opportunity to state their own case before any decision is reached
- give employees the right to be accompanied to a disciplinary hearing by a fellow employee of their choice
- ensure that, except for gross misconduct, no employee is dismissed for a first breach of discipline
- ensure that disciplinary action is not taken until the case has been fully investigated
- ensure that employees are given an explanation for any penalty imposed
- provide a right of appeal and specify the procedure to be followed.

ACAS is expected to publish a new recommended disciplinary code later in 2000.

The implementation of disciplinary procedures

A form of implementation of disciplinary procedures as shown in Figure 13.4 should meet all the requirements.

> The Employment Appeal Tribunal held that *a disciplinary hearing is not a full scale trial as in a court of law. Nonetheless, there must be a careful examination of all relevant matters and the investigation must not be so hastily or cursorily carried out that important evidence is overlooked.*
>
> Johnson Matthey Metals *v.* Harding (1978)

The hazard of not having or failing to use proper procedures was shown in the following newspaper report.

> A lecturer was dismissed for gross misconduct based on alleged sexual impropriety with one of his students. At the employment tribunal the Chairman said *'No sexual allegations were established. In our view the investigation was wholly inadequate and any finding on it was unfair. The investigative approach was unscientific. We therefore find the dismissal decision to be unfair.'* The lecturer received substantial compensation.
>
> Unnamed applicant *v.* City of London Polytechnic (1996)

Written documentation

Following are points of relevance about written documents:

Formal written warning

This will set out the details of the offence and the possible consequences if the offence is repeated. The employee should also be told that this is the first formal stage of the disciplinary procedure.

Final written warning

This will set out the details of the offence. The warning may place the employee 'on notice', e.g. an employee who has frequently been late might be warned that any unjustifiable lateness during the next six weeks will result in a full disciplinary hearing. Otherwise the employee will be told that a repeat of the offence will lead to disciplinary penalty, e.g. dismissal.

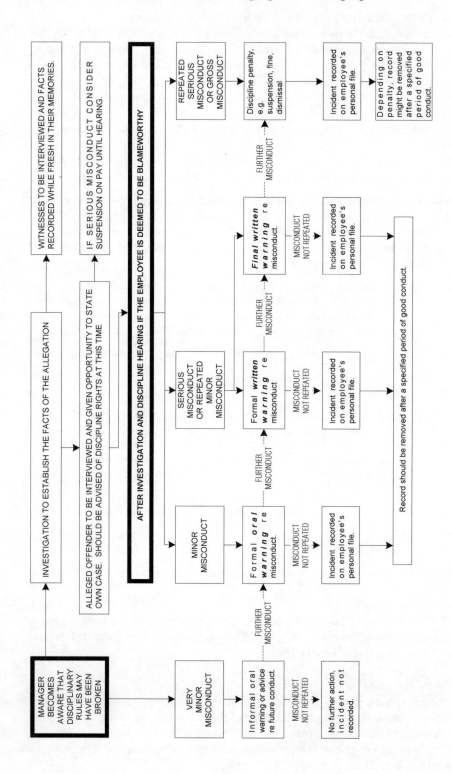

Figure 13.4 Disciplinary procedure

Result of disciplinary action

This is a written document given to an employee found guilty of a breach of discipline rules containing:

- the result of the hearing
- the effect of any penalty awarded
- any right that the employee has to appeal against this finding and how he can make the appeal.

Discipline records

Discipline records should be maintained by the employer, and they should:

- detail breaches of disciplinary rules by employees
- detail the action taken and the reasons for decisions made
- note whether the employee appealed against any disciplinary decision
- record the outcome of any appeal and any subsequent developments.

These records must be regarded as confidential and must be safely stored and treated as any other confidential documents.

Written records should be retained for at least six years. Thus, if any matter is being pursued through either courts or tribunals, written evidence will be available giving the details of all actions taken at every stage of the discipline proceedings.

Penalties

The sanctions or penalties that may be imposed upon an employee must be clearly stated in the disciplinary code, and must conform to the terms of the contract of employment. Whatever penalty is invoked it must be reasonable in all the circumstances.

Except for gross misconduct calling for instant dismissal, no employee should be dismissed for a first breach of discipline. Such a case will almost invariably be construed to be an unfair dismissal. The penalties following due disciplinary proceedings could be, amongst others:

- dismissal or requirement to resign
- suspension without pay for a period of time
- transfer to another section or location
- demotion
- non-payment of a pay increment.

> The Employment Appeal Tribunal held that *if an employee is told that he will be dismissed if he does not resign, then a resignation because of the threat is treated in law as a dismissal.*
>
> Allders International Ltd. *v.* Parkins (1981)

The discipline code used in a practice should follow the guidelines laid down in the ACAS Code of Practice I: Disciplinary Practice and Procedures in Employment, as mentioned earlier this code is currently (May 2000) being rewritten.

Grievance procedures

When those who represent the organisation (managers and supervisors) are dissatisfied with the conduct of an individual employee the disciplinary procedures are used. When an individual employee is dissatisfied by the way he is treated, a different method is used to air the complaint. This is usually referred to as the *grievance procedure*.

Desirably, all organisations should have a formalised grievance procedure. Unfortunately not all do but at the other extreme some organisations have a system whereby any worker with a grievance can always gain immediate access to senior management on a face to face basis.

A reasonable grievance procedure should:

- be laid down in writing
- state to whom grievances must be taken in the first instance (usually the immediate supervisor)
- give an aggrieved employee the right to be accompanied by a trade union representative or a colleague
- state clearly how an employee can pursue a grievance if it is not resolved by the first interview (The next stage might be seeing the supervisor's supervisor or a more senior manager.)
- prescribe a specified time limit by the end of which the employee can expect to be told the result of his complaint
- arrange for all meetings and/or discussions concerning the complaint to be properly minuted and for all parties to receive a written record of the proceedings.

Many of the things that cause concern to employees can be dealt with on an informal basis. This will only happen if the manager takes positive steps to listen to complaints and take appropriate action. A minor complaint left unresolved soon becomes a major issue. Suitable advice papers are available from ACAS.

Part V
Consumer Protection and Product Liability Law

- Consumer protection
- Product liability
- Medicinal products

Chapter 14
Consumer Protection and Product Liability

Consumer protection – general points

In years gone by the buyer was responsible for ensuring that the goods he bought were of a required standard. If he bought a 'pig in a poke' he could not take the seller to court to obtain redress. The legal phrase describing this idea is *caveat emptor* or 'let the buyer beware'.

In the past the criminal law was used in cases of fraud and in limited cases relating to the standards of food and drink, especially ale and beer, and later, drugs. In the main the laws regulated transactions as a part of the law of contract and no real account was taken of consumers as such.

Since the early 1970s there has been a change of emphasis in these matters. Many new laws (mostly beyond the scope of this handbook) have been enacted to give increasing protection to the individual consumer. Several of the laws have created new criminal offences.

From the 1970s the European Union has taken a lead in this particular area of law and a number of Directives were made during the 1980s. United Kingdom law has been brought into line with these Directives thus giving considerably more protection to consumers than they previously had.

Two phrases that should be identified are used in this area of law.

- *Product (or consumer) safety:* laws using this phrase create criminal offences and alleged offenders may be prosecuted regarding defective or unsafe products.
- *Product liability:* laws using this phrase relate to civil actions for compensation that can be taken by anyone who is injured by a defective or unsafe product.

Increasingly GPs are supplying things outside the terms of their NHS responsibilities, not only medicinal products but other items as well. Indeed, one GP was reported as having a coffee shop with a liquor licence in the same building as the surgery.

The sale and supply of any items could result in criminal or civil liability if any of the consumer protection laws are breached and at worst this could result in the GP being the defendant. At the least he could be called as a witness in proceedings taken against either the wholesale distributor or the producer of the goods.

In any of these cases all appropriate records from the practice would probably have to be produced in court. This is a very strong argument for ensuring that all administrative records are kept accurately and remain accessible for several years.

Criminal liability

The Consumer Protection Act 1987 creates criminal offences for producing or supplying unsafe products as shown in Figure 14.1. In simple terms the word 'producer' means the manufacturer or anyone who modifies or repairs the product in any way. The 'distributor' is anyone who passes on the product unchanged from the way it was received. In most cases GPs will be 'distributors' unless they alter the product before supplying it to the patient.

There are many different regulations that define the standards for particular products together with statutes regulating specific products such as the Food Safety Act 1990. Several, but not all, place strict liability on producers and/or distributors, which means that it is only necessary for the prosecution to prove that a defined standard for the product has not been met. A case showing the stringency of this test involved food production; the case was under a now repealed statute, but the principle remains valid.

> A company producing several million tins of peas per week was convicted after one tin was found to contain a very small caterpillar. The case was appealed to the House of Lords where it was said that *it was not enough for the company to show that they took all reasonable care to avoid the presence of extraneous bodies in the tins. This was an offence of strict liability so the appeal against conviction was rejected.*
>
> *The Lord Chancellor observed that to interpret the law less strictly would make a serious inroad into the consumer protection legislation that Parliament had enacted and continued to extend.*
>
> Smedleys *v.* Breed (1974)

Medicines Act 1968

This Act replaced all previous legislation in controlling the manufacture, importation, supply and prescription of medicinal products following the thalidomide tragedy.

The Act and its regulations define the safety requirements of medicinal products. It places strict controls on where and by whom they can be sold and should be read in conjunction with the terms of the General Product Safety Regulations 1994.

Definitions

Medicinal product as defined under the Act means:

- any substance or article used for medicinal purposes.

Medicinal purposes means any one of the following:

- treating or preventing disease
- diagnosing disease
- contraception

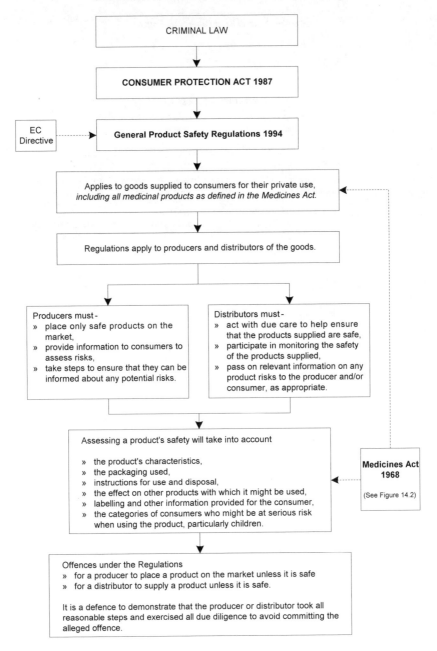

CRIMINAL LAW

CONSUMER PROTECTION ACT 1987

EC
Directive

General Product Safety Regulations 1994

Applies to goods supplied to consumers for their private use, *including all medicinal products as defined in the Medicines Act.*

Regulations apply to producers and distributors of the goods.

Producers must -
» place only safe products on the market,
» provide information to consumers to assess risks,
» take steps to ensure that they can be informed about any potential risks.

Distributors must-
» act with due care to help ensure that the products supplied are safe,
» participate in monitoring the safety of the products supplied,
» pass on relevant information on any product risks to the producer and/or consumer, as appropriate.

Assessing a product's safety will take into account

» the product's characteristics,
» the packaging used,
» instructions for use and disposal,
» the effect on other products with which it might be used,
» labelling and other information provided for the consumer,
» the categories of consumers who might be at serious risk when using the product, particularly children.

Medicines Act 1968

(See Figure 14.2)

Offences under the Regulations
» for a producer to place a product on the market unless it is safe
» for a distributor to supply a product unless it is safe.

It is a defence to demonstrate that the producer or distributor took all reasonable steps and exercised all due diligence to avoid committing the alleged offence.

Figure 14.1   Consumer protection law – criminal law

● inducing anaesthesia
● temporarily interfering with the normal operation of a physiological function.

Figure 14.2 illustrates the main points of the Act.

   The details of the mode of sale of particular products are specified in Regulations made under the authority of the 1968 Act. A recent example of such was

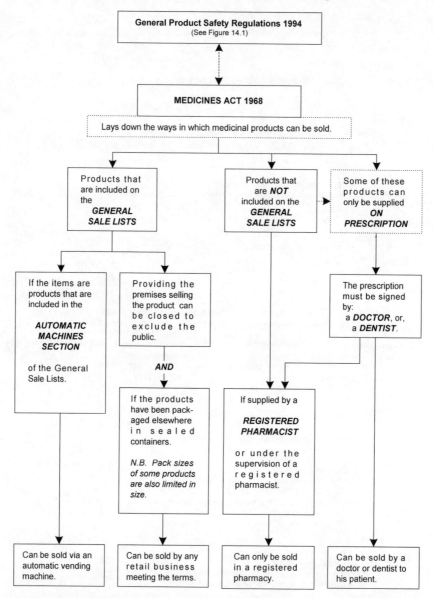

Figure 14.2   Medicines Act 1968

The Prescription Only Medicines (Human Use) Amendment Order 1997 that restricted the sale of paracetamol and aspirin in general shops to packets containing not more than 32 tablets.

The following case concerned the sale of a medicinal product that had a tragic outcome.

A four day old baby was prescribed a medicine to be made up by a chemist. A trainee pharmacist confused double strength chloroform water with concentrated chloroform that resulted in the preparation being 20 times too strong. His supervisor failed to check his work and in any case as she had only been qualified for two years she was not entitled to supervise. As a result of the mistake, when the medicine was administered to the baby he immediately became ill and died 18 days later. *Both of the defendants pleaded guilty to supplying a defective medicine* and were fined at the Crown Court.

R *v.* Taylor-Lloyd and Khattab (2000)

Prescriptions

The medicinal products that can only be supplied on prescription are those such as:

- substances given by injection
- most controlled drugs (except some very weak preparations), and
- any product that contains an item from a list of stated substances.

A prescription must be completed in a form regulated by law. The prescription form must be written or printed in indelible ink or carbon and must contain the following details

- the name and address of the patient for whom the product is prescribed
- the age of the patient if he/she is under 12 years of age
- the name and address of the prescribing doctor or dentist
- the date on which the prescription was made (it is invalid after 6 months)
- the signature, in ink, of the doctor or dentist prescribing.

Note that it is quite acceptable for someone such as a medical secretary to enter the details of a prescription. The doctor or dentist must then check that it is correctly completed before signing it in ink.

Medicinal products that are not on the general sale list, i.e. 'prescription drugs' can only be sold:

- from a registered pharmacy, sales being made by either a registered pharmacist or by a person acting under the supervision of a registered pharmacist
- by a doctor supplying a product that is needed for the immediate treatment of a patient before supply can be obtained from a pharmacy.

The sale of medicinal products is another example of 'strict liability' as was shown in this case:

A pharmacist was handed a forged prescription and he supplied the drugs thereon. He had been duped by the forgery and there was no evidence of either dishonesty or a want of care. The case was appealed to the House of Lords where it was held that *the offence under the Medicines Act of supplying prescription drugs without a prescription is one of strict liability. In consequence the conviction of the pharmacist was upheld.*

Pharmaceutical Society of Great Britain *v.* Storkwain (1986)

Doctors in rural practices may be authorised to sell prescription items to patients who live more than a mile from a retail pharmacy. In most of these practices the surgery receptionist provides the prescription items under the control of the doctor. A test case was brought by three pharmacists in an attempt to ensure that all dispensing was carried out either by the doctor or by a qualified pharmacist in these rural practices.

The Court of Appeal found in favour of the doctors and described the pharmacists' arguments as 'absurd'. The Court held that whilst *it was accepted that there is a public interest in the safe supply of medicinal products there is also a public interest in controlling the cost of the National Health Service. It is clearly wasteful of scarce human resources and money if a job that can perfectly well be done by a person with some basic training and ability to read has to be done by a doctor.*

R *v.* FHSA *ex parte* Elmfield Drugs Ltd (1998)

The major criminal liability of a GP under the Medicines Act would be in breaching the restrictions on the sale of medicinal products. However if the GP is involved in drug trials or has his own pharmacy there are many other regulations to which he must conform. The details of these regulations are outside the scope of this handbook.

The Medicines Act 1968 also legislates for:

- medicinal product licences and clinical trials
- registration of pharmacies
- homeopathic and herbal remedies
- forms of container and/or packaging to be used for medication products
- labelling and marking of containers and packages
- advertising of medicinal substances
- veterinarians and medicinal products used on animals.

Controlled drugs

Misuse of Drugs Act 1971

This Act and the regulations made under its authority make special rules concerning certain drugs referred to as *controlled drugs*. Controlled drugs are classified according to their harmfulness. The classification of the drugs involved affects the maximum penalty that can be imposed on an offender convicted of an offence under the Act.

- *Class A drugs* include heroin, cocaine, diamorphine, opium and ecstasy.
- *Class B drugs* include cannabis and cannabis resin, amphetamine and codeine.
- *Class C drugs* include bromazepam, diazepam and prazepam.

The above examples give a brief idea of the sort of drugs included in each classification. The full list of controlled drugs is very extensive and will be found in the 1971 Act together with the regulations that have amended the original list from time to time.

The Act and its regulations make rules regarding controlled drugs concerning:

- possession and supply of controlled drugs
- safe custody of controlled drugs
- the documentation of transactions
- keeping records and supplying information as required
- the inspection of records and procedures used
- regulation of the issue of prescriptions for controlled drugs
- the requirement for any doctor attending an addict to inform the authorities.

No doctor may supply addicts with drugs unless he is in possession of a licence.

It is expected that doctors licensed to hold and prescribe controlled drugs will familiarise themselves with the appropriate regulations, some significant points from which are considered below.

Storage of controlled drugs

All controlled drugs must be kept in a securely locked container that can only be opened by the doctor or with his direct authority.

> An *unlocked case in a locked motor car is not considered to be a 'securely locked container'* for the purpose of the Act.
>
> Kameswara Rao *v.* Wyles (1949)

Records of controlled drugs

A doctor possessing or supplying controlled drugs must maintain a register in a prescribed form. The register must:

- record details of all drugs that are obtained or supplied
- have recorded items entered in chronological order
- be divided into separate parts, each part relating to the transactions for one specific drug.

The items entered in the register must be:

- made on the day of the transaction or the following day
- made in ink or other indelible medium
- not cancelled, obliterated or altered and any corrections should be made by marginal or foot notes that must be dated
- kept at each place to which it relates (and if the doctor carries the drug to administer to a patient he must carry and maintain a register)
- kept for a minimum period of two years after the date of the last entry.

Prescriptions for controlled drugs

A prescription for a controlled drug has to be completed in a specified form and it must:

- be written in ink or other indelible medium by the person issuing it in his own handwriting
- be signed and dated by the person issuing it using his usual signature
- state the name and address of the person for whom it is issued
- specify the strength of the preparation, the dose to be taken and the quantity of the preparation in both words and figures.

Note differences to normal prescriptions for other medicinal products, page 219.

Civil liability

Product liability leading to civil claims for compensation might lie under different legal headings as illustrated in Figure 14.3.

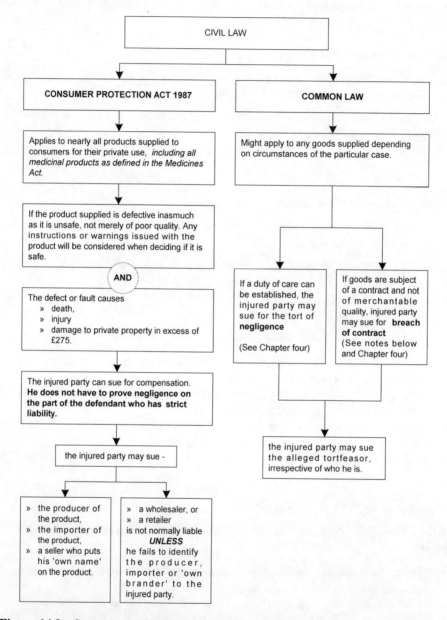

Figure 14.3   Consumer protection law – civil law

Consumer Protection Act

As will be seen in Figure 14.3, anyone injured by a defective product might have a claim for compensation against the producer, importer, etc. of the product.

Usually if the seller of the product is neither producer or importer so he will not have legal liability.

When an injured party intends to sue for compensation he has the right to know the identity of the producer or importer of the defective product. This information must be given to him by the person who supplied him with the product. If the information it is not provided when required the supplier or seller becomes liable and may become a defendant in the action.

In a practice containing a pharmacy, when dispensing for example, generic drugs supplied from more than one supplier, a record should be kept showing the source of the drugs supplied to each patient. Any deficiency in the records causing doubt about the origin of defective drugs could lead to the GP being held liable for the reasons given above.

Negligence

Before a landmark case heard in 1932 only the buyer of a product could sue concerning an injury caused by a defective product and this was done by an action for breach of contract. Any other person using or affected by the product had no legal means of redress. Following are brief details of this 1932 case.

> A woman and her friend visited a cafe where the friend bought her a ginger beer. The drink was brought to the table and some of it was poured into a glass of ice cream. Some of the ginger beer was drunk and the glass was topped up from the bottle but as this was done the decomposing remains of a snail fell from the bottle into the glass. The woman was not only shocked by the sight of the snail, she also developed gastro-enteritis and had to spend several days in hospital.
>
> As the law stood, because the woman had not bought the drink she was not a party to the contract of sale, consequently she had no case for a breach of contract. Nonetheless an action was started for damages by Mrs Donoghue against the ginger beer manufacturer Stevenson. She claimed that he had marketed a defective product that had caused her injury.
>
> The case went through the legal system and eventually ended in the House of Lords where Mrs Donoghue's case was upheld. *The first definition of negligence was made laying down the law that everyone has a duty of care towards any other person affected by their actions* (see page 35).
>
> Donoghue *v.* Stevenson (1932)

If a claim is made against the practice for negligently supplying an allegedly defective product that has caused an injury, the plaintiff will have to prove that the practice had a duty of care together with the other features of a negligence action as shown in Chapter 4.

The cause of the injury is not always attributable to the manufacturer of the product bought or used. Sometimes the supplier's carelessness will cause injury and thus he will be the defendant in the action.

> A woman contracted dermatitis as a result of having her hair dyed by her hairdresser. The manufacturer had issued instructions that the dye might be dangerous to certain skins and advised that a test be made before the dye was used. The hairdresser read the warning instruction but ignored it, made no test and dyed the plaintiff's hair. It was held that *the hairdresser was liable in this case and no liability could be attached to the manufacturer.*
>
> Holmes *v.* Ashford (1950)

Negligence actions regarding product liability are possible as shown in the case of *Holmes* above. Action under the Consumer Protection Act seems a likelier course for an aggrieved person because as shown in Figure 14.3 details of negligence do not have to be proven.

Contractual liability

When a patient/customer buys something at a practice, a contract is created between the buyer and the seller. The buyer will be the patient, but as the doctor is acting as an agent for the NHS, the NHS will be the seller in any incident that is questioned. However, if the doctor acts as a private individual providing goods or services to private patients outside the remit of the NHS, then the doctor will be the seller and the private patient the buyer. From the foregoing it is evident that in most practices any question of contract law affecting the doctor as a seller will not arise frequently. For general notes on contract matters look in Chapter 4.

The Sale of Goods Act 1979 (as amended) sets out the contractual obligations of buyers and sellers and defines the circumstances under which either party could sue the other for sub-standard goods. Likewise the Supply of Goods and Services Act 1982 provides similar regulation of contracts regarding the provision of services.

Although of little relevance to most general practices it is of interest to have a brief look at some of the important points covering the legal relationships between buyers and sellers.

When a seller advertises or displays a product for sale in a window or elsewhere this is called in legal terms an *invitation to treat*. Put into ordinary language it is an invitation to a potential buyer to discuss a sales transaction. An invitation to treat is not part of the contract process, therefore the potential buyer cannot insist that an item that is displayed with a particular price tag must be sold to him.

The first stage of the contract process occurs when the customer makes an offer by saying 'I want to buy that'. It is then up to the seller to accept the offer by agreeing to sell the product at a particular price. He might also demand that the price be paid in a particular way, thus he can reject the offer by refusing, say, to accept a cheque. Both parties then receive benefits or consideration from the transaction: the buyer receives the product and the seller receives the money.

As far as the seller is concerned, there are some points that he must adhere to when he is selling anything to a private individual as opposed to a commercial organisation. Briefly the important ones are as follows.

- If he makes an untrue statement about the quality, performance or detail of the product during the treating (sale negotiation) and if the buyer relies on that statement which is later found to be false, the contract may be cancelled. However, if the buyer has the opportunity to check the truth of the seller's statement before the contract is concluded, by for example carrying out a pre-sale check, then he will find it difficult to cancel the contract.
- The goods sold must be of satisfactory quality.

'Satisfactory quality' means that the goods are:

- fit for the purpose for which goods of that sort are normally supplied, bought and used

- of a reasonable standard considering
  - ○ any description made of the goods
  - ○ the price charged for them (a buyer should not expect the same standard of quality from two items, one of which costs a lot more than the other)
  - ○ any other relevant factor.

A relevant factor could be that the buyer has relied upon the seller's skill, knowledge and judgement on the suitability of a particular product and has accordingly accepted a recommendation by him.

Note that the definition of 'satisfactory quality' is not the same as the definition of 'a defective or unsafe product' under the Consumer Protection Act 1987. The factors defining a product's safety under the 1987 Act are shown in Figure 14.1.

Breach of contract

If either party does not meet the contractual obligations, the contract is breached. So, for example, if the buyer's cheque bounces, quite apart from any question of fraud, the buyer would have breached the contract and the seller is entitled to compensation for the losses he has incurred.

The seller has strict liability to ensure that goods sold are of satisfactory quality. This means that the buyer does not have to prove that any statement made by the seller was meant to mislead or deceive the customer. It is only necessary to show that he must have known that the statement was untrue or he did not care whether it was true or untrue. In other words it is not necessary to prove dishonesty or negligence to gain a remedy.

If the buyer suffers any harm or loss, including the inability to use the bought goods for their stated purpose, because they are not of satisfactory quality, he is entitled to redress. At the least he has the right to reject the product and claim a refund plus damages to cover any additional expense or injury from the seller in consequence of the breach of contract.

Note that a credit note against future purchases is not a sufficient remedy, although the buyer may if he wishes accept a credit note as recompense. The seller cannot insist that it is the only recompense that the customer can have.

Once the buyer has accepted the goods the transaction is complete. If he has dealt with the goods as though they were his own by using them for a period of time without returning them, he cannot claim a refund. He might be able to claim damages if any additional expenditure or injury is suffered arising out of his reasonable usage of the goods.

Note that because something is the wrong size or the wrong colour it is not in consequence 'not of satisfactory quality' and the buyer has no right of redress. In practice many shops are prepared to exchange such goods, but it is done as a customer relations exercise as there is no legal compulsion on the shop to act this way.

Once a breach of contract has been proved, the seller of the goods has strict liability and cannot evade responsibility by blaming the manufacturer. Normally there is a contractual arrangement between the manufacturer and the seller concerning this area of liability.

Contract exemption clauses

A seller can not try to evade liability by using small print that pretends to exclude a buyer's rights. For instance it is unlawful to display a notice that says that refunds will not be given for unsatisfactory goods or by purportedly restricting the buyer's rights in any way.

Part VI
Deaths, Coroners and Mental Health Law

- Sudden deaths and the coroner
- Mental health law

Chapter 15
Sudden Deaths and the Coroner

Deaths in the home

Deaths that occur outside private homes will be dealt with by the emergency services or by hospital staff. If the death occurs at home a practice manager might become involved in dealing with and advising relatives of the deceased.

Several documents have to be completed following every death as shown in Figure 15.1.

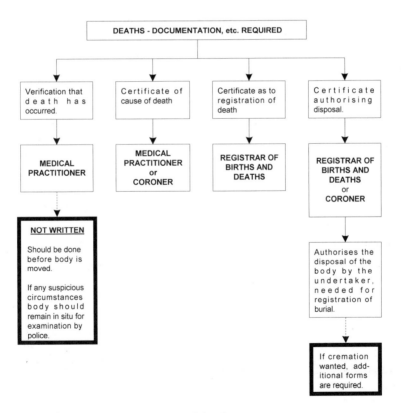

Figure 15.1   Documentation in respect of deaths

Verification of death

Only a medical practitioner can state that life is extinct, so the emergency services rely on doctors for their medical expertise. If verification is done casually or negligently the consequences may be serious for the following reasons.

- A body wrongly pronounced as dead may be taken to a mortuary and subsequent signs of life will cause professional difficulties for the doctor concerned. This has happened on occasions.
- Overlooking a suspicious sign may impede any subsequent investigation into the cause of the death.

Certificate of cause of death

This certificate is issued by a registered medical practitioner who has personally attended the deceased during his last illness. The certificate must:

- state to the best of the doctor's knowledge and belief the cause of the death
- give the date that he last saw the patient alive and this must be within the 14 days prior to the death
- be delivered forthwith to the registrar. It is usually given to the informant (the person giving notice of the death to the registrar) who delivers the certificate by hand but it might in some cases be sent by post.

There are special arrangements and forms for spontaneous abortion, stillbirth and neonatal death (death occurring within the 28 days from the birth).

These certificates and forms must be correctly and truthfully completed by the doctor as failure to do so can lead to prosecution under the terms of the Perjury Act 1911 as the following case shows:

> A GP falsely stated on a medical certificate that he had seen the deceased on the day of his death. He claimed that it was the custom in his practice for a partner to sign the certificate as long as another partner had seen the patient alive providing there were no suspicious circumstances. The Court of Appeal held that *total veracity in these matters is demanded in the interests of public administration and accordingly the doctor was guilty of perjury.*
>
> R *v.* Sood (1998)

Registration of death

Every death, and the cause of that death must be registered by the registrar of births and deaths for the sub-district in which the death occurred. Details are recorded in a register kept for that purpose and a copy of the entry can be provided on a special form usually referred to as the 'death certificate'.

Where a person dies in a house, the following persons are qualified to be informants regarding the death:

(1) any relative of the deceased person present at the death or in attendance during his last illness
(2) any other relative of the deceased residing or being in the sub-district where the death occurred

(3)   any person present at the death
(4)   the occupier of the house if he knew of the happening of the death
(5)   any inmate of the house who knew of the happening of the death
(6)   the person causing the disposal of the body (e.g. the undertaker).

It is the legal duty of:

(a)   the nearest relative, or of any other relative (as (1) or (2) above), or
(b)   if there is no such relative, then one of the persons mentioned at (3), (4), (5) or (6)

to give to the registrar within five days of the death the information necessary to register the death, and sign the register accordingly. After registration of the death the registrar will give the informant a certificate of registration of the death. However, the registrar can refuse to register the death and refer the matter to the coroner.

The death will be reported to the coroner by the registrar in any of the cases illustrated in Figure 15.2.

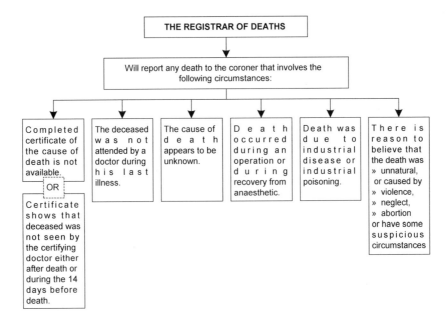

Figure 15.2   Registrar's reports to the coroner

The registration procedure described above is not necessary if the coroner decides to hold an inquest into the cause of death.

Certificate authorising disposal

This certificate is for the person in charge of the burial ground. A register of burials must be maintained and the details of this certificate are entered therein.

The certificate may be issued by the registrar in normal cases, and in other cases by the coroner.

Cremation

Cremation is tightly controlled by law and either two doctors or the coroner must authorise the procedure. If a doctor has any doubts about the cause of death of any patient then he should discuss the facts of the case with either the medical referee at the crematorium or the coroner before signing any of the approval forms. The rules for the approval of a cremation are illustrated in Figure 15.3.

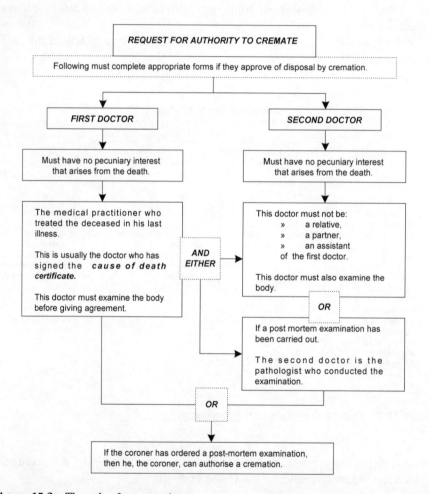

Figure 15.3   The rules for cremation

The procedure that must be implemented when someone dies at home is not simple but can be seen by following the details illustrated in Figure 15.4.

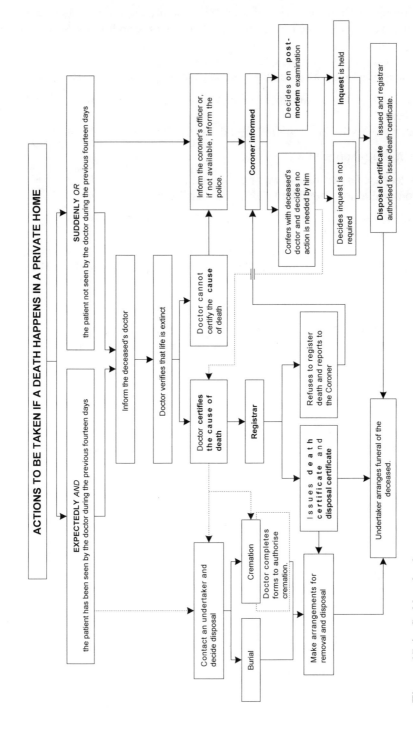

Figure 15.4 Sudden deaths

Coroners

Coroners act in England and Wales and are locally appointed. They must be either a barrister or solicitor of at least five years standing or have certain medical qualifications. (In Scotland, the Procurator Fiscal serves an equivalent function.) Their main duties are to look into abnormal deaths and in this context the coroner must enquire into and hold an inquest when necessary in cases of:

- all sudden, violent or unnatural deaths, or where there is suspicion that this is the case
- deaths where the law requires an inquest to be held

A sudden death happens when

- the deceased's last illness was not treated by a doctor, and/or
- a doctor did not attend him during the last 14 days of his life.

An unnatural death is a death contrary to the course of nature. In either case there is some uncertainty as to the true cause of death.

When he considers it to be necessary the coroner will order a post-mortem examination to help him in determining whether or not an inquest should be held.

Reporting deaths to coroners by doctors

There is no legal duty on a doctor to report any death to the coroner but they are advised to inform him when they attend any deaths in the following circumstances:

- sudden or unexpected deaths where the doctor cannot certify the real as opposed to the terminal cause of death, *or* where the doctor has not attended in the last illness or within the 14 days prior to death.
- abortions, other than natural
- accidents and injuries of any date if in any way contributing to the cause of death
- alcoholism, chronic or acute
- anaesthetics and operations – deaths while under the influence of anaesthetics and deaths following operation for injury or where the operation, however necessarily or skilfully performed, may have precipitated or expedited death
- crime or suspected crime
- drugs – therapeutic mishaps, abuse or addiction
- ill-treatment – starvation or neglect
- industrial diseases arising out of the deceased's employment, e.g. all diseases and poisons covered by the Reporting of Injuries, Diseases and Dangerous Occurrences Regulations 1995 (RIDDOR)
- infant deaths – if in any way obscure
- pensioners receiving disability pensions, where death might be connected with the pensionable disability
- persons in legal custody in a prison, detention centre or police cells
- poisoning from any cause – occupational, therapeutic, accidental, suicidal, homicidal or food poisoning

- septicaemias – if originating from any injury
- stillbirths – where there may be any possibility of the child having been born alive, or where there is suspicion.

Coroner's officer

In most cities and big towns a full-time coroner's officer is appointed. The responsibility for appointing this officer lies with the local authority for the area. In the past, a police officer has fulfilled the role but civilians are increasingly being appointed to the post. In rural areas the duties of the coroner's officer are often undertaken by the police officer attending the relevant incident.

The duties of this officer consist of:

- making the initial report of the death to the coroner
- carrying out enquiries and interviewing people as the coroner directs
- acting as a link between all interested parties and the coroner
- making arrangements for the inquest, e.g. ensuring the attendance of parties, witnesses, jury, etc.
- supervising the inquest proceedings and reporting its result as directed by the coroner.

Irrespective of where death occurs an inquest can only be conducted by the coroner in whose district the body lies. For this reason a body must not be removed from the district of one coroner to that of another except with the prior consent of both.

In cases where there is no body (destroyed or not recoverable) the Home Secretary can direct a particular coroner to hold an inquest.

Post-mortem examinations ordered by a coroner

The following are the general rules covering these examinations.

- The examination must be carried out as soon as reasonably practicable.
- The examination should be carried out by a suitably qualified pathologist. In the case of suspected homicide the pathologist must be approved by the Home Office.
- Interested parties must be informed of the time and place of the examination so that they can attend in person or be represented. 'Interested parties' are defined below under Inquests.
- The pathologist must preserve any body materials that bear upon the cause of death for forensic examination. The materials will be preserved for as long as the coroner directs.
- The pathologist's findings consequent upon a post-mortem examination should be reported only to the coroner. Some coroners authorise a wider distribution of the post-mortem reports, for example they may be given to the deceased's GP.

The arrangements for these matters will be undertaken by the coroner's officer.

Exhumations

The coroner has power to order disinterment if he thinks it is necessary to do so but this authority is only rarely used in cases of emergency. The normal way in which disinterment is authorised is by obtaining an order from either the Home Secretary or from a judge of the High Court.

Inquests

A coroner's inquest is a court of law but its procedures are different to all other legal proceedings in this country. It is said to be an 'inquisitorial' hearing which means that the coroner is not merely an impartial judge, but also has the power to question parties to the proceedings.

The purpose of the coroner's inquest is to:

- identify the name and abode of the deceased, and
- ascertain the causes of and the surrounding circumstances of the death.

Anyone who has a 'proper interest' can attend an inquest and he, or a lawyer representing his interests, can ask questions. The questions must be relevant and the coroner will decide whether particular questions are relevant or not.

Properly interested persons

Persons entitled to attend or be represented at an inquest are:

- a parent, spouse, child or anyone acting on behalf of the deceased
- anyone whose actions the coroner believes might be concerned with the death, accidentally or otherwise such as representatives of past employers in RIDDOR cases
- beneficiaries or underwriters of life insurance policies
- a lawyer representing the chief officer of police, but a police officer will have attended the post-mortem in cases where crime is suspected
- representatives of any government departments concerned in the circumstances of the death
- anyone who the coroner decides has a proper interest in the proceedings, such as hospital staff or doctors who attended the deceased.

Procedural points

During the hearing, lawyers representing parties to the inquest are allowed to ask questions that the coroner accepts as being relevant to the inquiry. However, they are not permitted to make speeches to the court.

Some rules of court procedure and evidence are not applicable at an inquest, for instance the coroner can accept hearsay evidence, which is not always allowable in other courts. See comments on hearsay evidence on page 133.

The coroner must always view the body before holding the inquest. If for any reason he does not do so the verdict of the inquest is quashed and a new inquest must be held. If the coroner sits with a jury, the jurors do not have to view the body unless they wish to do so or if the coroner directs that they should see it.

A coroner must hold an inquest in all the following circumstances:

● all violent or unnatural deaths
● all sudden deaths where the cause of death is unknown
● all deaths of persons who are held in prison or police custody, and
● when an inquest is required by law such as suicides, drug overdoses, etc.

The coroner has discretion to hold an inquest in the case of any death in which there is reasonable suspicion that death was unnatural.

In inquests involving the following, the coroner must sit with a jury, but in all other cases it is a matter for his discretion whether he calls a jury:

● cases involving murder, manslaughter or infanticide
● deaths arising out of use of a motor vehicle on a public road
● when the death is one reportable under RIDDOR
● when the death occurs in circumstances raising issues of public safety, e.g. food poisoning, deaths under anaesthetics, etc.
● deaths of persons held in custody, or
● other deaths requiring an inquest by law.

Inquest verdicts

At the conclusion of the inquest, the findings or verdict will be reached. This consists of the following information:

● the deceased's name
● the injury or illness causing the death
● the time place and circumstances in which the injury was sustained
● the conclusion as to the cause of the death.

There is no legally specified form for the conclusion as to the cause of death, but the Coroners' Rules 1984 lists 12 suggestions that coroners might use, as follows.

● *Natural causes:* sometimes this verdict has the phrase 'lack of care' appended to it and this has caused concern to the medical profession. It has been recommended that a more appropriate addition would be 'to which neglect contributed' in cases where neglect to provide medical attention did not make the medical condition worse but meant that there was no opportunity to cure it.
● *Industrial disease:* this will apply to any RIDDOR reportable diseases, but can also apply to other cases outside the regulations.
● *Want of attention at birth:* this does not apply to cases of negligence or intention to cause harm.
● *Stillbirth:* cases where a child is born dead and never had independent life outside the mother.
● *Attempted or self-induced abortion*
● *Dependence on drugs or non-dependent abuse of drugs:* this verdict relates to either the death of a drug addict from the poisoning effect or excessive dosage of a particular drug.
● *Accident:* an accident is something over which there was no human control.

- *Misadventure:* means that there was a deliberate but lawful act that unintentionally caused the death. The person causing the death is not criminally liable, but subsequently there could be civil liability in some cases.
- *Lawful killing:* means that the death was caused without criminal responsibility in such circumstances as self defence or perhaps caused during the lawful arrest of an armed man.
- *Unlawful killing:* covers all forms of homicide such as murder, manslaughter or infanticide committed by a criminally responsible person. Such verdicts lead to further action by other agencies and courts unless they are made after a named offender has been tried and found guilty in a criminal court.
- *Suicide:* means that the deceased took his own life. In the past suicide was a criminal offence that led to burial in unconsecrated ground and the forfeiture of the suicide's estate to the Crown. Nowadays the greatest legal significance will be concerned with the payment of death benefits from an insurance policy as the policy might be repudiated in cases of death by suicide.
- *Open verdict:* means that there is insufficient evidence available to come to any conclusion regarding the cause of the death.

If the coroner believes that action should be taken to prevent a recurrence of similar incidents he can say at the time of giving his verdict that he proposes to bring the matter to the attention of an appropriate authority.

No verdict can be handed down that appears to determine any person's responsibility at either criminal or civil law for the death. That matter must be determined by other appropriate courts.

There are special rules to be followed when a person has been charged with an offence relating to the death before the inquest is held by the coroner. In most of these cases the inquest will be opened and after evidence of identification it will be adjourned until the criminal proceedings have been completed.

Offences

It is an offence to fail to answer a summons to an inquest or to refuse to answer questions put by the coroner at an inquest.

It is an offence for a medical practitioner to fail to obey a summons from a coroner to attend an inquest.

Chapter 16
Mental Health Law

Terms used in mental health law

The major legislation in this area is the Mental Health Act 1983. The Act deals with admission to mental hospitals, the rights of patients admitted and matters concerned with the control of their property.

There are a number of definitions in the Act the following being the most important from a practice manager's viewpoint:

Mental disorder

Any illness, arrested or incomplete development of mind, psychopathic disorder and any other disorder or disability of mind.

Severe mental impairment

A state of arrested or incomplete development of mind that includes severe impairment of intelligence and social functioning and is associated with abnormally aggressive or seriously irresponsible conduct on the part of the person concerned.

Mental impairment

A state of arrested or incomplete development of mind (not amounting to severe mental impairment) which includes significant impairment of intelligence and social functioning and is associated with abnormally aggressive or seriously irresponsible conduct by the person concerned.

Psychopathic disorder

A persistent disorder or disability of mind (whether or not including significant impairment of intelligence) which results in abnormally aggressive or seriously irresponsible conduct by the person concerned.

Persons not covered by the Act

A person shall not be dealt with under this Act as suffering a mental disorder only for the reason of:

- promiscuity or other immoral conduct
- sexual deviancy
- dependence on alcohol or drugs.

Place of safety

This means any of the following:

- residential accommodation provided by a local authority
- a hospital
- a police station
- a mental nursing home
- a residential home for mentally disordered persons
- any other suitable place the occupier of which is willing to receive the patient temporarily.

A psychopathic disorder as defined above is deemed to be a condition that cannot be cured, although the behaviour resulting from the disorder can often be controlled by treatment. This aspect of the 1983 Act was examined in the following decision.

> To deprive citizens of their freedom when they had committed no crime was a drastic step, and the detention of psychopaths was lawful only where they were treatable. *An untreatable psychopath, however dangerous, could not be detained under the terms of the Mental Health Act 1983.*

> R *v.* Cannons Park Mental Health Tribunal, *ex parte* A. (1993)

See also the case of *Johnson* v. *United Kingdom* (1997), page 247.

The potentially serious implications of the above decision were shown in a later case.

> A man had seriously harassed a woman over a protracted time and in consequence she suffered from depression. At a second trial the man admitted the offence and acknowledged that he had 39 previous convictions that included offences of violence, rape and indecent assault. He was remanded in custody for psychiatric reports. Subsequently the court was told that although he had engaged in incidents of deviant and anti-social behaviour he was not mentally ill.
>
> The offender was sentenced to 3 years and 10 months' imprisonment but because of the time that he had already spent in custody he was released forthwith. The judge, who described him as an 'ongoing risk to the public', said *'It is now clear to me that the limitations and constraints of the Mental Health Act are regrettably such that I cannot make an order for your treatment'.*

> R *v.* Morris (1998)

Following the above case and other examples of anti-social behaviour of people suffering from psychopathic disorders, a joint Department of Health and Home Office discussion paper titled *Managing Dangerous People with Severe Personality Disorder: Proposals for Policy Development* was published in July 1999. It is reasonable to anticipate that new legislation will soon be introduced to constrain such people.

The Mental Health Act cannot be used by doctors as a means of coercing an adult of sound mind to receive medical treatment against his will as the following case demonstrated.

> A pregnant woman refused treatment and her decision would have resulted in the death of herself and her unborn child so she was detained under the Act and a caesarean section was performed. During the period of detention no specific treatment for any mental illness was prescribed.
>
> Subsequently the Court of Appeal held that the Mental Health Act should not be deployed to detain an individual merely because her thinking process was unusual even apparently bizarre, irrational and contrary to the views of the overwhelming majority of the community at large. *A person detained under the 1983 Act for mental disorder could not be forced into medical procedures unconnected with her mental condition unless her capacity to consent to such treatment was diminished.* Accordingly, the actions of the doctors in this case were unlawful.
>
> St. George's Healthcare NHS Trust *v.* S (1998)

The 1983 Act provides a national legal framework to regulate the ways of dealing with mentally disordered persons. Its provisions are locally implemented so although principles are the same everywhere there are variations in procedures from one locality to another. Note that the Act and local procedures specify such things as:

- forms to be completed by doctors when making recommendations
- the maximum interval that may elapse between a doctor examining a patient and making a recommendation, and the reception of that patient in hospital
- how soon after arrival at hospital a patient must be seen, etc.

Access to hospital or other location

The Act provides several different modes of access. The guiding principle is that the action must always be taken for the benefit of the patient or for the protection of other people.

Figure 16.1 gives a summary of the legal authorities contained in the Act: each of the sections is subsequently examined separately.

Informal or voluntary admission

This is the case when a patient seeks admission to a hospital without the compulsion of a legal order. Figure 16.2 shows the details of voluntary admission.

The power of the Mental Health Act is extended by the common law in some circumstances as shown in this case:

> A long-term patient had gone to live with carers but became particularly agitated following an accident at a day centre. The carers could not be contacted so the patient was taken into hospital where the doctor decided in-patient treatment was needed to stabilise the patient's condition. Had the patient resisted he would have been compulsorily detained but he was compliant. Subsequently it was claimed that the hospital was guilty of unlawful imprisonment.
>
> The House of Lords stated that a *mentally disordered person lacking any capacity to consent could be admitted to hospital under section 131 of the Act. Under the common*

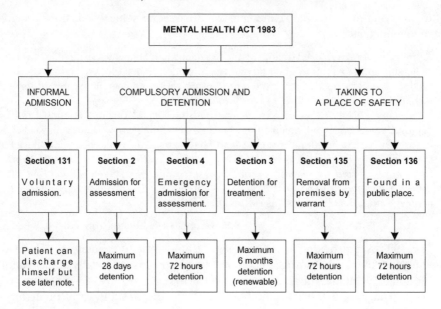

Figure 16.1 Mental Health Act 1983

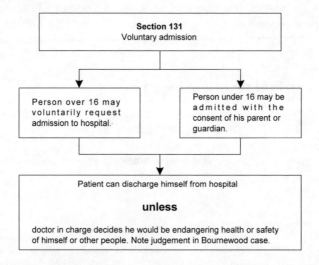

Figure 16.2 Voluntary admission

law doctrine of 'necessity' the actions of the medical staff, which in other circumstances would have been unlawful, were justified.

R *v.* Bournewood Community and Mental Health NHS Trust, *ex parte* L (1998)

This judgment implies that patients suffering from such conditions as Alzheimer's disease and severe learning difficulties who lack the ability to consent to or refuse treatment and who have been informally admitted could be detained for treatment when it is a necessity.

In 1993 the hospital and community care component of the National Health Service and Community Care Act 1990 was extended to include all community and outpatient mental health services together with mental health counselling. Community psychiatric nurses have been employed to rehabilitate and care for the mentally infirm in a community setting. From this it follows that whilst a patient can request admission into hospital under section 131, unless the condition is serious he is likely to be treated within the community.

Compulsory admission and treatment

In cases of people who are suffering mental illness and either their own health and safety or that of others is endangered, then they may be detained for assessment and/or treatment. Section 2 of the Mental Health Act deals with admitting people to hospital for assessment of their mental condition; the criteria are shown in Figure 16.3.

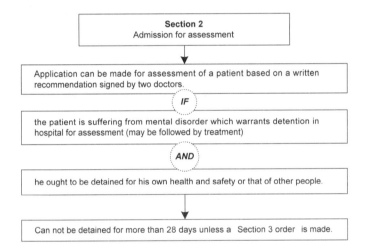

Figure 16.3   Assessment admission

Sometimes the need for admission is an emergency and assessment is needed as a matter of urgency, in such cases the power of section 4 would be used. The main points of this section are shown in Figure 16.4.

In cases of severe mental illness if the patient refuses to stay in hospital for treatment, the powers of section 3 may have to be used which is illustrated in Figure 16.5.

It will be noted that the section refers to 'psychopathic disorder' but the treatment envisaged must be likely to help the condition. The section must be read in conjunction with the judgments in the cases *R* v. *Cannons Park Mental Health Tribunal, ex parte A.* (1993) on page 240, and *Johnson* v. *United Kingdom* (1997) on page 247.

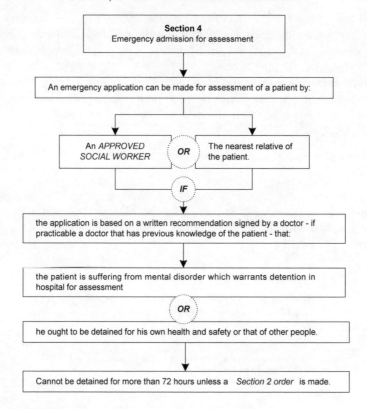

Figure 16.4   Emergency admission

Place of safety powers

If a patient is being illtreated in some way or if he has escaped from a mental hospital (including failure to return after leave of absence) then a magistrate can issue a warrant to the police for his detention and removal to a place of safety.

If a patient is absent from hospital for 28 days or more a warrant under section 135 becomes invalid. The patient can only be detained under the terms of section 2, 3 or 4 of the Mental Health Act.

Figure 16.6 shows the main points of section 135.

Police powers under the Mental Health Act

If, in a public place, the police find a person who they reasonably suspect to be mentally ill, they are empowered to detain him and take him to a place of safety.

If this person has committed a criminal offence all factors relating to the offence and the offender are considered and a decision will be made whether the patient should be prosecuted or handed over to the appropriate mental health authority.

Figure 16.7 shows the extent of these powers.

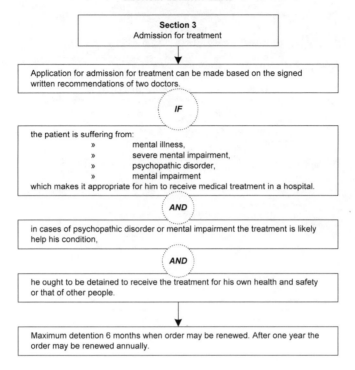

Figure 16.5 Admission for treatment

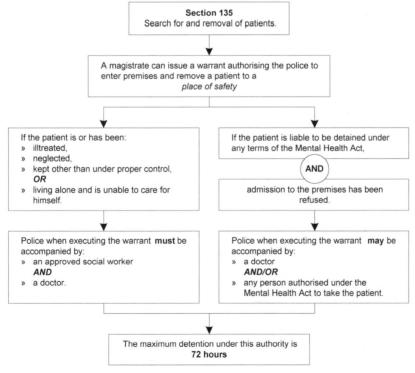

Figure 16.6 Search and removal of patients

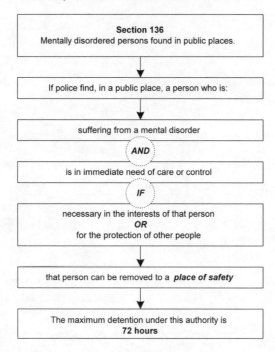

Figure 16.7   Police powers

The Mental Health Act – other matters

Besides the legal controls concerning the admission to hospital, etc. of mentally disordered persons the Act also covers the following matters concerning these patients:

- the treatment of, manner of dealing with and the discharging of patients from hospital
- patients who are absent from hospital without leave
- patients who have committed or are involved in criminal offences
- guardianship and the management of property and affairs of patients
- Mental Health Review Tribunals
- the functions of local authorities in respect of the Act.

The Human Rights Act 1998

The European Convention for the Protection of Human Rights states that:

'Everyone has the right to liberty and security of person, and can only be deprived of liberty in certain cases. One of the cases of lawful deprivation of liberty is the detention of persons of unsound mind.'

The Human Rights Act 1998 has been enacted by Parliament and it is expected to come into full operation in all courts in the United Kingdom in late 2000. All courts will be required to make judgments that conform to the Human Rights Convention.

To use the Mental Health Act 1983 as an excuse to evade the conditions of the Human Rights Convention will not be tolerated by the courts. The following case that eventually reached the European Court of Human Rights illustrates this point:

> Johnson was convicted of punching a woman in the street and was sentenced to imprisonment. He had previous convictions for unprovoked assaults. In prison he was assessed as suffering from schizophrenia superimposed on a psychopathic personality. After five years (the duration of the prison sentence), the Mental Health Tribunal considered his case. He was said to be free of any symptoms of mental illness, but needed a period of rehabilitation in a suitable hostel. Johnson was not released because suitable accommodation could not be found although genuine efforts were made to place him.
>
> The Court of Human Rights held that *after it was decided that Johnson was free of any symptoms of mental illness the failure of the authorities to release him constituted a breach of the Convention in that he was unlawfully detained.* Johnson was awarded £35,000 in damages against the United Kingdom government.
>
> Johnson *v.* United Kingdom (1997)

This different approach will ensure that doctors will not be able to use the Mental Health Act as a justification for forcing beneficial treatment on to an unwilling patient who is of sound mind.

Appendix A
Legal Authorities

This handbook contains legal information taken from many Acts of Parliament, Regulations, and the reports of cases heard in courts and tribunals. These sources are listed for the information of any reader who wishes to research particular topics in greater depth which may be done by consulting appropriate legal textbooks covering the particular area of interest.

Statutes, Regulations, etc.

Following is a list of the most important Acts of Parliament, etc. consulted during the preparation of the handbook. It is not a formal table of statutes as found in a legal textbook as it merely shows the range of authorities that are covered herein.

Regulations, Orders and Rules are shown under their 'parent' Acts but it should be noted that there are many more of them than are listed here. Where an Act or Regulation is shown with the phrase 'as amended' it means that later legislation has altered or extended the original, but these amending enactments are not listed in the interests of brevity.

The chapter(s) that have used information drawn from a particular enactment is/are shown in the right hand column.

Case Decisions

As with the list of statutes, this is not the same as a table of cases to be found in a legal textbook. Many of the examples quoted have been taken from ordinary newspaper or other reports, and in consequence they must not be treated as formal law reports. Additionally, some reports relate to cases from lower courts or tribunals. They cannot likewise be regarded as being legally significant as other courts in differing circumstances could make other decisions.

The purpose of the citations is to show the reader how the law has been construed on a day to day basis and they should be taken as indicators and not as authoritative statements of the law. Appropriate cases have their formal legal references given.

Allders International Ltd. *v.* Parkins [1981] IRLR 68

Balgobin *v.* Tower Hamlets London Borough Council [1987] IRLR 401
Bartholomew *v.* London Borough of Hackney [1999] IRLR 246
Bliss *v.* SE Thames Regional Health Authority [1987] ICR 700, CA
Bracebridge Engineering Ltd. *v.* Darby [1990] IRLR 3
Brenton *v.* Mid-Glamorgan County Council (1996) *The Times* and *Daily Mail* 25/5/1996
Brown *v.* Rentokil Ltd. (1998) Case C-394/96 *The Times*, Law Report 2/7/1998
Burrett *v.* West Birmingham Health Authority [1994] IRLR 7
Burton and Another *v.* De Vere Hotels (1996) *The Times*, Law Report 3/10/1996
Bux *v.* Slough Metals [1974] 1 All ER 262

Carlson *v.* Post Office [1981] IRLR 158
Carmichael and Another *v.* National Power PLC (1999) *The Times*, Law Report 23/11/1999
Castledine *v.* Rothwell Engineering Ltd [1973] IRLR 99
Clark *v.* Commissioner of the Police for the Metropolis (1999) *The Times* and *Daily Mail* 17/9/1999
Clark *v.* Novacold Ltd. (1998) *The Times*, Law Report 11/6/1998
Coote *v.* Granada Hospitality Ltd. (2000) *The Times* and *Daily Mail* 28/1/2000
Crees *v.* Royal London Mutual Insurance Society Ltd. (1998) *The Times*, Law Report 5/3/1998
Cresswell *v.* Board of Inland Revenue [1984] ICR 508
Crummey *v.* Hughes (1993) *Daily Telegraph* 2/12/1993 and 27/12/1993; *GP News* 11/2/1994

Dekker *v.* VJV Centrum [1991] IRLR 27
Denco Ltd *v.* Joinson [1992] 1 All ER 463
Dietman *v.* Brent London Borough Council [1988] IRLR 299, CA
Diocese of Hallam Trustees *v.* Connaughton, EAT (1996)
Donoghue *v.* Stevenson [1932] AC 562 (HL)
Dryden *v.* Greater Glasgow Health Board [1992] IRLR 469 EAT

East Lindsay District Council *v.* Daubney [1977] ICR 566
Easter *v.* Hain (1998) *The Times* and *Daily Mail* 5/9/1998

Eggleton *v.* Asda Ltd. (1995) *The Times* and *Daily Mail* 20/4/1995
Egg Stores (Stamford Hill) Ltd *v.* Leibovici [1976] IRLR 376
Ely *v.* YKK Fasteners Ltd [1994] ICR 164

F.W. Farnsworth Ltd. *v.* McCoid (1999) *The Times*, Law Report 31/3/1999
Franxhi *v.* Focus Management Consultants (1999) *The Times* and *Daily Mail* 16/6/1999

Gaskin *v.* United Kingdom [1990] 12 EHRR 36
Gilbert *v.* Midland Bank Ltd. (1998) *The Times* and *Daily Mail* 2/9/1998
Glasgow Corporation *v.* Taylor [1922] 1 AC 44
Greaves *v.* Kwik Save Stores Ltd. (1998) *The Times*, Law Report 5/3/1998

Halfpenny *v.* IGE Medical Systems Ltd. (1999) *The Times*, Law Report 4/1/1999
Halstead *v.* Marshall of Wisbech Ltd. (1989) EAT 5/10/1998 cited in *Waud's Employment Law* (1998)
Hammond *v.* West Lancashire Health Authority (1998) *The Times*, Law Report 5/3/1998
Handels-og KFD *v.* Dansk Arbeijdsgiverforening [1992] ICR 332, ECJ
Hare *v.* Murphy Bros [1974] ICR 603
Harling *v.* CL Plastics (2000) *The Times* 26/2/2000
Holland *v.* Glendale Industries Ltd. (1998) *The Times*, Law Report 28/5/1998
Holmes *v.* Ashford [1950] 2 All ER 76
HSE *v.* Forbo Kingfisher (1993) *Independent* and *Daily Mail* 25/3/1993
HSE *v.* Norfolk and Norwich Health Care Trust (1998) HSE Press Release E280:98 of 17/12/1998
HSE *v.* Spindle Select Ltd. (1996) *The Times*, Law Report 9/12/1996
HSE *v.* Swindon and Marlborough NHS Trust (1997) *The Times* 4 and 21/8/1997
Hudson *v.* Ridge Manufacturing Co Ltd. [1957] 2 QB 348

Isle of Wight Tourist Board *v.* Coombes [1976] IRLR 413

Johnson Matthey Metals *v.* Harding [1978] IRLR 248
Johnson *v.* Nottinghamshire Combined Police Authority [1974] ICR 170
Johnson *v.* United Kingdom (1997) ECHR Case No. 119/1996/738/937
Jolley *v.* Sutton LBC (2000) *The Times*, Law Report 24/5/2000
Jones *v.* Smith (1995) *Mail on Sunday* 8/10/1995
Jones *v.* Tower Boot Co. Ltd. (1996) *The Times*, Law Report 16/12/1996
Joyce *v.* Morrissey and Others (1998) *The Times*, Law Report 16/11/1998

Kameswara Rao *v.* Wyles [1949] 2 All ER 685
Kaye *v.* Caldwell (1999) *Independent* 29/5/1999
Kenny *v.* Hampshire Constabulary (1998) *The Times*, Law Report 22/10/1998
Khanun *v.* Mid-Glamorgan Health Authority [1979] ICR 40
King *v.* The Hundred of Hoo Nursery (1998) *The Times*, Law Report 10/6/1998

Leverton *v.* Clwyd County Council [1989] ICR 33, HL
London Borough of Lambeth *v.* Commission for Racial Equality [1990] IRLR 231
London Underground Ltd. *v.* Edwards (1998) *The Times*, Law Report 1/6/1998
Lynch *v.* Martin (1993) *GP News* 9/11/1993 and *Pulse* 29/1/1994

Macarthys Ltd *v.* Smith [1980] ICR 672
Mennell *v.* Newell and Wright (Transport Contractors) Ltd. (1996) *The Times*, Law Report 2/5/1996
Morse *v.* Wiltshire County Council (1998) *The Times*, Law Report 11/5/1998

Notcutt *v.* Universal Equipment Co. (London) Ltd. [1986] ICR 414, CA

O'Brien *v.* Prudential Assurance Co.[1979] IRLR 140

O'Neil *v.* Symm and Co. Ltd. (1998) *The Times*, Law Report 12/3/1998
Orphanos *v.* Queen Mary College [1985] 2 All ER 233

Pape *v.* Cumbria County Council [1992] 3 All ER 211
Pharmaceutical Society of Great Britain *v.* Storkwain [1986] 1 WLR 903
Pickstone and Others *v.* Freeman PLC [1988] 3 WLR 265
Polkey *v.* A.E. Dayton Services Ltd. [1988] ICR 142
Popat *v.* Shonchhatra (1997) *The Times*, Law Report 4/7/1997

R *v.* Bournewood Community and Mental Health NHS Trust, *ex parte* L (1998) *The Times*, Law Report 30/6/1998
R *v.* Bow Street Stipendiary Magistrate, *ex parte* Government of the USA (1999) *The Times*, Law Report 7/9/1999
R *v.* Cambridge District Health Authority, *ex parte* B (1995) *The Times*, Law Report 15/3/1995
R *v.* Cannons Park Mental Health Tribunal, *ex parte* A. (1993) *Independent*, Law Report 1/9/1993
R *v.* Chief Constable of Thames Valley Police, *ex parte* Cotton [1990] IRLR 344
R. v. Department of Health, *ex parte* Source Informatics Ltd. (2000) *The Times*, Law Report 18/1/2000
R *v.* FHSA, *ex parte* Eimfield Drugs Ltd (1998) *The Times*, Law Report 16/9/1998
R *v.* Morris (1998) *The Times* 22/8/1998
R *v.* Nimmo (1998) *The Times* 30/6/1998
R *v.* North Derbyshire Health Authority, *ex parte* Fisher (1997) *The Times*, Law Report 2/9/1997
R *v.* Salford Area Health Authority, *ex parte* Janaway (1988) *The Times*, Law Report 2/12/1988
R *v.* Secretary of State for Health, *ex parte* Pfizer Ltd. (1999) *The Times*, Law Report 17/6/1999
R *v.* Sood (1998) *The Times*, Law Report 24/3/1998
R *v.* Taylor-Lloyd and Khattab (2000) *The Times* and *Guardian* 2/3/2000
Rainey *v.* Greater Glasgow Health Board [1987] IRLR 26
Re Shannon (1997) *The Times* 22 & 24/4/1997 and *Daily Mail* 22 & 24/4/1997
Rees *v.* Apollo Watch Repairs PLC (1996) *The Times*, Law Report 26/2/1996
Ridout *v.* TC Group [1998] IRLR 628
Rowley *v.* Walkers Nonsuch Ltd. [1997] Unreported, quoted by Barrow and Duddington, *Briefcase in Employment Law*
Roy *v.* Kensington, Chelsea & Westminster FPC [1992] IRLR 233, HL

Smedleys *v.* Breed [1974] AC 839
Smith *v.* Gardner Merchant Ltd. (1998) *The Times*, Law Report 23/7/1998
Snowball *v.* Gardner Merchant Ltd. [1987] IRLR 397
Spencer *v.* Paragon Wallpapers Ltd [1976] IRLR 373
St John of God (Care Services) Ltd *v.* Brooks [1992] IRLR 346
St. George's Healthcare NHS Trust *v.* S (1998) *The Times*, Law Report 8/5/1998
Strathclyde Regional Council *v.* Porcelli [1986] IRLR 134
Sutton & Gates (Luton) Ltd *v.* Boxall [1979] IRLR 486

Tarling *v.* Wisdom Toothbrushes (1997) Industrial tribunal, unreported
Tomlinson *v.* Folding Caravan Centre (1998), *The Times* and *Daily Mail* 5/9/1998
Toon *v.* Jersey European Airlines (1999) *The Times* 15/5/1999 and *Daily Mail* 10/6/1999
Tottenham Green Under Fives Centre *v.* Marshall [1989] IRLR 147
Treganowan *v.* Robert Knee & Co. Ltd [1975] IRLR 113

Unnamed applicant *v.* City of London Polytechnic (1996) *Daily Mail* 9/2/1996

W *v.* Edgell and Others (1989) *Independent,* Law Report 10/11/1989; [1989] 1 All ER 835, CA

Walker *v.* Northumberland County Council [1995] IRLR 35

Webb *v.* EMO Air Cargo (UK) Ltd. (No.2) (1995) *The Times,* Law Report 20/10/1995

Western Provident *v.* Norwich Union [1997] NLJ 1277

White *v.* Minnis and Another (1999) *The Times,* Law Report 18/1/1999

White *v.* White (1998) *The Times,* Law Report 13/7/1998

Williams *v.* Watsons Luxury Coaches Ltd. [1990] IRLR 164

Wood *v.* Thimmegowda (1996) *Daily Mail* 13/3/1996

Unknown title, environment law case described in *Practice Manager,* October 1997, page 14.

Unknown title, gross misconduct 1 quoted by BMA lecturer.

Unknown title, gross misconduct 2 quoted by BMA lecturer.

Unknown title, gross misconduct 3 quoted by BMA lecturer.

Appendix B
Getting Further Information on Legal Matters

There are a number of locations that provide information on health matters that have a legal connotation. In some cases the information is free, in others the materials have to be paid for. Website addresses are given, and for many queries they may provide a suitable starting point. Telephone numbers and postal addresses are also provided in some cases but it should be noted that these are often only applicable for ordering publications and no other purpose.

Sources of Information

Advisory, Conciliation and Arbitration Service (ACAS)

Publishes booklets on matters concerned with employment law and relationships in the workplace. Some are free and can be downloaded, other more comprehensive publications are priced. Details of all publications and how to order them are on the website.

Website: www.acas.org.uk/
Telephone: 01455 852225
Address: ACAS Reader Ltd.
           P.O.Box 16
           Earl Shilton
           Leicester, LE4 822

Association of Medical Secretaries, Practice Managers, Administrators and Receptionists

This site provides information of particular interest to members of AMSPAR. Details of AMSPAR courses held throughout the UK are given.

Website: www.amspar.co.uk/
Telephone: 020 7387 6005
Address: Tavistock House North
           Tavistock Square,
           London, WC1H 9LN

British Medical Association

Most of this site is restricted by password to BMA members but the site does contain some documents of interest on topics such as confidentiality that can be downloaded by non-members. Documents may be ordered by non-BMA members but they must be paid for.

Website: web.bma.org.uk/public/pubother.nsf/webdocsvw
Telephone: 020 7703 6380
Address: BMA House
           Tavistock Square
           London, WC1H 9JP

Commission for Racial Equality

Information is available on race relations law and other matters concerned with race relations. Some publications can be downloaded from the website, others are priced and must be ordered.

Website: www.cre.gov.uk/
Telephone: 020 7828 7022
Address: Elliot House
              10–12 Allington Street
              London, SW1E 5EH

Data Protection Commissioner

The website provides information and guidance on the implementation of the Data Protection Act 1998. Additionally both free and priced publications are available.

Website: www.open.gov.uk/dpr/dprhome.htm
Telephone: 01625 545745
Address: Wycliffe House
              Water Lane
              Wilmslow
              Cheshire, SK0 5AF

Department for Education and Employment

There is some information on the website but of most value are the free publications supplied from the offices of the Employment Service. These publications cover nearly all aspects of employment legislation and practice managers are strongly recommended to acquire the booklets that are relevant to their own circumstances. The publication of these booklets is now undertaken by the DTI.

Website: www.dfee.gov.uk/

Consult telephone directory for telephone number and address of local offices of the Employment Service.

Department of Health

This is a comprehensive site designed for the use of health professionals. It contains a mass of information including press releases, list of publications and much other health-related material. It also carries DoH circulars that can be downloaded. Additionally the site provides links to other health-related sites.

Website: www.doh.gov.uk/
Fax: 01623 724524
Address: Department of Health
              P.O. Box 777
              London, SE1 6XH

Department of Trade and Industry

The DTI is an enormous department with responsibility for an immense range matters. The DTI home page is at www.dti.gov.uk/ and on this page is a dropdown menu that gives access to the many different departments. Of most interest to practice managers are the following sites.

DTI employment relations
This site contains information on all aspects of employment relations regulations and has many documents that can be downloaded. Of considerable help at this website is a list of

telephone numbers to get help on specific matters such as maternity leave, the Working Time Regulations and so on. The site is worth visiting merely to see what is on offer so that in time of need you know where to go to for some information.

Website: www.dti.gov.uk/er/index.htm

DTI consumer protection regulations

Although of less interest to the practice manager than the previous site, all of the regulations concerning consumer protection will be found here, together with telephone numbers for further assistance.

Website: www.dti.gov.uk/cacp/ca/regs.htm

Disability Rights Commission

Most of the information on this site is designed to help disabled people. There is information about the Disability Discrimination Act of value to a practice manager who has any disabled staff. Various other publications can be downloaded.

Website: www.disability.gov.uk/
Telephone: 0345 622 633, or
            0345 622 688
(Have the reference number of the publication required available.)
Address: DDA Information
          FREEPOST
          MID 02164
          Stratford-upon-Avon, CU37 9BR

Equal Opportunities Commission

This body deals with all equal opportunities matters. The site has information about employment practice, parental leave, sex discrimination and equal pay legislation. A range of publications are available, those that are free can be downloaded, priced publications must be ordered.

Website: www.eoc.org.uk/
Telephone: 0161 833 9244
Address: Customer Contact Point
          Overseas House
          Quay Street
          Manchester, M3 3HN

General Medical Council

The site contains information about professional matters concerning doctors. There are papers of interest to practice managers that may be downloaded concerning topics such as confidentiality, management in health care, access to GP's records for financial audit, etc.

Website: www.gmc-uk.org/
Telephone: 020 7580 7642
Address: 44 Hallam Street
          London, W1N 4AN

Government Information Service

This is a very useful website. It provides access to all government departments, local government offices, and other official organisations.

The site has an alphabetical list of several hundred organisations, and a functional list of government tasks. Clicking on to the appropriate title gives access to the site sought.

Website: www.open.gov.uk/

Health and Safety Executive

Information about the requirements of health and safety at work law. The website has a large number of electronic pages that can be downloaded. Some are of particular value when they explain recent changes to health and safety law. There is a full listing of all HSE publications, both those that are obtainable free and those that are priced. Priced publications can be ordered over the internet if required.

Website: www.hse.gov.uk/
Telephone: 01787 881165
Address: HSE Books
             PO Box 1999
             Sudbury
             Suffolk, CO10 6FS

Health Service Ombudsman for England

The site gives details of how complaints against the NHS can be made to the Health Ombudsman and details of what he can investigate. The site contains forms that can be completed and then posted to his office for him to consider.

Website: www.health.ombudsman.org.uk/
Telephone: 020 7217 4051
Address: Millbank Tower
             Millbank
             London, SW1P 4QP

The contact details for complaints against the NHS in Wales are:
Telephone: 029 2039 4621
Address: Pearl Assurance House
             Greyfriars Road
             Cardiff, CF1 3AG

The Stationery Office

This site contains Acts of Parliament and Regulations (referred to as Statutory Instruments) from 1996 as they are enacted by Parliament. Most of them are difficult to read unless you are very familiar with the area of law concerned. However for the last couple of years the site has carried explanatory notes for each new Act of Parliament, and these documents can be very helpful. See as an example the explanatory notes to the Health Act 1999 which is considerably easier to read than the Act itself. Documents on the website can be downloaded without charge. The site gives details how to obtain printed copies, including the prices of individual items.

Website: www.hmso.gov.uk/

Many bookshops act as agents for The Stationery Office; look in the local telephone directory for details.

Institute of Healthcare Managers

A site for the use of members of the IHM containing professional information of interest. Some documents can be down loaded by non-members.

Website: www.ihm.org.uk/
Telephone: 020 7460 7654
Address: 7–10 Chandos Street
             London, W1M 9DE

Medical Defence Union

This site gives limited access to non-members and full access to members. It contains a lot of useful professional information including on-line library facilities that give access to specialised publications and case studies. Some of this information can be downloaded by non-members.

Website: www.the-mdu.com/
Telephone: 020 7486 6181
Address: 3 Devonshire Place
             London, W1N 2EA

National Association of Primary Care

This site contains much information relating to primary care matters, including reports, papers, etc. concerning current issues. Documents can be downloaded by non-members.

Website: www.primarycare.co.uk/
Telephone: 020 7636 7228
Address: NAPC
             Lettsom House
             11, Chandos Street
             Cavendish Square
             London, W1M 9DE

National Institute of Clinical Excellence

This site provides comprehensive information about NICE and how it operates. There is a lot of technical information together with links to other sites containing information of similar professional interest. Documents can be downloaded.

Website: www.nice.org.uk/

NHS Executive

This site provides information about NHS Executive organisations, information, publications and statistics. They can be downloaded.

Website: www.doh.gov.uk/nhs.htm

Royal College of General Practitioners

The site is primarily designed for members of the RCGP but it contains a number of RCGP Blue Books on a series of topics of interest to practice managers. One example deals with clinical governance in primary care. These documents can be downloaded.

Website: www.rgcp.org.uk/publicat/bluebks/advice.htm

Wales

Welsh government departments can be accessed via this website.

Website: www.wales.gov.uk/

Search engine

Readers familiar with the Internet will be aware of the use of search engines. For those less familiar, a search engine is a program that can be used to find websites of interest to the user. Details of the area of interest are typed into the search engine and it will then find locations in which those typed details appear. Although simple in description it takes some practice to get the best results from search engines.

There is one search engine that the author commends to all practice managers using the Internet. The address is:

Website: www.medisearch.co.uk/

The website contains an enormous range of medical topics and has the added benefit that it is simple and straightforward to use. All practice managers having access to the Internet are recommended to visit this site to see the range of information and links that are available.

Newspapers

Sometimes an item of interest such as a court case or an official statement catches your attention but it might be difficult to know where to look for further details. A good starting point could be the broadsheet newspapers. They all give access to some back editions and with some of them the search facilities are very good even if you only know a name or a date. All will ask you to 'subscribe' in some way or other. This does not involve you paying any money or undertaking any obligation other than giving your name, address and if appropriate, email address. In return you gain full access to the back editions.

Guardian	www.newsunlimited.co.uk/
Independent	www.independent.co.uk/
Daily Telegraph	www.telegraph.co.uk/
The Times	www.the-times.co.uk/

They vary in their coverage of stories and one of the four might provide better information than the others when looking for matters of particular interest.

Index